FRENCH ENTRÉE

NORMAN

An *Eat and Sleep* Guide

FRENCH ENTRÉE 17

NORMANDY

An *Eat and Sleep* Guide

Patricia Fenn

Quiller Press

First published 1997 by Quiller Press Ltd
46 Lillie Road, London SW6 1TN

Copyright © 1997 Text: Patricia Fenn
Illustrations and maps: © 1991 and 1997 Quiller Press Ltd
Wine Section text: © John Doxat

Line drawings: Ken Howard, Tony Cooke and Patricia Drennan
Area and port maps: Helen Humphries and Paul Emra

ISBN 1–899163–17–4

Printed and bound in Great Britain by
Biddles Ltd, Guildford and King's Lynn

Every effort has been made to check the information
in this book and the advice which is given in good faith.
However neither the author nor the publisher can be
held responsible for holiday disappointments.

Contents

Notes on using the book - and an appeal

1 The area maps are to help the reader to find the place he wishes to visit on his own map. Each place is given a reference on the relevant area map, but they are not designed to replace a good touring map.

2 The 0 in brackets at the beginning of a telephone number should be used when dialling in France, but when making calls from outside the area, e.g. from UK, dial 0033 then the nine digits omitting the 0.

3 o.o.s. stands for 'out of season'; cl. for 'closed'. Other abbreviations, such as f for francs, are standard.

4 L, M or S in the margin stand for 'L' = Luxury, 'S' = Simple and 'M' for those in between.

5 H stands for Hotel; R for Restaurant and C for Chambre d'hôte in combination with 4 above, ie (H)S, (R)L etc.

6 stc means service and taxes are included (*service et taxes compris*).

7 The ➡ symbol means the establishment fulfils exceptionally well at least one of the author's criteria of comfort, welcome and cuisine.

8 Ⓜ stands for parking.

9 Credit cards are so generally accepted that they have been omitted. Mastercard/Eurocard/Visa are the most popular.

10 The figures given in the address, eg. 62000, are the postal codes, which should be used in all correspondence.

Author's appeal

In order to keep *French Entrée* up to date I need all the latest information I can get on establishments listed in the guide. If you have any comments on these or any other details that might supplement my own researching I should be most grateful if you would pass them on.

Please include the name and address of establishment, date and duration of visit. Also please state if you will allow your name to be used.

Patricia Fenn
Quiller Press
46 Lillie Road
London SW6 1TN

RAISONS D'ÊTRE

The first Normandy book, French Entrée 3, was published in 1985. Further editions followed over the intervening years, but now in 1997 it is evident that there have been so many changes that only a completely new book will do. This is it.

It is new in that every one of the entries have been re-visited by me and re-assessed, but not new in that it relies on twelve years' experience of the region and on hundreds of letters from readers relating their experiences. These are one of the book's unique assets. On the day I visit, there might have been an unprecedented disaster in the kitchen, or the patron might now recognise me and make a special effort. Neither of these occurrences is typical, but a thick file of thumbs up or down fills in the gaps in between.

Look at the number of **NEW** signs in the margins and it will be evident how many exciting additions I have been able to make. Sadly some old faithfuls have bit the dust, and with a recession greatly fiercer than we in Britain seem to realise, and a general disinclination of the young to take over family businesses, I expect more to follow.

The aim of the book remains the same - to paint a comprehensive picture of Normandy's hotels, restaurants, scenery and diversions, and then to leave the reader to decide what is right for *him*. The assumption is that we all have different priorities at different times. Take the kids and we're talking budget. Take the bride and the sky's the limit.

Look elsewhere for a quick symbolised reference guide or one for a particular income group. Snatch up this one if you want to know *exactly* what's on offer before *you* make the choice.

ARROWS

These are to point you in the right direction - to the bullseyes. Pick of the bunch, they are chosen because they fulfil superbly well at least one - and preferably all - of the over-riding criteria - welcome, good food, comfort and situation. Other entries may be there simply because there is none better in that particular town; the arrows are there because they have been tried and tested and proved to be winners.

ENTRÉE TO THE ENTRÉES

Hotels and restaurants are graded into three categories: L for Luxury, M for Medium and S for Simple, but always the prime criterion for recommendation is value for money. Service with a smile scores top marks. Few chain hotels are included because (a) they are not difficult to locate without any help from me and (b) I happen to prefer a degree of individuality and owner-management to even the most efficient plastic uniformity.

To spend a night in a L hotel you should expect to spend around 500-700f for the room and find it equipped with every necessity. Bathrooms will be luxurious, often offering a jacuzzi and certainly a bath as well as a shower. Look for the ones that have a Michelin star attached to their restaurant - anything in this category should take their food seriously, and not just charge a lot for superficial gloss. Often there will be cheaper, less luxurious rooms, and these are well worth investigating if you like the trappings - the comfortable *salons*, the good restaurant, the swimming pool, the smooth service - without wanting to spend too much on the room. Remember though that the extras will push up the bill - breakfast, drinks at the bar, wine with dinner. If it's a special occasion it's worth going for the hotel's best, and even at top prices - around 1,000f - you will be doing a far better deal than in the U.K. where beds, not rooms, are charged for.
L restaurants are another matter and every visitor to France should try and budget to sample them. Lunch menus offer particularly good value, with a talented chef cutting costs to rock bottom in order to fill his restaurant. There are several listed where a four-course meal need only cost around £15. When you get to the double Michelin stars, like La Bourride in Caen, you are talking about 330f for dinner, but even here there is a lunch menu at 190f.

The M category covers the majority of hotels, safe and not too expensive. The cost should be between 200f and 400f, and my selection is nearly always owner-managed, bringing in the personal touch which we all appreciate above gloss. Rooms will be well-equipped, usually with telephone, T.V., good hanging space and with any luck some efficient lighting (but this is France). They will have *en suite* bathrooms with bath or shower, and you should have a choice of twin or double beds and the use of a garage.
M restaurants range from the typical French *bourgeois* style, with draped curtains, well-upholstered chairs, *patronne* likewise, and a clientele of local worthies, businessmen during the week

and families for the sacred Sunday lunch gathering, to the small but tasteful new venture of a young couple anxious to get established. In the first group you will probably eat traditional French dishes, prepared by a *patron/chef* who knows what his regulars like and is not over-keen to experiment; in the latter there may be a new Michelin star chef striving for recognition, who may well enjoy extending the range of established cuisine with new ingredients and ideas from other countries. There is excellent reliable value to be found in this category, where a meal should cost between 80 and 180f.

It is the S category that causes me most pleasure and most pain. Pleasure because we all like a bargain and there is great satisfaction in discovering one probably not listed in other guides, and pain because obviously short cuts are a temptation. With S hotels I have to be particularly careful - one bad meal you can forget, a night with bedbugs you can't. There is a limit to just how simple you can get, so nowadays most people would expect *en suite* 'facilities', probably a shower not a bath for a price between 150f and 250f. There are some winners in this category, relying more on the owners' welcome and good will than on the frills, and these are the ones that the faithful Brits return to year after year.

S restaurants can imply a simple bucolic meal served at scrubbed tables in a farmhouse, one dish in a *brasserie*, a *crêperie*, a salad bar, or a basic town restaurant often attached to a hotel, where the *patron* cooks, and his wife and family serve to a devoted bunch of regulars, who rely on his *plat du jour*. These last are the ones to make for with an appetite but not if you require finesse.

TIPS FOR BEGINNERS

Maps and Guides   Good maps are essential and I must stress that those in the front of this book are intended only as an indication of where to find the entries. They should be used in conjunction with the appropriate Michelin maps: 231 covers all Normandy; 52, 54, 55 will deal with smaller areas.

   The red Michelin, apart from all its other virtues, has useful town maps.

Booking   Sunday lunch is the Meal of the Week, when several generations settle down together to enjoy an orgy of eating, drinking, conversation and baby-worship that can well last till teatime. You should certainly book then and on *fête* days. Make tactical plans and lie low, or it could be a *crêpe* and a bed in the car. French public holidays are as follows:

New Year's Day	France's National Day, 14 July
Easter Sunday and Monday	
Labour Day, 1 May	The Assumption, 15 August
VE Day, 8 May	All Saints' Day, 1 November
Ascension Day	Armistice Day, 11 November
Whit Sunday and Monday	Christmas Day

If you wish to book ahead and do not speak French, try and find someone who does to make a preliminary telephone call. If necessary, write in English and let them sort it out, but make sure when you get the confirmatory letter that you understand what you've booked. Many hotels nowadays will ask for a deposit. My method is to send them an English cheque; they then either subtract the equivalent from the bill or return the cheque.

   Make good use of the local tourist bureaux, clearly indicated in the centre of every town, where you will find English spoken. Let them do the booking for you if you have problems. This is the place to pick up maps and brochures.

Closing Times   The markets, like the rest of the town, snap shut abruptly for lunch. I regularly get caught out by not shopping early enough; if it's going to be a picnic lunch, the decision has to be made in good time. From 12 noon to 2.30 p.m. and sometimes 3 p.m., not a cat stirs. At the other end of the day it's a joy to find shops open until 7 p.m. Mondays tend to be almost as dead as Sundays and it's likely to prove a grave disappointment to allocate that as a shopping day.

It does not pay to be casual about the weekly closure (*fermeture hebdomodaire*) of the restaurants. It is an excellent idea to ensure that not every restaurant in the same town is closed at the same time, but do check before you venture. Thwarted tastebuds are guaranteed if you make a special journey only to find the smug little notice on the door. 'Sun. p.m. and Mon.' are the most common and often it will take a good deal of perseverance to find a possibility open then. "cl. o.o.s." means closed out of season (usually from October to Easter).

Changing Money

Everyone has their pet method, from going round all the banks to get a few *centimes* advantage, to playing it the easy and very expensive way of getting the hotel to do it. It depends on how much is involved and how keen a dealer you are as to how much trouble is worth it. I change mine on the boat, where I have always found the rate to be very fair. If you get caught outside banking hours, the *bureaux de change* stay open late.

Telephoning

In October last year the French numbers changed. Some brochures have not been brought up to date, so it is worth checking that they now include 9 digits.

The new addition to the Normandy codes is the figure 2 inserted in front of the old 8 digits. This means that if you are telephoning France from England you would dial the international code 00, then the country code 33, then 2 followed by the number. If you are phoning within France you should insert 0 before the 2, and this the format I have used in the book, on the assumption that most of the reservations will be made from France.

Bring Home

The list of Best Buys doesn't change much. Obviously wine, but not the more expensive varieties which are, surprisingly, cheaper in England. Be a lager lout and take as much as you can carry. Coffee is much cheaper; jams, plain chocolate, stock cubes are worth considering, as are electrical goods, ironmongery, kitchen gadgets, and glassware. Best of all are impulse buys in the markets.

Breakfast

A sore point. The best will serve buttery croissants, hot fresh bread, home-made preserves, a slab of slightly salted butter, lots of strong coffee and fresh hot milk, with fresh orange juice if you're lucky. The worst - and at a price of between 20 and 50f this is an outrage - will be stale toasted bread, a foil-wrapped butter pat, plastic jam, a cup of weak coffee and cold sterilised milk. Synthetic orange juice can add another 10f to the bill. If you land in an hotel like this, get out of bed and go to the café next door.

Tipping Lots of readers, used to the outstretched British hand, worry about this. Needlessly - 's.t.c.' should mean what it says - all service and taxes included. The only exception perhaps is to leave the small change in the saucer at a bar.

Garages and Considerably older and wiser since I started travelling so often,
Parking I now have sympathy with readers who insist on a garage. I can only advise removing any valued belongings, however tiresome that may be, and taking out adequate insurance.

What's Next? Unlike previous French Entrées, there are no *chambres d'hôtes* in this book. They were so popular that an entire book: *Bed and Breakfast in France* had to be devoted to them. The second edition, which covers the whole of France, is now being prepared and should be published this year. It's a good idea to mix and match - say use this book for hotels en route and the other for a base for a longer stay. Following the FE policy, every one of the 400 odd entries has been vetted, half of them by me.

Other Entrées Entrée to Malta
Entrée to Majorca
Entrée to Algarve
French Entrée 8 The Loire
French Entrée 10 South of France
French Entrée 11 Paris
French Entrée 12 The North of France
French Entrée 13 Provence
French Entrée 14 Brittany Encore
French Entrée 16 Gardens of France
French Entrée 17 Nomandy
French Entrée 18 Chambres d'hôtes in France
Entrée to Florida
Entrée to Halkidiki
Entrée to Catalunya

None of these, and especially F.E.16, would have been possible without readers' help. Please write to Patricia Fenn, c/o Quiller Press Ltd., 46 Lillie Road, London SW6 1TN, if you have any comments, favourable or otherwise, and stating if you object to being quoted. I do try and answer each letter personally but please be patient!

NORMANDY

Normandy is BIG. And diverse. Five *départements* ring the changes from rustic to sophisticated, seashore to city, tourist-orientated to bosky bucolic, dusty plain to lush valley, gastronomy to take-away, *Relais et Châteaux* to *chambres d'hôte*, *autoroute* to farmyard track. Back your fancy or sample a medley.

Calvados is the *département* best known to British tourists, and the one that offers most variety within its borders. Its *préfecture* is **Caen**, three-quarters destroyed in the war but still a good choice for a short city break, combining culture (the superb Mémoriale museum for Peace, William the Conqueror's castle, two great abbeys, Gothic churches, university, more museums), with gastronomy (one of Normandy's pair of Michelin two-star restaurants and numerous others), a superb Sunday market, and proximity to ferry port and sea.

Deauville is a one-off, epitomising *fin-de-siècle* elegance, millionaires' studs and race meetings, designer shops, classy hotels, glamorous *Parisien* customers, miles of sand. The sand is the only one of these attributes that extends to next-door **Trouville**, but it has others. More *en famille* than naughty weekend, hotels that open year round rather than six frantic weeks like its neighbour, real fishermen unloading real fish into a real market patronised by real Frenchmen. Brassy, cheerful, colourful Trouville.

Honfleur is special. Without doubt my No.1 choice for a weekend 'away from it all', especially now that the elegant new Pont de Normandie connects it with Le Havre so speedily. So photogenic. Great for a stroll round the quays, and then another getting to know it better, and then another into the quiet twisting mediaeval streets. Too busy at summer weekends, too expensive on the surface but not if you know where to go, infinitely rewarding if you enjoy sitting in cafés admiring the view, both human and scenic.

Deviate a km or two on either side of the autoroute that speeds across Calvados linking Normandy's two great cities Caen and Rouen to find another Normandy. Here is picturepostcardland:- brown and white Normandy cattle, authentically eyepatched, black and white Normandy cottages authentically thatched, time-warped hamlets, gnarled apple trees, green valleys, primitive farms, 'cider routes'. And Deauville is *how* far away? You must be joking.

Bayeux is another good choice for a short break. Better than ever now that its centre has been pedestrianised, it not only has the historic tapestry and cathedral to offer but a pleasant and animated character.

The **Suisse Normande** is an extension of Calvados southwards. Not really very Swiss but unmistakably different. The wide and wonderful river Orne cuts through deep escarpments and offers all manner of water-sports. It's all craggy peaks, green valleys, unspoiled villages, with a higher ratio of French to English tourists than that nearer the coast.

And of course there is the Calvados of the D. Day landings. **Arromanches** is full of ghosts, evoked by the wreck of Mulberry Harbour and the D. Day museum, but a visit there will make you thoughtful rather than sad.

Seine Maritime Caen's age-long rival, head of Upper Normandy - **Rouen**. He who is tired of Rouen must be tired of life. Less shattered than Caen by wartime devastation, still blessed with street after street of enchanting mediaeval buildings (some skilfully restored admittedly), a superb cathedral and other distinguished churches, and a heart which it is easy to find and love, more restaurants than you or I could ever exhaust and a population that loves to sit outside and supply the typically Gallic atmosphere, it is a city that alone merits the journey to Normandy.

Head north for the typical Caux (chalk) landscape of rolling plains that drop abruptly into the sea. Beaches are pebbly, white rocks are familiar from many an Impressionist painting, rivers carve their way to the sea via fertile valleys. Here are some of France's premier fishing fleets - Fécamp, Le Tréport, Étretat, salty, breezy, colourful, where the fish has at least a chance of being fresh. **Dieppe** is the Channel port with most colour, good market, good shops.

As its name implies, this is the *département* of the Seine, whose banks are well worth following, on either side. **La Bouille** is an unexpected jewel dropped down from the thundering *autoroute* between high cliffs. A sunny lunchtime could not be better spent than in one of the waterside restaurants here, a stone's throw from the mammoth barges.

Take a *bac* across to **Jumiéges** with its historic abbey ruins and then follow the almost circular loop of the river along the *Route des Fruits*, where stallholders sell whatever their various fruit trees most recently produced.

Eure takes up the river where Seine-Maritime runs out, via the fabled **Les Andelys** and the castle of Richard the Lionheart, **Giverny** and Monet's gardens are not far away, and great forests sheltering picturesque excursion towns like **Lyons-la-Forêt**. Nearer the estuary is **Pont Audemer**, built over rivulets of the river Risle and the little-known strange marshland of La Brière. The river from which the *département* takes its name flows through unspoiled countryside, with good picnicking on its banks. The *préfecture* is **Evreux**, a lively city with ancient cathedral that survived the bombardment. Paris is only an hour or so away, so restaurants become more sophisticated.

La Manche is not at all sophisticated. This is bucket n' spade territory, with golden sands and golden family holiday memories. **Carteret** has the lot, plus a picturesque river estuary and the Manche's only Michelin star. **Granville** is bigger, a real fishing port, with real fishy restaurants and a cheerful bustle down by the sea, while up in its *Haute Ville* the ramparts enclose another world, hushed and secretive.

Inland, the lanes, farms and hamlets remain resolutely rural. Even more so is the dramatically wild NW corner, where the Atlantic rollers pound against fearsome granite cliffs - the highest in Europe. You could be in Cornwall. Great for windswept walks.

To the north-east are to be found the delightful fishing villages of **St. Vaast-la-Hougue** and **Barfleur**, animated by yachtsmen, coloured by salty old characters on wobbly bicycles. More lovely walks. Further down the peninsula are the windswept landing beaches whose names are written in the history books. And let us not forget Normandy's No.1 tourist attraction, on the border with Brittany. For centuries **Mont St Michel** has drawn pilgrims from all over the world, and it still does. **La Merveille** they call it and that about sums it up. Get there early or late to catch the magic, and witness the rushing in or out of the tides over the salt marshes - faster than a galloping horse.

That leaves the **Orne**, the least tourist-orientated, the most elegant, the domain of the spa, the forest and the horse. The National Stud has been here since the beginning of the 18C, covering over 1,000 hectares, with ten different breeds represented. Other aristocratic creatures crop contentedly behind private white stud fences. In the early morning you can come across them at exercise, their breath steaming in the misty air, or perhaps later on in the day stepping out proudly in front of a trap. Their owners spend half the year in Paris and the rest here in large gabled houses or family châteaux. The lovely Perche region, which deserves to be better-known, has given its name to a breed of horse, the massive *Percheron*.

This is a *département* for leisurely pursuits, untainted by tawdry commerce. Golf is *big* and getting bigger, and huntin', shootin', fishin' are everyday pursuits, with a sports shop in every small town displaying rod and gun. Where the Manche is pre-war old-fashioned, with kiddies in sunhats and dresses tucked in knickers, **Bagnoles de l'Orne** harks back to Edwardiana; large hotels with white sugar icing façades house the '*curistes*'. Ladies and gentlemen saunter round the lake to take the waters, all is green, peaceful and very refined. **Alençon** is the main town, famous for its lace, but some of the smaller towns have interesting specialities too. In lively little **Mortagne** it is the black pudding, important enough to have its own annual festival.

MARKETS

French markets are more than just a utility, they are part and parcel of the French scene, and everyone loves them. It is worthwhile making a special detour to visit some of the best, which will spill out of the main market square into neighbouring streets and ensure that the bars round the square are kept very busy indeed.

Take your time strolling round the colour and hubbub and experience the pleasure of buying from someone who knows and cares about his wares. The man selling you a kitchen knife will be an expert on knives and will want to know what you need it for; the cheesemonger will choose for you a cheese ready for eating today or in a couple of days' time, back home. trust them. Choose for yourself the ripest peach, the perfect tomato and buy as little as you need and no more, so that you can buy fresh again tomorrow.

Principal Markets:

These are the market days supplied by the French Tourist Office, but please note that some of the markets only operate in the summer months, some are morning only, some afternoon only and some all day. it is worth checking locally before you set off.

Calvados

Sun: Cabourg, Caen, Clécy, Grandcamp-Maisy (summer only), Noyers-Bocage, Pont d'Ouilly, Port en Bessin, Tilly sur Seules, Trouville, Villerville.

Mon: Pont l'Evêque, St. Pierre sur Dives, Vierville sur Mer.

Tues: Balleroy, Bloville, Caen (rue de Bayeux), Courseulles, Deauville, Dives sur Mer (summer), Dozulé, Grandcamp Maisy, Mondeville, Ouistreham (bourg), Thury-Harcourt, Villers sur Mer, Villerville, Vire.

Wed: Arromanches (summer), Bayeux, Berniers, Bonnebosq, Cabourg, Caen (bd. Leroy), Creully, Evrecy, Isigny, Lisieux, (Hauteville), Luc sur Mer (summer), Méry Corbon, Orbec, Thaon, Trouville, Villers Bocage.

Thurs: Le Bény Bocage, Blangy le Chateau, Bretteville sur Laize, Caumont l'Eventé, Condé sur Noireau, Douvre, Houlgate, Lion sur Med (summer), Livarot, Merville Franceville (summer), Le Molay Littry, Mondeville, Trouville.

Fri: Blonville (summer), Caen (pl. St. Sauveur), Cambremer, Colombelles, Courseulles, Deauville, Langrune, Lisieux, Ouistreham (Riva Bella), Trevières, Villers sur Mer, Vire.

Sat: Amfreville, Arromanches (summer), Aunay sur Odon, Bayeux, Beaumont en Auge, Beuvron, Dives sur Mer, Falaise, Fleury sur Orne, Grandcamp Maisy, Honfleur, Isigny, Lisieux, Louvigny, Luc sur Mer, Ouistreham (bourg), St. Sever, Touques, Troarn, Verson.

Manche

Sun: Octreville, Hauteville sur Mer (summer).

Mon: Carentan, Torigni, St. James, Bricquebec.

Tues: Villedieu les Poêles, Cherbourg, Bréhal, Quettehou.

Wed:	St. Hilaire du Harcouët, La Haye du Puits, Marigny, St. Pierre Église.
Thurs:	Coutances, Cherbourg, St. Mère Église.
Fri:	Les Pieux, Valognes, Picauville.
Sat:	Avranches, Granville, Mortain, Périers, Barneville, Carteret, Gavray, St. Lô, Montebourg, St. Sauveur le Vicomte, St. Vaast la Hougue.

Eure

Sun:	Houlbec-Cocheral, Gisors, Evreux, Ezy-sur-Eure, Ferrières-sur-Risle, Perriers, Pont de l'Arche, St. Pierre du Vauvray.
Mon:	Les Andelys, Beaumesnil, Bourg Achard, Gisors, Le Neuborg, pont Audemer, Thiberville.
Tues:	Beaumont le Roger, Beuzeville, Damville, Fleury, Gaillon, Montfort, Montreuil-l'Argillé.
Wed:	Barre-en-Ouche, Bretauil, Étrapagny, Evreux, Garennes, Ivry-la-Bataille, Lieurey, Louviers, Le Neubourg, Le Nonancourt, Routo, St. Georges-du-Vièvre.
Thurs:	Brionne, Conches-en-Ouche, Evreux, Lieurey, Lyons-la-Forêt, Pacy.
Fri:	Bec Hellouin, Broglie, Cormeilles, Gisors, Pont Audemer.
Sat:	Bernay, Bourgtheroulde, Charleval, Evreux, Ivry-la-Bataille, Louviers, Mainneville, Quilleboeuf, Rugles, Verneuil.

Seine-Maritime

Sun:	Angerville-l'Orcher, Biville, criel, Darnetal, Gourney, Grande Couronne, Harfleur, Le Petit Quévilly, Rouen, Sotteville, Ste. Etienne-du-Rouvray, St. Nicholas d'Aliermont.
Mon:	Bolbec, Buchy, Cany-Barville, Harfleur.

Tues: Bellencombre, Bihorel, Bois Guillaume, Bonsécours, Boos, Dieppe, Ducalir, Elbeuf, Foucarment, Francqueville-St.-Pierre, Goderville, Gournay, Grand-Quevilly, Harfleur, Petit-Quevilly, Rouen, Sotteville, Ste. Adresse, St. Etienne-du-Rouvray, Le Tréport, Yerville.

Wed: Bacqueville, Bihorel, Bosc-la-Hard, La Bouille, Canteleu, Dieppe, Gonneville-le-Mallet, Grand Quévilly, Harfleur, Lillebonne, Mesnil-esnard, Mont-St. Aignan, Petit Qévilly, Rouen, St. Etienne-du-Rouvray, Valmont, Veules-les-Roses, Yport, Yvetot.

Thurs: Bihorel, Criel, Dieppe, Elbeuf, Étretat, Fontaine-le-Dun, Forges-les-Eaux, Harfleur, Londonières, Montivilliers, Pavilly, Sotteville, St. Etienne-du-Rouvray, St. Saens.

Fri: Auffay, Bihorel, Blangy, Bois-Guillaume, Clères, Criquetot, fauville, Gonfreville-l'Orcher, Gournay, Grand Quevilly, Harfleur, Notre-Dame-de Gravenchon, Rouen, Ste. Adresse.

Sat: Aumale, Barentin, Bihorel, Canteleu, Caudebec, Dieppe, Doudeville, Elbeuf, Envermeu, Fécamp, Harfleur, Malaunnay, Macourmel, Neufchatel, Petit-Couronne, Petit-Quévilly, Rouen, Ry, St. Etienne-du-Rouvray, St. Martin-de-Boscherville, St. Roman-de-Colbosc, Le Trait, Le Tréport.

Orne

Sun: Alençon, Argentan, Céton, Couromer, Domfront, Montilly, Mortrée.

Mon: Briouze; Remalard, Tinchebray; Vimoutiers (p.m.).

Tues: l'Aigle, Alençon, Argentan, Athis, Bagnoles de l'Orne, Nocé, Ciral, Pervenchères; Soligny la Trappe (all day).

Wed: Damigny, Flers, Longny au Perche, La Mêle sur Sarthe, Le Theil sur Huisne, Ste. Colombe, Tessé la Madeleine.

Thurs:	Alençon, Bellême, Bretoncelles, Céauce, La Ferté Macé, La Ferté Fresnel, Le Merlerault, Messei, Moulins la Marché, Puytanges Pont Écrepin, Trun.
Fri:	Argentan, Condé sur Huisne, Courtomer, Domfront, Écouché, La Chapelle d'Andaine, La Forêt Auvray, Tourouvre, Vimoutiers.
Sat:	Alençon, Almenèches, Bagnoles de l'Orne, Bretoncelles, Flers, Mortagne au Perche, Rânes, Le Sap, St. Georges des Groseillers, Sées; p.m.: Carrouges, Gacé, Mortagne au Perche.

NORMAN FOOD

Our Norman cousins are fishermen and dairy farmers by tradition and inclination. No surprise to find that Norman cuisine centres round the produce of the sea and the cow. Simple, fresh, local is the key. The Norman larder overflows with tender lamb from the salt marshes, thick yellow cream from the indulged Norman cow, with lobsters from the Cotentin rocks fit for the best tables in Paris and sole brought flapping from the Dieppe catch. Vegetables proliferate in this natural market garden (where they say a stick poked in the ground will burst into leaf overnight) and a surplus of apples and pears plop to the ground for want of picking.

The products of cow and apple - butter, cream, cider and Calvados - appear repeatedly (some might say monotonously) in the cooking. *Sauce normande* can literally cover a multitude of sins. At worst it can be merely cream sloshed indiscriminately, with no attempt to blend and enhance; at best an unctuous glossiness made by whisking the cream and butter into a cider sauce and used to coat, not drench, the vegetables or fish. The fecund *Pays d'Auge* gives its name to a sauce combining both cream and apple. The two most common bases are chicken and veal escalope, but turbot *vallée d'Auge* is a traditional dish for first communion celebrations around Étretat. The Caux area of Upper Normandy is potato country and you can expect to see them included in any dish labelled *Cauchoise*, along with the cream.

A familiar sight in the apple orchards is a fat pig happily rooting amongst the windfalls. When his time comes to be despatched by the local *charcutier* some of his more obscure parts will go into a variety of sausages, like the smoked *andouilles* from Vire, or the *boudin noir*, coloured with blood and enriched with cream. Black pudding to you or me. The strong flavoured liver of the pig goes into *terrines*, along with the pork fat, their richness spiked with a lacing of Calvados.

From Rouen comes *canard rouennais*. I don't know anyone in Normandy nowadays who sticks by the rules and smothers the duck so that its blood is retained but duck presses survive, which squeeze the bones to supply the juice to enrich the red wine and calvados sauce. The bird should be a special variety, half domestic, half wild and the Hôtel de la Poste at Duclair used to be famous for serving it in fourteen different ways.

Mussels breed abundantly along the coast and the tiny juicy variety from these cold northern waters have far more flavour than the inflated southern kinds. The Norman way of serving them of course is to add cream to the broth. If you see '*dieppoise*' attached to a dish it will involve the baby grey shrimps hauled in at Dieppe. I prefer *marmite dieppoise*, a fish stew using white fish, shelled mussels and peeled shrimp and made piquant with spices (echoes of Dieppe's early eastern seafaring forays) to the overrated *bouillabaisse* made from the bony Mediterranean fish. *Tarte aux pommes* is the ubiquitous dessert, in legions of shapes and guises. Many is the slice of blackened cardboard pastry topped with thin leathery apple slices I've choked on in the interests of French Entrée. *Tarte aux demoiselles Tatin* is often found in Normandy but don't let them tell you its origins are local - it was in the Loire that the blessed Tatin daughters accidentally burnt and caramelised the sugar and turned the tart upside down to hide their carelessness.

NORMAN CHEESES

Prime in all France are Norman cheeses. The northern grass is lushest and the bespectacled Norman cows that chew it are promotional poster clichés. To be true Norman they must be brown and white with a brown patch over at least one eye.

Many French will reject a cheese because it is not 'in season'; the date that the cows are put out to pasture and the length of time it takes to make the cheese comes into their consideration. Just as wine buffs know the soil and microclimate of every vineyard and how long the wine will take to age correctly, so will the cheese purist know at what season the grass sprouts, (not once but twice a year) and when the meadows break into flower. He will know about individual cheesemaking methods within an area sometimes no larger than a few fields.

There are really only four outstanding names to remember:-Camembert, Pont l'Evêque, Livarot and the cream cheese loosely referred to by the name of the area from which most of them derive - Neufchâtel. However, within these varieties there are many distinctions and it's worthwhile remembering what to look for.

Camembert

There are around 2,000 brands of Camembert produced in France but of course no Camembert is as good as Normandy Camembert and the best of all is that which comes from the Auge country between the rivers Touques and Dives. Chalk and cheese is the difference between the commercial and the unpasteurised *fermier*. The best has an appellation V.C.N. (*véritable Camembert de Normandie*) and it's well worth any extra francs involved. Certainly the cheese is named after a village near Vimoutiers, where a monument stands to Marie Harel, generally credited with having 'invented' this delicacy in 1791 (but local lore has it that farmers' wives in the area had been perfecting its smooth creaminess for generations before). Napoleon III was presented with a cheese specially made for him in the village of Camembert in 1855 and he liked it so much that he kissed the waitress. Fifty years later a Monsieur Ridel designed the familiar little circular wooden box, so that the cheese could be packed and enjoyed at some distance from the farms.

Trust your nose when choosing the perfect Camembert, but it isn't easy to describe smells in cheesy terms - 'Like the feet of a god' was one off-putting attempt. Correctly it should bulge but not run when cut, but British taste tends to prefer it riper than the French and I certainly like mine oozing a bit. Best seasons are late spring, autumn and winter.

Pont l'Evêque

Probably the oldest cheese in Normandy and still made almost entirely in the farms of the *pays d'Auge*, with commercial producers trying to emulate. Small, squat, soft and tender, with golden rind, it has a pronounced tang, should feel supple when pressed and smell 'savoury with some bouquet' as the king of the cheese-makers, Pierre Androuet, puts it. He also advises avoiding one with a 'cowbarn odour', which shouldn't be too difficult.

The generic name for the square cheeses of Lower Normandy is *Pavé d'Auge*. They are all at their best during summer, autumn and winter.

Livarot

Another cheese with a long history, probably devised, like so many good things, in a monastery. It has a stronger, spicier smell than Pont l'Evêque, due perhaps to its being aged in airtight cellars lined with hay. If you hear a cheese referred to as a 'Colonel' it will be Livarot, the five bands of sedge which enclose it evoking the five service stripes. Best seasons are late spring, autumn and winter.

Neufchâtel

The group of cream cheeses loosely termed Neufchâtel, after the town, come from north of the Seine in the *pays de Bray*. They make a tempting sight on the market stalls, in towns like Gisors, in their varying shapes and sizes - hearts, discs, obelisks. Look out for *triple boudard*, supposed to be the shape of the bung of a cider barrel, with a very pronounced fruity flavour. Its best season, like all these creamy cheeses, is late autumn.

My own weakness is for *Brillat-Savarin*, which comes from Forges-les-Eaux. This one not only looks but smells appealing, which is more than can be said for most, with a downy white rind and delicate creamy nose. It is not for the cholesterol-conscious - a triple cream with a wicked 75% fat content. An upstart little cheese, it was invented by the grandfather of Pierre Androuet between the wars.

Farms selling their own produce, cheese, cider and Calvados, can be identified by their green and yellow sign: *Vente de Produits Fermiers*. Following the indications in the pays d'Auge for the *Route du Fromage* makes a good excuse for an excursion, and penetrates deeply into the most gorgeously bucolic countryside. You can pick up leaflets at local tourist offices or from the producers themselves.

Good markets at which to enjoy selecting the perfect cheese are at St. Pierre-sur-Dives on Mondays and Livarot on Thursdays.

NORMAN DRINK

Cider and *Calvados* are to the apple and to Normandy what wine and brandy are to Bordeaux. You cannot eat a cider apple - far too mouth-puckering - but you can see the trees throughout Normandy, wizened and bent with their load of tiny red apples. If you explore some of the side roads in the Auge region you will come across signs indicating *Route du cidre*. There is one from Beuvron-en-Auge, which leads through delightful little villages set on hilltops above the sloping orchards, with *dégustation cidre fermier* signs on every farm gate. Quite an experience to sit in the farm kitchen at the scrubbed table and sample the golden liquid.

In autumn the presses go from farmer to farmer, each extracting from the neat glowing piles the juice which he will then mix with a proportion - usually about a third - of sweet apple juice to make his own blend of *'cidre bouché'*. Left to ferment in the bottle, this is the champagne of cider. An everyday version, a kind of cider plonk known as *petit bère*, is made by adding a lot more water and passing the lot back through the apple pulp again.

Lovers of German *Spätlese* wines would appreciate that the best cider comes from the latest apples, with a touch of frost to concentrate the flavour.

Like wine-making there is a lot of judgement and a little luck in producing a good vintage, but perhaps in Normandy the farmers attach more importance to considerations like the moon being in the right quarter and the wind blowing from the right direction before perfect bottling can be achieved than would their aristocratic counterparts in Épernay.

Young Calvados is for stronger stomachs than mine. Not for nothing has the glass of the firewater offered between course been named a *trou normand*. It may well make room for more food but you can actually feel it burning the hole! However, a mature Calva, stored in oak for ten to fifteen years, is another matter - a smooth, golden, fruity and distinctly soothing *digestif*. Look for an *appellation contrôllée* label as an indication of quality - and don't drive afterwards!

GARDENS

I must confess that, keen gardener though I am, I have hitherto adopted a take-em- or-leave-em attitude to French gardens. We are so richly blessed with superb gardens in England that those across the Channel seemed second-rate. Usually they were over-formal, with stiff flowers in stiff rows in front of stiff hedges, and colours were chosen to contrast fiercely rather than blend seductively. Nowhere did I find the artful contrivance of the best English gardens, where the impression is that nature not the gardener made the choices. Border edges were precise and any clump that dared spill casually over was smartly reprimanded with the shears.

Only recently have I been persuaded to look again, so I cannot claim to be an expert or have a comprehensive experience of Normandy gardens, but some of those I did visit would alone merit the journey for the dedicated gardener. The Seine-Maritime département is particularly well-endowed, but brochures and maps for the whole region are freely available at tourist offices – and also see our own *Entrée to Gardens of France* by Barbara Abbs.

These are my favourites, very different but both memorable:

Le Clos du Coudray is near the village of Loeuilly at the crossroads of the D6 and the D25, north of Rouen and beyond the pretty village of Clères. It has made wonderful use of the concept of treating the garden as a series of rooms, so that there is always a delicious surprise round the corner. There are trickling streams, lakes, arches, arbours, roses tumbling over specimen trees, a thatched cottage, pergolas, deep rich borders and cascades of flowers from May to October. Many of them are unusual and certainly new to me and the exceedingly good news is that you can buy a selection in the well-organised garden centre attached. Some seemed cheap, some (particularly the roses) expensive, compared with prices back home, but at least take a notebook and note the favourites. There is a good café if you want to make a day's outing, but allow a couple of hours minimum to do justice to the garden.

Le Clos de Coudray, 76850 Etampuis, Seine Maritime (0)2335.34.196.85. Open from Thursday to Monday from 10 a.m. to 7 p.m. in summer; from 10 a.m. to 5.30 p.m. from March 1st to April 15th and in November. Entrance 35f.

Les Jardins d'Angelique are to be found NE of Rouen. Take the D42 direction Lyons la Foret, exit at Montmain to the hamlet of Pigrard and the garden is on the right.

When their daughter Angelique died, Gloria and Yves Lebellegard decided that her most fitting memorial would be a beautiful garden, peaceful, serene, always changing, always growing. They have achieved their aim here. It is the kind of garden that you or I, given almost unlimited time, patience and dedication, might even imitate. There is nothing grand or commercial about this one, but the atmosphere is very special. Yves and Gloria are always on hand to show you round their treasures, not in a supervisory way, but more as fellow-enthusiasts. Yves' particular joy is roses, a passion which I share, so I learned a lot. Some of the names are the same, some quite different and he is keen to learn the English versions, so that he can buy from specialists like Peter Beale and Charles Austin. He is a gentle, kind man, who insisted that we ate our picnic in the shade of an arbour and then gave me some cuttings to take home. They will be the happiest of souvenirs.

Jardins d'Angelique, Hameau du Pigrard, 76520 Montmain, Seine Maritime. (0)2335.79.08.12, open from 1st May to 15th October every day except Tuesday, from 10 a.m. to 7 p.m. Entrance 20f.

Map 6E   **ALENÇON** 61000, Orne. 220km from Le Havre

(M) *Tues., Thurs., Sat., Sun.*

Just the right size for a town – large enough to contain a variety of shops, bars, restaurants, not so large that covering it on foot becomes a problem. Narrow, ancient cobbled streets, mellow stone courtyards, black Norman timbered houses, window boxes full of geraniums, pedestrianised centre, all guarded over by the massive Église de Notre Dame, a very agreeable place to pass an hour or so.

Lace has been manufactured in Alençon since 1665, in competition with the fashionable Venetian lace. You can still buy the local product in the Lace Museum, which shares a building with the town's art gallery. Alas, the art of lace-making is dying and now a scrap of the intricate work costs a good deal.

Alençon makes an excellent touring centre, from which to explore lower Normandy, especially the Perche region, with delightful little towns like Sées and Mortagne. Within a short drive in any direction are the forests – Perseigne, Écouve, Andaine, with the Alpes Mancelles and the National Park of Normandy-Maine to the west. Chate d'Ô, Médavy and le Pin d'Haras, the national stud and stunning 18C château, are pleasant excursions to the north.

The problem is that I cannot find a hotel within the town that I could heartily recommend. Le Grand St. Michel, 7 rue du Temple, is probably the best bet, certainly central, but do not expect too much with a price tag of 145-260f on the rooms.

Au Petit Vatel (R)M
72 pl. du Cdt Desmeulles (0)233.82.64.58 cl. Sun. p.m.; Mon. 28/7-17/8

Popular as much for the *chef-patron* – Michel Lerat – as for his cooking. A genuine welcome precedes every meal with a good deal of kissing for the locals.

The dining rooms are pretty and pink, the cuisine is traditional Norman, but never dull. Fish are particularly good news, as too are the desserts.

Menus from 118f.

Escargot Doré (R)M
183 av. Gen Léclerc (0)233.28.67.67 cl. Sun. p.m.; Mon. 30/6-29/7

An unpromising site on the outskirts of the town on the busy Le Mans *nationale* but at least it solves the parking problem. L'Escargot is a sprawling stone building, becoming quite smart nowadays. It offers a 98f menu good enough for Michelin to award it a red R (particularly good value).

Au Jardin Gourmand (R)S
14 r. Sarthe (0)233.32.22.56 cl. Sun. p.m.; Mon.

NEW In a narrow side street (park before you get here), a tiny unpretentious restaurant that would probably be my first choice in the town nowadays. 70f buys a *gateau* of potatoes, wickedly rich and melting, a *feuilleté* of red mullet, cheese, and Tiramisu, accompanied by that test of whether a restaurant really cares – homemade bread. There is also that rarity amongst French restaurants, an interesting vegetarian menu.

In line for an arrow.

Le Bistrot (R)S
21 r. Sarthe (0)233.26.51.69 cl. Sun. and Mon.; 14/4-20/4. 4/8-25/8

NEW Bang opposite Jardin Gourmand. This is the restaurant that Charles-Henry de Valbray (see below) recommends to his visiting friends and clients. It certainly has bags of atmosphere, a real bistro, decorated with old photos, and tin Ricard signs, with a lively bar.

The *Menu du Marché*, a mere 69f, featured all the old Parisian bistro favourites – *tarte a l'oignon, langue de boeuf* with a piquant sauce or *tête de veau*, and *crème brûlée* to finish.

Great to see two young-at-heart newcomers to the town, but shame that one of them couldn't have helped out us starving tourists on a Sun./Mon.

➤ **Château de Saint-Paterne**
72610, St. Paterne. 3 km SE of Alençon on the D311 Chartres road. (0)233.27.54.71 Fax (0)233.29.16.71 cl. Jan.

St. Paterne is not a particularly attractive suburb and seems to be becoming more and more engulfed in factories and road works. The autoroute is scheduled to pass right through it, with an exit there.

All the more delightful then to find this oasis, set in 120 acres of woods, flowers, and the fruitful vegetable garden that supplies the kitchen with freshest and best.

The 15C château, reputed to have been the love nest of Henri IV, was inherited by its present owner Charles-Henry de Valbray, when he was in his early twenties. Perhaps if he had been older he might have been daunted by the task of restoring the crumbling building, finding furniture and fabrics and granting it a fresh lease of life as something between a chambre d'hôte and hotel. If it is the former I am quite prepared to cheat a little to include it in this hotel guide just because I'm doing my readers a favour; I'm prepared too conveniently to ignore the fact that half the property lies within the Sarthe departement. You'll thank me for it.

Apart from the youthful energy that allowed C-H to tackle some of the more expensive construction tasks himself, he had other advantages – a brother who runs the successful Château de Briottières in the Loire (See *Bed and Breakfast in France*) who could pass on useful tips, an attic full of neglected treasures begging to be restored and put to good use, and, most of all, an inherent good taste which ensured that the natural elegance of the château should be enhanced by his choice of curtains and furniture rather than drowned.

Perhaps a childhood spent under a Mediterranean sun influenced him in favouring bright cheerful colours – yellow for sun and blue for sea. Of his seven rooms I like best the cheapest – 550f, twin beds, feminine rose-spattered chintz, bath – and the most expensive – 800f, sunshine-yellow draped four-poster, elaborately pleated and swagged, French Revolution design curtains (which C-H admits are highly inappropriate in this aristocrat's residence), antique bath, shower and loo – but all the rooms are spacious and have their own bathrooms.

Dinner is an occasion not to be missed. Eaten in the extravagant light of thirty candles and expertly cooked by the multi-talented Charles-Henry, it is served by loyal local ladies, like the ever-smiling, invaluable, Marie-Denise who are only too willing to contribute to the renaissance of the château which was always the heart of the village that St. Paterne used to be. Four courses, apéritif, coffee and wine cost 250f. There is a new eating experience at the Château, the Auberge du Château, which has been created out of a previously disused wing. The walls have been colour-washed in terracotta and the theme is Provence, an instant pick-me-up in northern France. The speciality will be tapas and it will be open to non-residents. I look forward to the first reports.

There is always something new to report on St. Paterne and this time it is not only the Auberge, but the gîte that C-H has arranged in a circular erstwhile *pigeonnier* by the entrance gate. It's charmingly conceived in bright colours, quite different from the elegance of the château furnishings. With a well equipped kitchen and bathroom, it would make a comfortable base for a longer stay. 1300f a week. And C-H is working on converting another bedroom in the château itself for 1998, which I'm sure will be just as exciting as the others.

Arrowed of course.

ALPES MANCELLES

To the south-west of Alençon lies a particularly attractive area little known to British tourists. The name is misleading – these are granite walls rather than snowy peaks, enclosing the valley of the Sarthe, but nonetheless making a dramatic impression of rock, heather, and sparkling water, in contrast to the several forests – Perche, Andaine, Perseigne – which are alternative excursions in this lovely area.

The best-known, and recognised as one of France's prettiest villages, is St. Cénéri, 14 km SW of Alençon by the D101. The river is crossed by a picturesque stone bridge, and an 11C Romanesque church stands guard above the gorge. Old stone houses are wreathed with many flowers to welcome the tourists who drive out at weekends to eat and drink at one of the cluster of bars and restaurants above the river. The Lion d'Or used to be called the Auberge des Peintures, because penniless painters would gather there and offer a painting (many of which still decorate the walls) to pay for their lunch.

Map 3H   **LES ANDELYS** 27700, Eure. 40 km SE of Rouen

Ⓜ *Mon.*

Les Andelys because there were originally two distinct areas, le Petit Andely to the west and le Grand Andely to the east. But who cares about that, or about any other part of the town than the bit that faces on to the river. Here the Seine is at its most magical. The river loops and curves dramatically, set in its chalky white escarpment. The Gaillard castle towers above and contributes considerably to the romantic scene.

This was the chosen site for the fortress built by Richard the Lionheart, Duke of Normandy, and subsequently King of England, in 1196, barring the way to Rouen from the French king, Philippe-Auguste. So massive was its foundation, so formidable its site that it held Philippe at bay for seven years, by which time King John had succeeded to the English throne. Philippe assembled all his formidable resources and eventually the castle yielded to his battering.

A visit to the ruins is a must, whether you approach them by a long puff up the hill behind the Tourist Bureau or by car, 3 km via le Grand Andely. The view is literally breathtaking. Far below the curves of the Seine lie shining to left, to right and to centre; Le Petit Andely nestles in the crook and the river barges passing slowly in and out of the range of vision, as though pulled by an invisible string, add animated perspective.

Les Andelys

➤ **La Chaine d'Or** (HR)L-M
27 r. Grande (0)232.54.00.31 Fax (0)232.54.05.68 R cl. Sun. p.m.; Mon. and Jan. H cl. Sun.; o.o.s.; Mon. and Jan.

The progress of the Chaine d'Or has been ever onwards and upwards since I first wrote about this little auberge right on the banks of the Seine. The young (well it was a dozen or so years ago) M. and Mme Foucault have worked long and hard to achieve the success of a Michelin star in their restaurant and a *Complet* sign up more often than not in their hotel. They start off with an enormous advantage. The view over the Seine from some of the bedrooms and the restaurant is pure picture-book; Les Andelys is near enough to Rouen and indeed to Paris to provide an ideal weekend getaway, and the hotel and restaurant are both well-known and well-loved.

The eight bedrooms have been steadily upgraded over the years and although I may regret the passing of the faded old furniture and the fin-de-siècle decor, I have to concede that the plumbing is better than of yore. The cost is now between 410 and 550f and there are two apartments at 780f. It is well worth paying for a room with a view if you can get hold of one.

The restaurant is the more important factor here, with dozens of covers and the tables by the windows eagerly sought. The cooking by Francis Chevalliez is sophisticated – a *croustillant* filled with soft boiled eggs and asparagus tips, oysters in a champagne sauce, chocolate soufflé with a jasmine sauce – making the cheapest menu, at 138f, a bargain for such skilled presentation. Prices leap after this, so it is a good idea to consult the menu before committing yourself.

An arrow for a comfortable hotel, with good food and one of the best sites in Normandy.

If the restaurant is full or beyond your budget there is consolation at hand. There could hardly be a better picnic site than here by the river, where there are stone benches and shade. Or, almost opposite the hotel:

Mistral (R)S
26 r. Grande (0)232.54.09.00 cl. Mon.; Tues.

NEW   So-called because the owners, Jacques and Michel Pesty, come from Provence and their tiny restaurant/*salon de thé* is themed accordingly. The decor zips you down to the south immediately. Cloths are yellow provençal prints, walls are stark white and there is a little creeper-covered patio at the rear to make the most of every glimpse of sun.

Dishes are in character – a *soupe de pistou* (35f), an *anchoiade* 42f, sardines 40f; the 98f menu includes a *brandade*, *confit* of goose that has cooked for five hours or a garlicky *daube*. They had just opened when I called. I wish them luck.

Several readers, frustrated by the increased prices of their old favourite, La Chaine d'Or, and still in love with Les Andelys, have tried the Hotel de Normandie not far along the river bank. The general view is that it's not bad, the view is just as good, and quite affordable. It has certainly smartened up a bit recently but I found the couldn't-care-less attitude of the staff a turn-off and suspect that a certain amount of cashing-in on the position goes on. Anyhow, the rooms cost 300f with bath and there is a lovely terrace running down to the water. (0)232.54.10.52.

Map 5E   **ARGENTAN** 61200, Orne. 59 km SE of Caen

Ⓜ *Tues., Sun.*

Once an attractive town, famous for its lace, but badly damaged during the Mortain-Falaise pocket action. Two fine churches survived, but needed extensive restoration. St. Germain dates from the 15th century and is bordered on its south side by the remains of the 14C castle of the dukes of Alençon. A fine Flamboyant porch opens on to the rue St. Germain. St. Martin is still under scaffolding. It's a sizeable town, with a good market in the main square, and plenty of bars and shops.

L'Auberge de l'Ancienne Abbaye (R)M
25, r. St. Martin (0)233.39.37.42 cl. Sun. p.m.; Mon.

NEW   Chef Arnaud Viel was a finalist in the *Championat de France* dessert competition, so whatever you do leave some room for afters. *À la carte* they cost 45f apiece – mango braised in spices, a *gratin* of figs with pistachios.

The Auberge is in an extremely old timbered building near St. Martin. Inside the dining room is cheerfully yellow and blue. Menus are 89f for lunch, 115f for dinner – say *tartare* of salmon, saddle of hare, cheese and those fabulous desserts.

La Renaissance (HR)S
20 ave. de la 2ème. (0)233.36.14.20

Excellent value here in a little restaurant near the station run by Véronique and Olivier Lecocq. The 92f menu includes wine as well as dishes like fillet of beef in red wine sauce or a *choucroute* of fish.
Rooms with bath cost 265f.

Map 3C   **ARROMANCHES** 14117, Calvados. 31 km W of Caen, 11 km E of Bayeux

Ⓜ *Wed.*

This once sleepy little seaside town will forever be assured of a place in the history books as the site chosen for the sensational Mulberry Harbour which made possible the 1944 landings – probably the most extraordinary feat of daring and maritime skills of the whole war. Not until you have visited the splendidly evocative museum and the new *cinéma circulaire* on the hill above the town, where the almost incredible story is related, can you possibly appreciate the concept and scale of the venture. Many *caissons* of the artificial harbour still protrude from the sea like a huge semi-circle of basking whales. More are washed up on the beach, black and menacing, with the word 'Danger' painted on them – an understatement if ever there was one.

One cannot reprove Arromanches from profiting from its wartime fame and the part that the people of the town played in the landings. They are rightly enormously proud of their role and in 1994 gave the veterans a huge welcome. Now the tourists invade the little town, climb to the *pointe d'orientation*, and are strangely silent as it begins to dawn on them how it must have been. Hotels, restaurants and bars abound to cater for them.

The beach here is wide, wonderful and very animated. The tide recedes for several kms, leaving plenty of firm sand for walkers, joggers and more esoteric sports; the sand yachting looks just as much fun as wind surfing and a good deal less wet, and there is a fascinating machine called Speedsport – a three-wheeled buggy which careers along the sands powered by a parachute. One misty morning I drew the curtains and saw two horses trotting ahead of Boadicea-like chariots; their drivers, in characteristic backward-leaning stance, guided them towards the sea and in a moment they were lost in the greyness. Ghosts? Perhaps.

► La Marine (HR)M
(0)231.22.34.19 Fax (0)231.22 98.80 cl. 15/11-15/2

Never growing too big for its well-known boots, the Marine remains a family-run hotel, in a prime position overlooking the sea and Mulberry, serving good food, especially fish. The rooms are not particularly large but are well-equipped and comfortable. Ours, 122, probably the best, boasting three windows overlooking the watery panorama, had peach curtains and flock wallpaper, lots of cupboard space and the usual appalling French lighting.

The restaurant, always full at summer weekends, is large and very pleasant, decorated in appropriate blue and green sea colours, making the most of its picture windows and the seascape they reveal. Cooking is reliable – nothing flashy but good quality, I recommend the second menu at 120f, which provided us with oysters, steak and dessert. Breakfasts are taken in the adjoining bar, which can get a bit smoky.

Private parking round the corner, a bit tight if you bring the Roller. We got locked out at 10.30 p.m. and had to rely on some guests to let us in, so make sure you take your key with you. 30 rooms at 270-350f (worth paying for the ones with sea views). Menus from 90-190f.

If you want to sleep peacefully and eat well in an M category hotel overlooking the sea, La Marine would take a lot of beating. Arrowed for long-term reliability and reader-popularity.

See Tracy-sur-Mer.

Map 4C   **AUDRIEU** 14250, Calvados. 13 km SW of Bayeux

Signed to the south of the N13 between Caen and Bayeux, on the D158

Château d'Audrieu (HR)L
(0)231.80.21.52 Fax (0)231.80.24.73 R. cl. Mon. Jan and Nov-Dec. H. cl. Jan. and Nov-Dec.

A stunningly beautiful 18C château, perfectly symmetrical. It is set in immense grounds, surrounded by ancient trees and flower gardens and there is a heated swimming pool.

Château d'Audrieu

There is little trace today of the horrors and destruction of the Normandy landings when for six weeks the château was in no-man's-land, attacked by British and Canadians from one side and by Germans from the other. 27 shells landed on the building, but the golden Caen stone resisted most of the blast.

Assuming that most customers for the L bracket can afford that little bit extra to pay for a really special room, I usually counsel going for nothing but the best but here the newly converted attic rooms at 700f are probably the best value. If you really don't care a fig, the apartments cost 2,000f.

Cooking meriting a Michelin star from Alain Cornet, trained at Senderens, is something to remember. He uses local produce, from sea and market, and embellishes it with imagination and skill. Sea trout with juniper berries, *tête de veau* with *andouille* from Vire are examples. Menus start at 200f.

The same family have run the château for many years and many readers look forward to seeing them every year for their annual Normandy fix.

Map 2H   **AUMALE** 76390, Seine-Mar. 22 km E of Neufchatel-en-Bray

---

The market in this centre of the dairy farming industry takes place on a sloping tree-lined square, hung about with many flowers. The town has many attractive boarded and timbered houses and an ancient market hall.

Hotel du Mouton Gras (HR)M
2 r. Verdun (0)235.93.41.32 cl. Mon. p.m.; Tues; 23/8-10/9

One of the most attractive buildings of all – 17C, classified, heavily beamed and set round a courtyard – houses this family-run hotel. Inside is predictably dark and cosy with lots of beams, copper pans, red check tablecloths and mock oil lamps. Josette Gauthier takes care of the hospitality while husband Jean concentrates on the cooking. The food is traditional Norman, in generous quantities. Menus start at 100f.

First and foremost this is a restaurant, with a good local reputation for Jean Gauthier's cooking and a *Complet* sign up at the weekend, but there are six comfortable rooms in a barn annexe across the courtyard which cost from 200-300f. Readers have approved of both food and beds, but objected to the high cost of wines.

Le Monton Gras
Aumale

Villa des Houx (HR)M
av. Gén de Gaulle (0)235.93.93.30 Fax (0)235.93.03.94

NEW

Don't be put off, as I nearly was, by the outside of the Villa des Houx. It looks huge, and is eccentrically timbered like a Disney pastiche of a Norman building, with gables, towers, balconies and whatever. In fact there are only thirteen rooms, all big and airy, with good bathrooms and excellent value for the standard of comfort, at 270-350f.

Newcomers Alain and Michele Mauconduit have a hard task ahead of them persuading customers to eat here in what they call a *restaurant gastronomique* rather than at the long-established, bags-of-character Mouton Gras. In fact the dining room was empty when I visited and the formal waiters standing around, hoping for customers in the over-large dining room depressed me so much that I fled. Menus from 98f.

I think this would be an excellent place to stay, however. I would welcome reports.

Map 5B   **AVRANCHES** 50300, Manche. 126 km S of Cherbourg

 Sat.

Sited on the main approaches to Brittany and Mont St. Michel,
Avranches is a popular overnight stop. Sadly, although it is a lively
enough town with plenty of bars and *brasseries* down in the lower
section by the castle, it has no outstanding restaurant to
recommend.

In 1944 General Patton launched his victorious 3rd Army attack
from Avranches and American soil was subsequently flown over to
form a square for the Patton Memorial, which thereby stands on
American territory.

On the Place Daniel-Huet, past the garden of the Sous-
Prefecture, is La plate-forme, where Henry II knelt in 1172 to do
public penance for the murder of Thomas à Becket. There's a fine
panorama of Mont St. Michel from the terrace at the end of the
square. Another good viewing point of the Mount and surrounding
countryside, river Sélune threading through, is from the Jardins
Publiques above the main town; the gardens are a blaze of all the
unflower-like flowers so dear to French gardeners' hearts. Cannas,
cacti, begonias, tortured into unnatural cohabitation, dazzle the eye
with their strident orange, purple and fuchsia-pink. Gertrude Jekyll
would have turned in her grave at the vulgarity, but the gardens are
certainly a cheerful, cool retreat and the Avranchins are extremely
proud of them. For connoisseurs of the bizarre, a visit to the basilica
of St. Gervais might prove interesting. There in the Treasury rests
the skull of St. Aubert, holed by the reproachful finger of St. Michel,
grown impatient at Aubert's dilatoriness in building the usual tribute
to the saint on the summit of Mont Tombe, later Mont St. Michel.

➤ La Croix d'Or (HR)M
83 r. Constitution (0)233.58.04.88 Fax (0)233.58.06.95

A 17C Relais de la Poste, now an extremely pretty little hotel. Lots
of polished copper, oak armoires, big fireplace, set the tone in the
flagged entrance hall and the stone walls of the dining room are
relieved by the cheerful yellow and blue decor.

The son of the previous owners has now taken over and it's all
much more professional, bustling and, I imagine, prosperous. As
this is the only restaurant worth considering in the town you can
imagine how busy it gets. I did feel the friendly welcome was
somewhat lacking – a complaint inherited from the former regime,
but it was nearly lunchtime when I called.

A lovely surprise awaits you behind the hotel. There is a burst of
colour from the hydrangeas, hollyhocks, lavatera filling the
courtyard, around which are set the 29 rooms. The temptation to do
these up has mercifully been resisted, so that the prices remain very

reasonable – 260f for the smallest with shower and 365f for one with two beds. They are a good size and simply but attractively decorated with flowery chintz fabrics, all looking out on to that lovely garden and assured of tranquillity. Menus start at 75f (lunch only), then 105-250f. Demi-pension 280-360f per person.

Croix d'OR, Avranches

Le Jardin des Plantes (HR)M-S
10 pl. Carnot (0)233.58.03.68 Fax (0)233.60.01.72

As its name suggests, at the top of the town by the botanical gardens. The *brasserie*-style restaurant is certainly very popular and perhaps I am doing it an injustice in suggesting that the Croix d'Or is the only good restaurant in town. It's a bustling friendly place, with a jolly landlord behind the bar who didn't turn a hair when I asked to see the rooms during the busy lunchtime period. Buffet meals cost 40f or 69.50f and the *plat du jour* plus dessert is 65f. The rooms are in an annexe at the rear and vary considerably. I was very impressed with the 280f version – a big room with bath and a view of distant water.

A good choice perhaps for a miserable day when all you want is company, good cheer and a plateful of something hot to cheer you up. Good for families too.

Map 6D   **BAGNOLES-DE-L'ORNE** 61140, Orne. 39 km SW of Argentan

---

Ⓜ *Tues., Sat.*

As the name suggests, a spa town, very well known for the treatment of circulation problems and *maladies des dames* Very efficacious I was repeatedly told. 50% of the visitors are *curistes* from all over the world. The Brits are very fond of the place, admiring the turreted and beamed architecture of the style dubbed Anglo-Norman, and many of them are buying property there, some in the prominent Residence du Lac, an old *palais* in prime position overlooking the lake.

It's all very tidy, very green, very manicured, with an extremely short season. Most of the hotels close for at least three months of the year, but are booked well ahead for the summer. There are so many of them that it's hard to imagine them all full, but that is the case in July and August. At other times of the year you have plenty of choice.

It is essential to pick fine weather in which to visit the little town. Given sunshine, it is very pleasant to walk around the central lake, sit outside the peach coloured casino with a drink in hand, or even take a ride in a *calèche* (pony trap). Alongside the lake you can hire ponies and horses and take off accompanied or solo. On pleasant weekends the Parisians pour into the town and the cafés and restaurants become lively and colourful; at other times the town can appear deserted and desolate. Most visitors eat in their hotels, so the restaurant scene is not good.

It's an excellent choice for a peaceful break, either overnight on a long journey or for a longer restful stay. Out of season the proprietors will be very pleased indeed to see you.

➤ **Bois Joli** (HR)M
12 Philippe du Rozier (0)233.37.92.77 Fax (0)233.37.07.56 cl. Wed.; Thurs. lunch o.o.s.; Jan.

The exception to the shut-up rule. They may not have many guests but they do have practically the monopoly o.o.s., and they look after them very well indeed. The bedrooms are delightfully old-fashioned,

Hotel Bois Joli,
Bagnoles de l'Orne

with high ceilings and masses of space. Ours, with pale blue colour scheme, and overlooking the lake, is known as the Pompidou room, after a previous incumbent. Excellent value at 550f. Others, all in Empire style, all different, cost 350f. But the real surprise here was the food. Hotels with 20 bedrooms, 19 of them empty, tend to send the chef home and open a tin for the isolated diners. Not so at the Bois Joli. Our 85f dinner was both imaginative and generous. Pigeon stuffed with *foie gras*, Norman sausages cooked in cider are the house specialities. The *patron* and his wife could not have been more accommodating.

Perhaps the Bois Joli's heyday was fifty or so years ago – the public rooms are a bit faded – but, like Bagnoles itself, it is a very good recommendation for a more elegant age. Arrowed for good value in both bed and board.

Lutétia (HR)M
Blvd. Paul Chalvet (0)233.37.94.77 Fax (0)233.30.09.87 cl. 15/10-1/4

See what I mean about the long winter in Bagnoles? I stayed in the Lutétia on a previous visit and loved the quiet tastefully decorated rooms, the luxurious bathrooms, the glassed-in terrace overlooking a pleasant garden, dotted with expensive recliners, and Madame Tramontana's benign supervision. I don't suppose any of that has changed but this time, on a spring visit, the hotel was firmly closed so I cannot personally vouch, and the arrow must go.

There are 30 rooms, from 295-400f, some in the annexe, some in the main building, which is a villa in a peaceful residential area not far from the town centre. If it's still as good as I remember it, this is excellent value.

Menus from 135f.

Capricorne (HR)M
allée Montjoie (0)233.37.96.99 Fax (0)233.38.19.56 cl. 5/10 – Easter

The hotels in Bagnoles tend to be either Gothicky or aggressively modern. The Capricorne falls into the latter category. It is tucked away in a quiet corner overlooking the lake. Rooms are functional but attractively furnished, and well-equipped. Readers have been well pleased. 280-400f rooms, and meals start at 105f.

➤ Manoir du Lys (HR)M
Rte de Juvigny (0)233.37.80.69 Fax (0)233.30.05.80

3 km out of town, surrounded by the forest, on the D335, is this half-timbered manor house, which has earned consistent praise from FE readers. A great part of this must be attributed to the management, in the very capable hands of the Quinton family. As the car drives up, some member of staff will rush out to carry the bags and direct the driver to the car park, Madame Quinton or her daughter will be there at reception, and son Franck will be busy in the kitchen. The family are constantly improving the property. There is a steady programme of renovation and re-building, and when I stayed there in March the new swimming pool was taking shape nicely. There is already a tennis court. In summer tables are set outside, and the feel-good factor is high.

The 23 rooms have a wide price differential – from 300f to 780f. As they all have good bathrooms and are well equipped, I would counsel the cheaper ones, which are decidedly the best value.

Franck's cooking is sophisticated and the service in the pretty dining room is suave, so the cheapest menu, Le Petit Normand, at 130f (155f with an extra cheese course) is excellent value. No choice – which is what keeps the price down – but trust the chef.

For us it was a well-flavoured *Tête de Porc* (which is what we used to call brawn), a *sauté* of venison in a dark sticky sauce and a wickedly rich *crème brûlée*. Fish appears on the 195f menu – bass with a tomato mousse, monk fish roasted and served on a base of spinach and wild mushrooms – and the desserts get more adventurous, like a selection of apple-based dishes.

Arrowed as a popular hideaway run by a caring family.

Map 5B   **LA BALEINE** 50650 Hambye, Manche. 3 km SW of Hambye; 22 km SE of Coutances

---

In a maze of country lanes due west of the Abbey of Hambye. The distance seems much further than that indicated on the signposts – you could be miles away from civilisation. La Baleine itself is pure picturebook, with a highly photogenic bridge crossing the river Sienne and a country kitchen advertising the home-made sausages and smoked hams, for which the region is renowned. There's a sign here for *La Route de la Table* which sounds promising but which I did not have time to investigate further. Anyone who has, please tell.

➤ **Auberge de la Baleine** (HR)S
(0)233.90.92.74 cl. Wed o.o.s.

What was once the village school has been transformed into a bar/hotel/restaurant, still very simple and the centre of village life. It's the restaurant not the rooms that you should come here for – the four bedrooms , which share a bathroom, are very basic, but cheap (125f), clean and south-facing.

The cooking on the other hand merits an entry in Gault-Millau, not noted for including modest country inns in their prestigious guide. *Chef-patron* is Patrice Barriée, aided and abetted by his wife Valerie. Patrice's cheapest menu merits a considerable detour, especially for mid-week lunch which offers four courses, ¼ pichet of wine and coffee for an incredible 55f. The evening menus hardly break the bank either – four courses again will set you back 78f, but you can go up to 195f if you give Patrice his head on dishes like a *sauté de crevettes* flamed in whisky, or a *filet* of duck cooked in cider and calvados.

A really special place, arrowed for exceptional cooking at exceptional prices.

Map 4C   **BALLEROY** 14490, Calvados. 16 km SW of Bayeux

Ⓜ *Tues.*

Like a stage set, with one wide main street of weathered grey stone houses, all of a period, leading down to the focal point, the Château de Balleroy. It was built in the 17C by Mansart for Jean de Choisy, whose descendant, the Marquis of Balleroy, sold it to the late Malcolm Forbes, the American publishing tycoon.

Château de Balleroy.

Manoir de la Drôme (R)M
(0)231.21.60.94 cl. Sun. p.m; Mon; 1/9-7/9; 8/2-20/2

My, how the Manoir has came on since readers first alerted me to the talent in this nice old stone house on the village outskirts. From simple delights to Michelin star in a very short space of time.

Menus start at 160f (another considerable change!) and feature M. Leclerc's specialities, like three kinds of duck liver *pâté*, a *fricassé* of sole, again with *foie gras* and a wonderful chocolate tart with sweet red wine.

I think the Manoir needs a re-assessment. While I thought the arrow was well deserved for a simple *auberge*, with simple *auberge* prices, the goal posts have now moved. I find the cooking a touch too rich, with expensive ingredients used when less prestigious ones would have been better. More reports please.

Map 2B   **BARFLEUR** 50760, Manche. 28 km E of Cherbourg

Just one wide main street lined with granite houses leading down to the colourful fishing port. It makes a pleasant outing to drive here and walk round the harbour past flowery cottage gardens in the Cour Ste. Cathérine, to check out the plaque commemorating the departure of William the Conqueror in 1066 for the conquest of England, and to visit the 17C chapel at the harbour extremity. There's even a sandy beach here. Richard Lionheart also contributed to Barfleur's page in the history books by embarking from the port on his way to be crowned our king. You could extend the drive to visit the lighthouse at the Pointe de Barfleur, and climb the 365 steps to view the panorama which covers the whole of the east coast down to the cliffs of Grandcamp and stretching over the vicious rocks that guard the entrance to the harbour.

➤ **Hotel Le Conquérant** (H)M
16 r. St. Thomas Becket (0)233.54.00.82 Fax (0)233.54.65.25 cl. 15/11-1/2

In the main street but calm and peaceful, thanks to an unexpected large and leafy garden at the rear, where it is most agreeable to sit and sup. Breakfast is served here whenever the weather permits. Otherwise it's around the inglenook fireplace in the cosy dining room.

The building is a 17C manor-house converted by the father of the present owner, Catherine Delomenede and her husband Pierre. The sixteen bedrooms (two in the garden, with terrace) are comfortable and equipped with British t.v. At 200f to 360f I think they provide a superb base for exploring the region and would be high on my list of favourites.

The lack of a restaurant is not serious since the food at the Moderne round the corner is so good, but Madame Delomenede will provide light meals and *crêpes* if requested. Menus (soup, omelette, salad, *crêpes* etc.) from 75f. Room with washbasin from 170f, with shower 280f or 300f overlooking garden, with bath 300f, with shower and twin beds overlooking garden 350f.

An arrow for a faithful favourite.

Hotel Moderne (HR)M
(0)233.23.12.44 Fax (0)233.23.91.58 cl. Tues.; and Wed.; o.o.s.; 15/1-15/3

This strange ochre-coloured building with oriental-looking dome, has had a new lease of life since the present owners, the le Rouliers, took over.

Evrard le Roulier is a fine chef who takes delight in the prime fresh ingredients available in his region, and the dining room not the bedrooms is the *raison d'être* for this establishment. It is large and airy and used by local gastronomes as well as tourists. The platter *de fruits de mer* is a wonder to behold, but more modest spenders should look no further than the 85f menu – excellent value.

Nothing much seems to have happened to the eight bedrooms since I first stayed there ten years ago, a fact reflected in their price of 140-230f. I would counsel sleeping at Le Conquérant and eating here.

Map 3E   **BARNEVILLE** 14600 Honfleur, Calvados. 6 km SW of Honfleur

---

Even if you have no intention of staying in Barneville, take the pleasant drive west of Honfleur along the Côte de Grace, then swinging inland on the D62 and D279 amid deeply rural and very green Norman countryside.

Auberge de la Source (HR)S
(0)231.89.25 cl. 1/11-15/2

There are no recommendable simple hotels in Honfleur and a town base can be noisy, so this little Logis de France could be a valuable asset. It is looking considerably smarter these days, under the jurisdiction of M. and Mme. Legeay, all freshly painted black and white, with the pretty garden well under control, and there are plenty of white tables and chairs under the trees from which to listen to the discreet tinkle of the stream from which the Auberge derives its name. A very peaceful spot to came home to.

There are sixteen rooms, mostly in the annexe building, comfortably equipped. Demi-pension is insisted upon but the cooking is good, so for those who do not fancy turning out in the evening, the deal is a good one. Prices for two people per day are: 640f with shower, 700f with bath, or 860f with a jacuzzi.

Map 3A   **BARNEVILLE-CARTERET** 50270, Manche.. 35 km SW of Cherbourg

---

It's all very confusing. There is the port and seaside resort of Carteret, there is the inland market town of Barneville-Carteret and there is Barneville Plage, which is more residential. Here we are talking about the little town, more dedicated to the French than to passing tourists.

Hotel de Paris (HR)S
pl. de l'Eglise (0)233.04.90.02

More confusion. As the Hotel de Paris, under the management of M. et Mme Poitvin, this modest little hotel was recommended and approved of by many readers. It was then sold to M. Appaire and changed its name to Les Embruns and was so-so. Now, the good news for us consumers is that the nice Poitvins have returned and we are all back in business.

Rooms are in an annexe-wing at the rear of the hotel, so escape traffic noise. They are without doubt simple but perfectly adequate and with all mod cons. Choose bath or shower, double, twin, disabled, from 140-260f, making a very cheap base in this relatively expensive area.

M. Poitvin still cooks and his *menu terroir* offers wholesome and generous sustenance. Menus from 52-120f.

Map 3D   **BAVENT** 14860, Calvados. 7 km SW of Cabourg by D513 and D95A

In other words, not in the village of Bavent at all but the other side of the main road. Look for the sign.

Hostellerie du Moulin du Pré (H)M (R)L
(0)231.78.83.68 Fax (0)231.78.21.05. cl. Sun. p.m. and Mon. except July, Aug. and fêtes; 4/3-18/3; Oct.

An interesting one. Plus points are the undeniable prettiness of the setting – a flowery garden with stream running through, old farm implements scattered on the lawn, fresh white paint, birdsong – and the interior – heavy beams, big log fire, cosy atmosphere, and the reliable cooking of Jocelyne Holtz. Not such good news are the prices – the only menu is 250f – and the fact that the rooms are pretty basic. I was wondering whether this should be the time, after many years inclusion, to forget about the Hostellerie. But rule no.1 is to take advice from the locals, who visit regularly and have ears to the ground, rather than the experience of an isolated occasion, and here they were unanimous. 'Isn't it rather expensive?' I suggested. 'Yes,' was the unanimous reply, 'but worth every franc.' So lie back and enjoy it.

The menu is likely to include items like *bavarois d'avocat aux huitres pochés, flan de langoustines au coulis de crustaces, soupe de fruits rouge*, so you are paying for sophisticated expertise in the kitchen. I was very pleased I had only to stagger upstairs afterwards, however unsophisticated the bathroom.

10 rooms 220-350f.

Map 3C   **BAYEUX** 14400, Calvados. 28 km W of Caen

Ⓜ *Wed.*

I cannot think of any town that has changed so much over the past decade as has Bayeux. Pre-pedestrianisation, it's one long main drag was a noisy, dangerous, fume-ridden nightmare, with pedestrians nervously proceeding Indian-style along narrow pavements, and drivers becoming increasingly frustrated. All that has changed and now it is possible to stroll, window shop, drink coffee, watch the world go by and appreciate this delightful town. Some of the side streets are beginning to get the message too and cafés are opening up in newly-cleaned stone, traffic-free enclaves. One of the prettiest is near the square designated for parking for the Tapestry, where a little stone bridge crosses the river. Perfect for peaceful picnicking, with plenty of benches thoughtfully provided. Otherwise there is a good *crêperie*, Le Triskell, whose terrace overlooks the water-wheel that churns up the river, or an interesting Italian restaurant with the sensible asset of a heated terrace. On a blustery July day it meant that we could still enjoy the view and fresh air without a shiver.

The city had the good fortune to escape the devastation that removed so much character from other less fortunate Norman towns, by virtue of serving as a hospital town during the 1944 fighting and by being the first French town to be liberated. Restoration work of the town's treasures is constantly in progress. The old noblemen's houses and ancient smaller dwellings have been spruced up; iron balconies gleam with fresh paint and the grime-free Caen stone now glows a creamy gold.

The city's greatest asset is of course the tapestry of Queen Mathilde, housed in an erstwhile seminary in a quiet square, well signed from all directions. Try and get there early or late so that you don't have to crane over burly German shoulders or shuffle round in a slow Japanese gaggle. Don't even think of trying to polish it off in less than two hours and that's pushing it. I've never yet met anyone who did not rate the experience as less than wonderful.

On the first floor is a mock-up of every detail of the work and a clear description in English and French of what is going on. The critical scenes – Harold's oath, Edward's death, Harold's coronation, the Norman invasion, William's bravery, Harold's death – are all emphasised to make identification easy when you do eventually get to see the actual tapestry. Check the times of the showing of the 15 minute film to make sure you don't have a long wait for the English version. And then at last, suitably awestruck, into the dark passage where this priceless account of the customs, clothing, food, events of 900 years ago, recorded so vividly, awaits you. Don't miss the English moustaches!

Bayeux is fortunate in having another string to its cultural bow – the magnificent Norman Gothic Cathédrale Notre Dame. Only the towers and crypt remain from the original church which was completed in 1077 by Odo, William's companion in arms who proved so turbulent that he met a sticky end at William's instigation. This is not the place for a lengthy description of its many virtues, but take it from me that a half-hour here will be well spent. Even the much denigrated *bonnet* which 19C 'improvers' thought would be a suitable cap for the central tower makes an unmistakeable landmark from within the town and from far and wide around it. The cathedral is set in the oldest part of Bayeux, well worth exploring to admire half-timbered houses and quiet courtyards.

Hotels and Restaurants: Bayeux is an excellent choice for a base at any time of the year, with plenty to admire in indifferent weather, and fortunately its hotels and restaurants recognise the fact and stay open for most of the winter months.

➤ **Hotel d'Argouges** (H)M
21 r. St. Patrice (0)231.192.88.86 Fax (0)231.92.69.16

Facing onto a huge square not far from the town centre and a
Relais du Silence, the nice old 18C *hotel particulier* is approached
through an archway. I like it better than ever, perhaps because the
owners Marie Claire and Daniel Auregan are so welcoming. There
is an annexe next door, approached via a large garden, where the
rooms are slightly cheaper than in the main building. There are 23
altogether, varying considerably, so it is worth discussing your
preferences. In the annexe they cost 280f overlooking the courtyard
and 350f over the garden, and in the main building 350f courtyard,
450f garden. Secure free parking.

Readers have been very happy to stay here for a reasonable
sum, enjoying the peacefulness in the town centre, so an arrow for
first choice in this must-see town.

Le Lion d'Or (H)M (R)M-L
71 r. St. Jean. (0)231.92.06.90 Fax (0)231.22.16.64 cl. 20/12-20/1

Now that the rue St. Jean is pedestrianised, this old coaching inn,
set back in a courtyard, is quiet enough to rate as a Relais du
Silence. It is Bayeux's best-known hotel and has been in the same
family for many years. Its fortunes have varied over that time. I
personally had my doubts about the justifiability of the Michelin star
from way back and now I see that it has been removed. That can
only be a good thing from the customer's point of view. No star is
far preferable to an ill-advised one. The latter situation leads to
complacency, the former, with luck, to a must-try-harder approach. I
believe that this could be the case here. With several new hotels
burgeoning in the town and surrounds the Lion d'Or must have
realised that it can no longer rely on its faithful (largely British)
clientele to go on supporting it without question. The daughter of
the previous owner is now in charge and there is a revitalised
atmosphere.

The decor previously disappointed – not my idea of what is
appropriate for an ancient provincial inn anyway. Now all the
bedrooms are being re-decorated and are pleasant and light. The
dining room is still a bit pompous but the service is good and the
cooking improving all the time.

Readers views have varied in the past – old-timers disillusioned,
newcomers still pleased to find such an atmospheric base in the
centre of town. I believe that it is time to forget old triumphs and
disasters and look at the Lion d'Or with fresh eyes.

26 rooms from 430-480f. 2 apartments at 600f or 1,000f.
Menus from 100-320f.

Churchill Hotel (see Restaurant l'Amirauté) (H)M
14 r. St. Jean (0)231.21.31.80 Fax (0)231.21.41.66

Centrally situated, freshly decorated and sound-proofed, with
benefit of good restaurant, integral to hotel but not under the same
management. A good bet if you like to eat in but not extravagantly.
There is a demi-pension arrangement.
31 rooms 300-460f. 1 apartment 520-680f.

l'Amaryllis (R)M
32 r. St. Patrice (0)231.22.47.94. cl. Sun. p.m.; o.o.s. and Mon. 24/12-10/1

NEW

Currently my number one choice in the town if good food is top
priority. New since FE9, l'Amaryllis is on the main western approach
road to the town, opposite a big parking square, and therefore lacks
the ambiance of the restaurants in the historic centre, but the
cooking makes up for a lot.
The 70f lunch menu is particularly good value; otherwise menus
start at 103f.

La Rapière (R)S-M
53 r. St. Jean (0)231.92.94.79 cl. Tues. p.m. and Wed. o.o.s.

The reverse of l'Amaryllis. Here the decor and atmosphere score
top marks, with the cooking a touch patchy. However, over the
eleven years since I first discovered this little restaurant, readers
have been well-satisfied and if you stick to the charcoal grills and
fish which are the house specialities, you can't go far wrong.
It's not really in the rue St. Jean at all, but tucked away in an old
courtyard. Stone walls, lace tablecloths, pink napkins, open fires, all
contribute to a feeling of well-being, and the warm welcome helps.
There is a 75f menu but I would go for the next one up, at 138f,
which buys nine oysters, an entrecôte steak, salad and dessert.
Wines are reasonably priced.
Good marks on the whole but I fear the arrow must go since
reports have not been unanimous.

l'Amirauté (R)M
14 r St. Jean (0)231.21.31.80 Fax (0)231.21.41.66

There are numerous little cheap restaurants at the bottom of the rue
St. Jean, with tables enticingly laid out on the pavement. If all you
need is a sandwich and lots of passing-by interest, this is the place
to head for. However anything more ambitious is fraught with
hazards. I think I'm fairly proficient in the art of menu-judging by
now but the usual stroll up and down, judging the clientele, the food

on their plates and the prices, let me down badly here and we ended up sadly disappointed with the kind of tasteless, badly presented food that alas is not uncommon nowadays in France.

All the more frustrating when just across the road is l'Amirauté, whose 58f menu offers honest simple fare that is just right for an inexpensive lunch. 58f bought *terrine*, omelette for me, *poulet Vallée d'Auge* for him, and a good apple tart. Of course there are far more ambitious menus up to 250f.

➤ **La Table du Terroir** (R)S
42 r St. Jean. cl. Sun. p.m.

NEW

And now for something entirely different. In the rue St. Jean is a butcher by name of M. Bisson, famous locally for his *charcuterie*, *terrines* and sausages. No ordinary butcher though, since he has had the brilliant idea of cutting out the middle man and dishing up his products in his own restaurant. Costs are kept to a minimum by using just one simple stone-walled room round the corner in the Allée d'Oranger, and the consumer benefits from the modest bill. Other restaurateurs must hate him.

You sit at long scrubbed tables and tuck into copious meat-based dishes. The French just love it, but it seems that the Brits have yet to discover the novelty. I don't know when M. Bisson does his butchering because he always seems to be in attendance in his little restaurant, but perhaps that's because it was brand new when I visited and he was still excited at his new venture. Can't blame him. On the 55f menu you can choose between juicy *terrines* or salad for starters, then a grill of whatever, then green salad or potatoes, then dessert or cheese. Bad luck vegetarians because even the salads are full of *pâté de foie*. The *grillade* comes hot (selection of grilled meats) or cold (house *charcuterie*). How's that for value?

You don't have to stick to the menu. Well worth sampling is the house speciality – *feuilléte Bayeusain*, which is a kind of upmarket Cornish pasty made with flaky pastry and more meat than veg. Or *paupiettes* of ham braised in cider, or roast pork or, perhaps best of all, a *gigôt* of *pré salé* lamb. Desserts understandably pale into insignificance but there is always a *tarte maison*. Arrowed for individuality and good value.

I must just put in a mention for a tiny bistro where I ate extremely well, le Petit Bistro (cl. Sun.; Mon.) in the rue de Bienvenu leading up to the cathedral. For 65f I enjoyed an asparagus *feuilleté*, a lobster *terrine* with crayfish sauce and spiced pears. The best in Bayeux? It might well be, but on my last visit there was a For Sale sign on the upper floor and as it was Monday I couldn't ascertain if this referred to the bistro too. Any reports welcome.

Map 4F   **BEAUMESNIL** 27410, Eure. 12 km SW of Bernay

 Mon.

l'Étape Louis XIII (R)M-L
Rte. de la Barre (0)232.44.44.72 cl. Sun. p.m.; Mon.

NEW   A special-occasion place, with the best cooking for miles around.
The *chef/patron* Christian Ravinel, is relatively new and is trying to
build up his clientele, so this is a good time to sample his bargain
98f menu (weekdays only alas).

He relies mainly on local ingredients and recipes, but cooked and
presented suavely and with no expense spared.

The Etape is as olde-worlde Norman as they come, with two
pretty dark cosy rooms, luxuriating in a big log fire on chilly nights. A
winter place I feel.

Menus: 98f (week), 195f.

Map 3E   **BEAUMONT EN AUGE** 14950, Calvados. 6 km W of Pont
l'Evêque by D118

 Sat.

A *village sauvegardé*, in other words protected. Very pretty, very
peaceful, rather more dignified and aristocratic than other pretty
Norman villages, more stately grey stone merchants' houses than
black-and-white farmers' cottages. Its situation comes as a surprise.
Walk across the grassy square and suddenly the ground drops
before you, disclosing a remarkable view of the Touques valley. A
gap in the far distance reveals the sea and Trouville, 15 km away.

Auberge de l'Abbaye (R)M
(0)231.64.82.31 cl. Tues.; Wed.; except July and Aug.; 3 weeks in Feb.

Not hard to find – this is a very tiny village and the auberge is bang
in the centre. Like the village, it is very pretty and very old – 17C. A
place for cold winter evenings I feel rather than summer lunches.
Ceilings are low, supported by columns, beamed walls are painted
red, giant twisted wine presses provide the decor.

Christian Girault's cooking is unrepentantly old-school. His 160f
menu revealed *tartare de saumon, carrée d'agneau*, cheese and
good desserts of the classical persuasion. No fireworks but good
ingredients, well-presented.

Menus at 160f, 240f, 280f. Good short wine list.

Map 6A   **BEAUVOIR** 50170 Manche, Pontorson. 5 km S of Mont St. Michel
          by D976

Just a name on the main road south.

Hotel Beauvoir (HR)M
(0)233.60.09.39 Fax (0)233.48 59.05 cl. 15/11-15/2

NEW   A pleasantly old-fashioned hotel which looks as though it has been
          catering for Mont St. Michel visitors for generations. Its virtue is that
          it does not regard this an excuse for a rip-off. The number of
          French people dining on the covered terrace testified to the regular
          value here, particularly of the substantial 90f menu.
              The rooms are fine, even if one regrets the flock wallpaper when
          a country print would have been more in keeping with the building's
          character. 18 of them cost from 280f with shower, to the biggest
          and best, with a bath, at 340f.

Map 3F   **LE BEC HELLOUIN** 27800, Eure. 24 km SE of Pont Audemer

Ⓜ *Fri.*

It's a lovely drive on the D130 through the Montfort forest, following
the river Risle to the great ruined abbey of Bec Hellouin. There's an
extraordinary peaceful feeling to the village, like a cathedral close,
even when it is thronged with visitors.
    The abbey, founded in 1034, has strong links with England, as
the commemorative tablet in the grounds will tell you. Duke
William's friend and counsellor, Lanfranc, was Instructor at Le Bec
and subsequently became Bishop of Canterbury. His secretary,
Gundulf, became Bishop of Rochester and architect of the Tower
of London. There are guided tours of the abbey, generally in
French, but the grounds are open to wander around, and those
prepared to climb 210 steps up St. Nicholas Tower will be rewarded
by a fine view of the Bec valley.
    There are several *crêperies* in the village, which readers have
recommended, a restaurant called Le Canterbury about which I
have heard absolutely nothing and a famous old inn:

Auberge de l'Abbaye (HR)M
(0)232.44.86.02 cl. Mon. p.m.; Tues. o.o.s.

Everyone takes a photo of the Auberge. It oozes charm, with
ancient beams and rustic antiquity, in a perfect setting above a
peaceful grassy square alongside the old church. I have been in

Auberge de L'Abbaye

and out of love with it for years – in because I'm a sucker for slanting squeaky floors, old fashioned flowery wallpapers, polished old family heirlooms, out because at times I felt (and readers agreed) that it was cashing in on its situation. Currently, denied an entry in either Michelin or Gault-Millau, I believe that it is reasserting itself, thanks to a refit of most of the rooms, the new entrance hall, and fresh paint around the courtyard where breakfast is taken in fine weather. Perhaps the jolt has been salutary and things are looking up. Always a good time to visit.

Some of the rooms are very pretty – the one I had in the front cost 390f and I had no grumbles, but one reader took issue with me when I described them as 'simple'. 'Simple my foot,' he wrote, 'I would call them basic.' As I say, they are in the process of being re-vamped, so care is needed when booking.

I haven't eaten there recently and the food would certainly have to improve to regain the old status.

I am reluctant to drop this old favourite and with the first signs of a new way of thinking, which included pleasant service and welcome, I'm going to be charitable. Any reports, particularly favourable, most welcome.

Rooms 300-390f (go for the best if you can).
Menus from 130f.

Map 3D   BÉNOUVILLE 14970, Calvados. 10 km NE of Caen

What was once a quiet village on the minor road leading to the sea is now surrounded by main roads and concrete, but it is still a good choice to stay near the ferry port. The old favourite, Manoir d'Hastings, which in its heyday boasted two Michelin stars, is still the landmark, but with new management there is a question-mark about the value for money. Recent reports welcome.

La Glycine (HR)S
(0)231.44.61.94 Fax (0)231.43.67.30 cl. Sun. p.m. from Oct to May

The youthful M. and Mme Decker have worked hard at improving their investment in what was once just a wisteria-covered bar. An entry in Michelin is their reward. Readers have been well pleased with the value here. The 25 rooms cost from 220-370f and menus start at 80f (mid-week). There is no choice at this level but if you fancy the dishes of the day you're in luck, because they include ideas like a *fricassé* of mussels with rosemary, half a chicken in *Vallée d'Auge* sauce and a *gâteau normand* with caramelised cream. Next one up, with more choice, is 98f but if you're eating at the weekend you will have to invest 130f for the *menu terroir*, with an extra course.
 Good value.

Map 4F   BERNAY 27309, Eure. 71 km S of Le Havre

 Sat.

I owe Bernay an apology. Not one of the previous editions of *Normandy* has even mentioned the place. I did have my reasons. It seemed ominous that a town of this size never merited a single entry in either Michelin or Gault-Millau (still doesn't, in the town itself), and a preliminary glimpse from the main road which follows the railway line and sidings looked highly unpromising, giving me the excuse to skip this one and get on with something more interesting. Even when my home town was twinned with Bernay and I could ask local dignitaries what they could recommend, there was much head scratching but little inspiration. My loss, because when this time, determined that no stone (or bistro) should be left unturned, I did investigate further I discovered that it's not at all bad. Maybe not worth a diversion, but if you should happen to find yourself nearby and in need of nourishment or a leg stretch, you could do far worse. I found it to be well provided with *brasseries*, three or four restaurants, two Logis de France hotels, and numerous bars.

The main shopping street is often traffic-jammed. Much nicer is the pedestrianised rue Gaston Folloppe, lined with old beamed buildings and leading down to the little river Cosnier. Plenty of alternative eateries here, with seating outside when the sun shines. I thought the cocktail bar *Le Piano* looked interesting, with a huge range of drinks and J.P.Bernais' wine bar *la Cour des Miracles*, with 100 whiskies and 40 calvados on sale. Tucked away behind the shop, through the courtyard, is an unexpected little bistro, good for light lunches – salads, home-made *foie gras*, cheeses, with a welcoming log fire on a cold March day.

Too cold alas for us to sit outside in the cobbled street, we chose instead to eat inside at:

Le Lapin Gourmand (R)S
r. Gaston Folloppe (0)232.43.42.32.10 cl. Sun.

NEW

Excellent value here in this little *charcutier/traiteur*. Something for everyone here, smart wine section next door to household necessities like Vim and dishcloths, take-away home-made *chacuterie*, plus eight simply-laid tables, all efficiently served by one efficient lady, wife of the *patron/chef*. You can order anything from the window display – quiches, *terrines*, ham, salads, home-made desserts, or choose something hot, freshly cooked. Husband had a fat ham omelette from a range which started at 20f and I enjoyed my large and lovely spinach and bacon salad for 25f. On the next table the parents, surrounded with their market shopping bags, tucked into steaks, while their children were blissfully into huge platefuls of golden crisp *frites*.

Ideal for a cheap lunch, with or without the kids.

Map 4E   **BEUVRON EN AUGE** 14430, Calvados. 30 km E of Caen, 15 km of Cabourg

---

(M) *Sat. p.m.*

Access: from Dozulé take the D85 then the D146 (or get pleasantly lost in the maze of country lanes).

If one had to select just one village to typify the Auge region Beuvron would be a strong contender. It not only has all the usual accoutrements of black-and-white timbered cottages, roses round the door, cider apple trees, black-and-white cattle, and farmhouses advertising their own cheese, but it centres on a superb example of ancient market *halles*. Far too good for animals and vegetables, it now houses a well-known Michelin-starred restaurant:

Le Pavé d'Auge (R)M-L
(0)231.79.26.71 Fax (0)231.39.04.45 cl. Mon.; Tues. o.o.s.; 2/12-15/1

Clever use has been made of the outstanding features of the heavily-beamed old market hall, so that one is impressed with its heritage but not over-awed. The Americans love it.

Jerome Bansard gives them exactly what they want – a meal full of flavours, often composed from local recipes and local ingredients (like the fish which is especially good) without too many surprises.

The cheapest menu at 130f is available on Sunday evenings – useful when so many restaurants are shut altogether, and on Saturday evenings, and lunch during the week. Otherwise it is 175f or 220f. The wine is not cheap but there is a commendable range of half-bottles.

La Boule d'Or (R)M
(0)231.79.78.78 cl. Sun. p.m.; Mon.; Jan.

Mme Duval proudly announces on her card that she has won the *Grand Prix National de la Tripe*, so I felt rather wimpish in ordering the *poulet Vallée d'Auge* instead. But it doesn't really matter – both dishes are typical of the region and both indicate the lack of pretension which is typical of this little restaurant. Nothing like so glamorous as its neighbour, le Pavé, but what it lacks in grandeur it makes up for in friendliness (and economy). Even in winter the interior is cheerful, with pink walls, pink napery, pink and green curtains and dark beams. We were served by the patron's niece, who had to keep rushing out to the street to reprove her son.

Just testing, I tried the only sophisticated dish on the 99f menu – the *terrine de petits légumes au poisson*. It looked good, but would have tasted better had it not been over-refrigerated. Husband did far better sticking to smoked ham – his plate overflowed with juicy mountain ham. My chicken was fine but his 'fish of the day', which turned out to be *lotte*, was better. Cheese board disappointing, *tarte aux pommes* unusually more like an English apple pie and none the worse for that.

I gather there are some rooms above the restaurant – all reports welcome.

N.B. The details supplied by the Boule d'Or state that the above are the closing days, but my notes say firmly that, because the weekends are so important, they close midweek. Best to ring and check.

There is another contender for Beuvron's culinary honours – la Forge, just opposite the Boule d'Or. Tablecloths are red check, food is cooked over the open fire. The reputation is that it is cheap, cheerful, smoky, fun, erratic, and that the patron is a 'character'. Any personal experiences?

Map 3E   **BEUZEVILLE** 27210, Eure. 15 km E of Honfleur, 14 km N of Pont l'Evêque

---

Ⓜ *Tues.*

Strategically sited, just off the autoroute, this small town makes an ideal staging post for basic shopping and, if you happen to be there on a Tuesday, a leg stretch round the market.

➤ Le Cochon d'Or (H)S (R)M
pl. du Général de Gaulle (0)232.57.70.76 Fax (0)232.42.25.70 cl. Mon.; Sun. p.m. Oct.-end Mar. and

➤ Petit Castel (H)M
(0)232.57.76.08 Fax (0)232.42.25.70 cl. 15/12-15/1

How good it is to see an old faithful not only continue to be faithful but to excel itself. There have been many changes here, particularly in the last few years, but they have been wise ones. The Cochon d'Or is greatly gentrified since it used to be our stop off the night boat for that first magical taste of France – coffee and croissants served in a Gaulois fug. Catherine and Olivier Martin, daughter and son-in-law of the previous proprietors, have taken over the reins and now the restaurant is very smart, with deep rose walls, flowery curtains and chairs, expensive carpets. Notwithstanding, when we dropped in and hesitantly asked for two coffees, M. Martin responded, 'I cannot refuse you.' Well he could have done. Many have. But here is a man out to please and that is high in my list of desiderata for a hotelier.

The whole set-up – modest rooms in the Cochon with a modest price tag, more luxurious rooms across the road in the Petit Castel – is equally to my liking. You are on a budget but still like your rooms spotless and the welcome warm? It's the Cochon for you. You want something smarter with new bathroom and view over garden? Make for the Petit Castel, to sleep and eat breakfast, then dine at the Cochon.

The re-furbishing of the Petit Castel goes on and the upgrading of the rooms is a continuous process. They have in common bright cheerful colours but otherwise are all different, so that you can specify double or twin bed, bath or shower, garden or road, and pay accordingly (but always assured of good value). In the Cochon the rooms are simple but infinitely better than many I've viewed at twice the price.

Best of all, because this all started off as a restaurant-with-rooms, rather than the other way round, the food has always been unusually good and is now better than ever, while prices have remained fair. It is good honest Norman cooking, unpretentious, copious and good value. That doesn't mean boring though. On the 103f menu for example you can choose a tart filled with mild sweet onions flavoured with thyme for a starter; the fish comes in various guises, with a Dover sole costing a reasonable 82f, and the *pâtisseries*, even on the 73f menu, is much more interesting than average.

Arrowed for its convenient position near coast and ferry, *gentil* management, good rooms, great value.

Rooms 180f in Cochon d'Or, from 255-320f in Le Petit Castel. Menus at 73f (not weekends), 103f, 150f and 220f.

Map H3   **BÉZANCOURT**, 76220, Seine-Mar. 10 km SW of Gournay by D316 and D62

A hamlet in lovely wooded countryside.

► **Château du Landel** (HR)M
(0)235.90.16.01 R cl. Sun. p.m.; Mon. 15/11-15/3

NEW   The 18C château was once a staging post on the pilgrims' route to Compostela. Now it is once again a peaceful relaxing haven for travellers.

It is the family home of M. and Mme Pierre Cardon who have converted the gracious rooms into a hotel with 17 individual bedrooms. Each room is totally different from its neighbour. You can choose a spacious luxurious example, dignified and elegant with brocade, or a smaller cheaper Mansard-window version, or a family suite. Ours was all pink and white, with the Toile de Jouy that the French love so much on walls, curtains and bed cover. This one had a well-fitted but tiny bathroom, others have larger bathrooms, smaller bedrooms, so if you get a chance to choose make sure you sort out your priorities. They cost from 450-700f.

The peacefulness is immediately striking as you approach the lovely building via a long drive. The grounds are extensive and delightful, the swimming pool is one of the best I have encountered in a hotel – large, well-heated and surrounded by plenty of

expensive recliners – and there is a tennis court in excellent
condition.

Chateau du Landel

M. and Mme Cardon are still very much in evidence and not
above making a bed or two when required but nowadays they leave
the day-to-day running of the hotel and the cooking to their son
Yves, who spent his childhood here. The 160f dinner menu yielded
haddock mousse, fillet of beef and a chocolate marquise, with a
choice of one alternative dish in each of the three courses –
admirably compact. The dining room is particularly attractive in
winter when the huge log fire blazes in the vast chimney. However,
fine weather would mean drinks on the terrace and a swim, so both
options are delightful.

I can hardly fault this one. The rooms are intrinsically lovely and
have been tastefully furnished and decorated, the grounds and
swimming pool are superb, the owners aim to please, and the
prices are good value for the quality. An arrow of course, but there
is one caveat. It was a Sunday night when I stayed at Landel and so
I have no first-hand experience of the food. Assistance please?

Map 3G **LA BOUILLE** 76530, Seine-Mar. 75 km E of Le Havre; 20 km W of Rouen

Ⓜ *Wed.*

La Bouille is a well-kept secret for many visitors who never think that a turn off the autoroute just one exit short of Rouen and a mere 3 km diversion could bring such rich rewards. If once they would wind down the corkscrewing hill to the peaceful little mediaeval village tucked between mighty river and sheltering escarpment they would be forever hooked.

They would discover beamy Norman cottages, a *crêperie* or two, a chemist, three hotels and several restaurants, but La Bouille's unique claim to fame is its proximity to a wide and interesting stretch of the Seine, where great barges and container ships pass astonishingly nearby, up and down to the docks at Rouen.

The *rouennais* of course have discovered the picturesqueness of the settlement long ago, as did the 19C landscape painters. This is a favourite Sunday excursion. There's a charming drive along the river bank to take the ferry across to Duclair and a little red *bac* chugs across from La Bouille too, to Sahurs, where's there's a café/bar by the water's edge and a modest Logis (see p. 203). But the No.1 treat is to book a table for lunch at one of the excellent restaurants for which La Bouille is known. The weather, of course, makes all the difference, so they tend to be packed out when the sun shines and deserted at other times.

When the gourmands have gone home it's a lovely place to stay on – peaceful, very near to the big city, which can be easily reached by whatever route you fancy. The easiest is to rejoin the autoroute, the quickest is to hold your nose and avert your eyes from the proliferation of heavy industry while following the road nearest to the river, via Moulineaux, Grande Couronne and Grande Quévilly, but the prettiest by far is to take the *bac* across the river and enjoy the little D51 for the first ten miles or so before it too gets immersed in the conglomeration.

St. Pierre (H)M (R)L
(0)235.18.01.01 Fax (0)233.48.59.82 cl. Sun. p.m.; Mon. o.o.s.; Jan.

When Bernard Huet was tragically killed in a car crash in 1995, heads were shaken and the end of the St. Pierre was prophesied. Bernard and Giselle had been such a good team – she up front, he taking care of the business side. Giselle has proved them wrong. After a terrible year, with her chef finding it too much to cope without Bernard's backing, she is now firmly in charge, with the help of her sister-in-law to do the books. The show must go on and she continues to welcome and advise, as tall, blonde, elegant and seemingly as cheerful as ever.

Just before Bernard died the whole of the downstairs area was redecorated. Out went the mauve and in came a more restful yellow and green – upholstery, carpet and curtains now in perfect harmony. The biggest change of all has been to the terrace, always La Bouille's prime viewing situation. Now there is a substantial sage-green trellis arrangement, providing the base for climbing plants and dividing up the area most attractively. On fine days the forty covers out here are keenly contested for.

The new young chef is shaping up well, showing imagination as well as confidence. The food is sophisticated and elegantly served, using prime expensive ingredients, especially seafood.

This is primarily a restaurant-with-rooms, but the rooms are a very good deal at a reasonable price. Make sure you get one of the three better ones overlooking the front though. You can lie in bed and watch the great ships pass by your window as if drawn by an invisible rope. Furnishing is vaguely oriental, with cane providing the character.

Arrowed for unique position, good cooking and comfortable rooms.

Menus from 160f (midweek).

7 rooms 300-350f.

➤ **Les Gastronomes** (R)M
pl. de Bateau (0)235.18.02.07 cl. Wed. p.m.; Thurs.; 1/2-15/2; 15/9-30/9

A pretty little doll's house, one room down, one up, the latter with view of the Seine if you crane a little. Rustic and cosy with tables outside if it gets a bit too cosy in summer.

The brothers Marrière are in charge, one in the kitchen and one doing the welcome bit, both charming. Jacques' cooking gets better and better – traditional but with individual trimmings, skilful sauces, The wine list and the service are beyond reproach and the atmosphere has been specially praised by readers, so the arrow certainly stays.

Menus from 145f.

La Maison Blanche (R)M
quai Hector Malot (0)235.18.01.90 cl. Sun. p.m.; Mon.; 15/7-6/8

Odile Rozada greets; Philippe, her husband, stays where he belongs – in the kitchen, from whence emerges a stream of simple dishes, simply cooked, conjured up from fresh ingredients – veal sweetbreads sautéed with port, salmon roasted in rock salt.

The old white house again overlooks the river, with a pleasant interior decorated with old furniture and ancient faience. A good stop for tea, this one, with that panoramic view thrown in.
Menus from 100f.

La Maison Blanche

Les Gastronomes

Map 5G   **LE BRETEUIL** 27160, Eure. 31 km SW of Evreux

Ⓜ *Wed.*

> The little town is almost surrounded by an arm of the Iton, forming a pool bordered by the public gardens. Adèle, daughter of William the Conqueror, was married in the 11C church here; the pillars in the transept date from William's reign, but the interior's most striking feature is the arcades in the nave, resting on twelve massive pillars built of *grison*, the red stone of the area. The Hôtel de Ville in the market square must qualify as the narrowest ever.

Le Biniou (R)S
76 pl. Lafitte (0)232.29.70.61 cl. Tues. p.m.; Wed; 19/8-3/9; 23/12-4/1

NEW

> I am always delighted to discover the Binious of this world. Small, unpretentious, welcoming, in the market square – that's my recipe for my kind of restaurant. It specialises in *fruits de mer*, and 125f will buy a platter that should keep you busy for a happy hour or so, but if you're not in that mood catch the 65f mid-week menu – fish mousse, steak *au poivre*, *tart du jour*, or the 110f version – 9 oysters, roast salmon, cheese, pineapple charlotte. You can't really go wrong.

Map 3E   **LE-BREUIL-EN-AUGE** 14130, Calvados. 21 km S of Deauville, 9 km N of Lisieux

> On the main road, the D 579; if time is no object, the D48 from Pont l'Evêque to Lisieux is a much more attractive route. Le Breuil, which fills in the gap between the two roads, has little to recommend it except:

➤ **Le Dauphin** (R)M
(0)231.65.08.11 Fax (0)231.65.12.08. cl. Sun. p.m.; Mon.; except Aug.

> The solid white building right on the road gives little indication of the pleasures within. The decor has been kept deliberately simple – white cloths, tiled floors, cane chairs, but the warmth is there, both in the comforting log fire (and Le Dauphin is at its best when it's a bit chilly outside) and in the welcome. *Chef-patron* Régis Lecomte has not allowed a royal visit (Her Britannic Majesty no less) to put him above welcoming his customers and to making a further round after they have finished their meal to check that all was *comme il faut* (and to collect their justified congratulations).

There is a photo of the Queen and a framed letter from Buck House saying how much she enjoyed her visit in 1987. All credit to whoever arranged the stop for having chosen exactly what I imagine was required – a typically Norman restaurant. I asked Régis why he thought he had been selected. 'Because I speak English I suppose', he disclaimed modestly.

Gratifyingly the prices have remained modest too. His 170f menu (not Sat.) is a snip for cooking of the very highest quality, well meriting the Michelin star. It featured one of the house specialities, a *barbecue d'huitres spéciales d'Isigny aux lardons*, which I had to try. Basically grilled oysters, but given exactly the right timing, flavoured with plenty of garlic but always retaining the oysters' delicacy, set in a thin bouillon full of savours. I stayed with the fish for the next course, a *pavé de morue roti* because cod has become my favourite fish since we have learned to cook it properly, and roast is a good way to do it, on a bed of spicy green lentils. Immaculate cheese board, then the *tarte aux pommes* by which all other *tartes aux pommes* should be judged – crispest pastry, melting apples, flavoured with lemon and served with a cinnamon ice cream. Perfection and worthy of two arrows.

Menus at 170f, 220f except Sat. p.m.

Map 5A   **BRÉHAL**, Manche. 10 km N of Granville

(M) *Tues.*

A small market town at the junction of several roads, left as a backwater after being bypassed by the D971.

➤ **Hotel de la Gare** (HR)S
1 pl. Ct. Godard (0)233.61.61.11

A little hotel (just nine rooms) in the centre of the town, with the friendliest atmosphere imaginable. One of my absolute favourites.

Responsible for the cheery atmosphere are the owners, Pierrette and Georges Coffre, who are particularly fond of English guests and are able to converse with them in their own language. Georges proudly showed me his garden behind the hotel. 'Who says we don't grow oranges in Normandy?' And there was living proof that indeed they do – tubs of citrus trees loaded with fruit. It's a calm green place to sit, take breakfast or a drink.

The rooms are very comfortable, and a double with a bath will cost you 300f. Those with showers are 280f. The garage is free.

Georges is *chef de cuisine* and this is a case where demi-pension is a good idea, because his cooking is generous and way above average (280f per person). Otherwise menus start at 78f, or 72f for lunch.

An arrow for just about everything.

'*Comfortable room just across the courtyard. Secure parking behind locked doors with a coded entrance. Reasonable three course dinner for 94f. Friendly and helpful staff.*'

Map 5A   **BRÉVILLE SUR MER** 50290, Manche. 3 km N of Granville

---

The beach here is a joggers' paradise – windswept dunes as far as the eye can see; there's a golf course too, with good sea views. But personally I would give it a miss and head straight for Granville. As the hotel scene there is a bit bleak, I was forced to look around the neighbourhood and found one possibility here on the main Coutances road.

La Beaumonderie (HR)M-L
20 rte. de Coutances (0)233.50.36.36 Fax (0)233.50.36.45

NEW   Newly opened as a hotel in 1995, this large Edwardian villa, freshly painted, is now looking very smart.

As well it should – this is definitely the most up market hotel in the area. Rooms are lovely; all twelve are different but tastefully furnished with luxury bathrooms. Everyone wants those with a sea view of course and they will set you back 600f, but there are cheaper ones (300f) at the front of the house, which is well removed from the road, behind a soothing garden.

There are two inestimable and rare assets here – a large heated covered swimming pool in the grounds, and a bar – Le Blues, described as the place to 'enjoy rare whiskies or home made cocktails round the fireplace at the English pub. Enjoy a wonderful plush atmosphere'. Well it's not *that* plush.

The Orangerie restaurant I have not tried, but it has a lovely view towards the sea, and is given lots of character by an umbrella-like roof and a big open fireplace. Menus start at 145f. Demi pension is 175f on top of the room price. More reports obviously needed, but this certainly fills the gap for a peaceful luxury hotel in this area.

Map 4F	**BRIONNE** 27800, Eure. 28 km S of Pont Audemer, 76 km E of Le Havre

Ⓜ *Thurs.*

Following the D39 along the left bank of the river Risle is a delightful way to approach the town, whose tourist attractions comprise a park on the river bank and the ruins of an 11C keep, from which the hotel takes its name.

Auberge du Vieux Donjon (H)S (R)M
pl. Frémont-des-Essarts (0)232.44.80.62 Fax (0)232.45.83.23 cl. Mon.; Sun. p.m.; o.o.s.; 15/10-31/10

Half-timbered, lots of flowers, pretty china, old beams, red ceiling in between, pleasant owners, inexpensive.

Serge Chauvigny's cooking continues to please most customers, though his prices have gone up alarmingly since I first wrote about him, leading to higher expectations and recently there have been mixed reactions. One reader rued the tinned veg (quite right too) and described the food as 'basic', the service as amateur, so the arrow will have to be suspended.

There are eight simple but comfortable rooms. Insist on one overlooking the courtyard because the ones in the front can be very noisy. The courtyard is a big attraction – most pleasant to sit here for breakfast, and dinner, or just to relax among the foliage after a hard day on the tourist belt.

'*Every bit as good as your recommendation. We can recommend the plateau des fruits de mer on the à la carte menu at 220f for two people; the set menu at 160f is also very good. Our only criticism is that the breakfast was very frugal – one baguette each with packaged butter and jam. Otherwise your arrow classification very well justified.*' Michael Stubbs

Rooms are 210-270f; menus from 78f (lunch); otherwise from 120f.

Map 5D	**BRIOUZE** 61220, Orne. 17 km SE of Flers

Ⓜ *Mon.*

A pleasant quiet little town with sloping market square.

Hotel Sophie (HR)S
pl. Albert 1er. (0)233.66.00.30 Fax (0)233.64.97.01 cl. Sat.; 15/8-31/8

NEW

The kind of modest, good-value little hotel that is fast disappearing from France, partly because of high taxation and partly because the children are not interested in the commitment involved in running a family hotel.

Here the patrons are aptly named M. and Mme Excellent. Didier is *chef* and cooks old-fashioned dishes like *gigôt*, *rosbeef*, and *côte de boeuf grillée*. But, surprisingly away from the sea, the speciality at Sophie's is fresh fish. When there is an *arrivée* (delivery); it appears on all the menus from 70f to 190f. For us it happened to be oysters and we weren't complaining.

Local popularity is a good indication of the value on offer here in the small dining room, red check cloths, lovely smells, and the bar to retreat to later.

The nine rooms are small and simple, with showers, perhaps not quite such good value at 250f, but the food is awaiting more reports for an arrow.

Map 4D   **CAEN** 14000, Calvados. 107 km W of Le Havre. 119 km SE of Cherbourg

---

Ⓜ *every day from Tues. to Sun. but Sun. is the big day*

Caen, capital of Lower Normandy, is a city of contrasts – the dismal post-war re-building and the magnificent monuments that survived, the grid of new streets and the winding alleys of the old, the antiquity of the abbeys and the castle and the youthful vivacity of the university in the city's heart.

Sad though it is to ponder that we shall never enjoy again the three-quarters of the buildings that crumbled in the wartime devastation, there remains enough of the old city to make a visit profitable. My advice would be to ignore the area south of the rue St. Pierre (apart from the excellent shops and restaurants), and to concentrate on two particularly attractive localities, never forgetting of course the abbeys and the castle, which is the focal point of the whole city. Just below it, in the paved Vaugueux area, the character is more fifteenth than twentieth century. The narrow cobbled streets and crazily-angled gabled houses have been carefully restored and a stroll around the antique shops and a coffee at a pavement café by the fountain makes a pleasant diversion.

Less touristy, less self-conscious, perhaps more typical of the 11C Caen that has been lost, is the area to the north of the rue St.

Pierre, where dignified patricians' houses, mediaeval beams and plaster, winding alleyways and a great leafy square, the Place St. Sauveur, deserve every visitor's attention. Turn up the rue Froide and wander at will, looking up as well as around. Interesting boutiques are springing up in these pedestrianised lanes, contrasting with the department and chain stores in the modern section, and some of the most rewarding restaurants have realised the appeal of the old buildings.

The rue St. Pierre itself has been vastly improved by pedestrianisation and it is now a calm stroll, window-shopping, most of the way towards the Hotel de Ville and one of Caen's great monuments, the Abbaye des Hommes.

For all its reincarnations since the 11C, Caen is still first and foremost William's town. References to the great Duke of Normandy and his Queen, Matilda, crop up repeatedly in the names of shops, streets and of course in the two great abbey churches. The Abbaye aux Hommes was William's outward sign of repentance for the sin he committed in marrying a blood relation, against the wishes of the Pope. In fact his cousin Matilda had shown some reluctance to the idea of marrying a bastard, causing William to drag her by her hair around her chamber until she was convinced. Convincing the Pope he left to his Secretary, Lanfranc (*see* Bec Helouin), who talked the pontiff into rescinding his prohibition of the match. It was a nice touch for the happy pair to build their spiritual memorials at opposite limits of the city, with the great fortified castle in the centre protecting them from their worldly enemies.

The monastery buildings, rebuilt in the 18C and now used as the Town Hall, protected the citizens of Caen during the bombardment of 1944; many thousands of them took refuge inside, and the complex was miraculously saved (as indeed was Matilda's abbey, the Abbaye aux Dames, though somewhat battered).

Only a slab before the high altar now marks the spot where William was buried. The tomb was ravaged once by the Huguenots in the 16C and again during the Revolution when his remains were thrown into the river. The dedication leaves no doubts about the priorities: 'Duke of Normandy, King of England'.

The building of his abbey began in 1077, romanesque, and was finished two centuries later, gothic, a striking contrast of styles within and without. Recently cleaned, the amber Caen stone is illuminated by light flooding through the three layers of windows, framed in graceful arches.

Matilda's abbey is less colourful, but impressive, as is her mausoleum inside.

Other points of interest are the capitals in the choir and the 11C crypt and the monastery, again rebuilt in the 18C; look out for the

Caen - Abbaye aux Hommes

remarkable fountains in the lavatorium, the cloisters and the double staircase.

Just outside Caen, well marked from all directions, is the *Mémoriale*, the museum for peace. If that sounds less than rivetting, especially for those not excited about the war, be prepared to be enlightened, inspired and very moved. The latest technology is used to bring the events to life, wraparound screens show contemporary films taken by both sides, skilfully representing both points of view, with powerful sound effects. Some of the photographs are harrowing, particularly those of the youthful Norman freedom fighters about to be hanged for their resistance. Allow more time that you could imagine necessary. Open every day from 9 a.m. to 7 p.m. and until 9 p.m. in July and August.

The best tip I can pass on concerning Caen is not to miss the market that fills the Place Courtonne and spills over on to the neighbouring quays. Sunday can be a difficult day to fill in northern France, especially when the sun is not shining, and a wander around the eclectic stalls that put on show so temptingly their offerings, literally from chalk to cheese, is a clever way to fill an hour or so. Cafés and bars in this area stay open to cater for market-day appetites.

Hotels: Oh dear. Keen though I am to suggest lodgings fit for this interesting city, which would make such a good base for a winter breakaway, I must admit the choice is slender. So slender that I am driven to include a chain hotel, since most of the rest are modern and characterless too. At least the Mercure has views over the yacht basin:

Hotel Mercure (HR)M
r. de Courtonne (0)231.47.24.24 Fax (0)231.47.43.88

Big rooms, well equipped, practical, central. 110 rooms from 460-550f.

Holiday-City Centre (HR)M
pl. Foch (0)231.27.57.57 Fax (0)231.27.57.58

NEW This is the old Hotel Malherbe re-furbed. Once I had got over the appalling name, I quite liked it and would now rank it as first choice in the city. Most of the rooms have pleasant aspects over the green expanse of the Hippodrome, perhaps ten minutes walk from the centre. Everything has been smartened up and the rooms are spacious and gracious. There is a restaurant, Le Rabelais, downstairs, where the food is not at all bad.

92 rooms from 350-580f.

In vain did I search for a smaller, cheaper hotel to recommend. To re-cap the last edition's suggestions, **La Moderne**, 116 bd. Mar. Leclerc (0)231.86.04.23, , which had gone from top of my list to bottom, has now been refurbished and its central position scores highly, but the English theme is not for me. (40 rooms from 320-630f.) The **Quatrans**, 17 r. Gemare (0)231.86.25.57, scored as many thumbs down as thumbs up; although the rooms are pleasant, the patronne was not. (36 rooms 170-260f.) **Le Relais des Gourmets**, 15 r. Géole, (0)231.86.06.01, apparently drew no takers at all I would have thought that its 28 luxury rooms at 380-580f were now good value, but need further reports.

Restaurants: Here the scene is brighter, with plenty of choice in all categories, including one of only three two-star Michelin restaurants in Normandy.

➤ La Bourride (R)L
1 r. du Vaugueux (0)231.93.50.76 cl. Sun. p.m.; Mon.; 4/1-14/1; 19/8-2/9

I have followed Michel Bruneau's career with interest and delight, since, fresh from Le Manoir d'Hastings, he set up here in the picturesque Vaugueux area, setting unparalleled standards of excellence among the pizza-bars and fast-food outlets. The first *macaron* followed swiftly and now the second ensures that his tables are always full. So if you are planning a treat, make sure you book ahead. I can hardly fault the experience. I like the inside of the galleried restaurant as much as I like the venerable exterior; I like the intimacy of its scale – so tiny that you feel privileged (but never cramped); I like not being required to add a drink at the bar on to the bill – no pursed lips if you prefer to go straight to your table, I like the raised fire on cold winter nights and the gentle classical music that soothes rather than blasts. I like the *amuses gueules*, a taste of the joys to come rather than a mass production job. And of course I like, very much indeed, the food.

Michel never loses sight of his Norman origins and there are always plenty of regional delicacies on the menu. But with the touch of genius that makes you place your trust in the man, even if he offers you sausages. Which he does – *charlotte d'andouille* is one of his favourite specialities, and is guaranteed to convert even the most hardened sausage-phobe. If you wish to sample the definitive *tripes à la mode de Caen, poule vallée d'Auge,* or *tarte aux pommes* this is the time to order them. The only snag is that any subsequent encounters are bound to disappoint.

Quality like this does not come cheap. Unless of course you take in the mid-week (or Sat. lunch) 196f menu, which is a true bargain. Otherwise it's 350f or a dizzying 480f. You could always order just one dish from the *carte*, if you have that kind of restraint, but at any level expect the wine to match the food in cost and standard.

Arrowed for some of the best cooking in Normandy.

➤ **Le Carlotta** (R)M
16 quai Vendeuvre (0)231.86.68.99 cl. Sun; 15 days in Aug.

NEW

Restaurants gastronomiques are all very well but my favourite kind of restaurant is the *brasserie*. I love them because they are so very French, so very flexible, so very full of character. You eat or drink what you want, when you want, without any kind of pretension or fuss. Sadly, like many other good things that one took for granted in France, the good ones are becoming rare. *Brasserie* is becoming synonymous with fast food outlet and a smoky, noisy den serving cheap microwaved food is not at all what I have in mind. Here in Caen is a gem, a paragon in the species. Carlotta in fact is so excellent that it breaks the usual *brasserie* rule that you don't have to book. Here, especially at lunchtime when the local businessmen settle down at their favourite tables, you would be asking for disappointment in assuming you could sit down immediately. But whether you book or whether you wait, it will be well worthwhile.

This is the very essence of *brasserie*-dom. Here are the leather *banquettes* the art deco lights and murals, white napery, waiters in black suits and starched aprons, some even sporting moustaches. The dishes are equally traditional – roast duck, beef tartare, *tête de veau* – plus wonderfully fresh fish, all served in portions to satisfy pre-Weightwatcher appetites. Mine could not handle the menus, admirable though they were: 92f bought six oysters, roast veal and *pâtisserie maison*, or the *Menu Affaires* offers just two courses with wine for 110f. The *hommes d'affaires* looked very happy with their *filet de boeuf* and *pâtisserie*, washed down with honest red. No, I settled for a simple sole, which proved to be simply the best. Cooked in butter and served with potatoes mashed with garlic, parsley and lemon and a tomato stuffed with *ratatouille* for a very reasonable 85f. Save room if you can for the desserts and particularly the *assiette gourmandes*, a platter of *nine* different puds like *profiteroles*, pistachio sorbet, *nougat glacé* with cherry sauce, *tarte Tatin*. At 38f too good a bargain to pass by.

Arrowed for lively, buzzy atmosphere, excellent honest cooking.

Le Boeuf Ferré (R)M-S
10 r. des Croisiers (0)231.85.36.40 cl. Sat. lunch; Sun.

In one of the oldest, most attractive streets in Caen. To find it, turn up the rue Froide and take a right. The original Boeuf Ferré was so successful that it overflowed into a satellite next door. Same menu, different door, similar decors, with raftered ceilings and stone walls. Both have a youthful, animated atmosphere (sometimes, with regrettable piped pop) and are particularly popular with local office workers at lunchtime. It is easy to see why the place is so well patronised. The 99f menu offers excellent value – like a *terrine* of sea trout with chive cream sauce, then fresh salmon with sorrel, topped up with wickedly calorific *profiteroles*. The 120f has more choice and includes a complimentary Kir.

l'Ambroisie (R)M-S
11 r. des Croisiers (0)231.50.30.32 open every day

Opposite the Boeuf and originally benefitting from its overflow. Now it thrives on its own reputation and, because it is still trying hard, I think I like it even better than the opposition, which may have become too popular. Certainly it's quieter, more elegant in an understated way, with good service. On the 75f menu I enjoyed smoked trout, *pièce de boeuf* and strawberries.

Le Pressoir (R)M
3 ave. H. Cheron (0)231.73.3271 cl. Sun. p.m.; Mon.; 4/8-26/8

This attractive little restaurant near the hippodrome has gone from strength to strength since I first wrote about it and classed it as (S). It now has an entry in Michelin and the cheapest menu price has almost doubled at 115f. This is still good value, however, and the cooking continues to be gratifyingly unpretentious, with items like *cassoulette* of mussels, grilled beef, *sole meunière*. It's a charming little restaurant with an ancient cider press justifying its name, old copper utensils and authentically worm-eaten furniture.

➤ Le Dauphin (R)M
29 r. Gémare (0)231.86.22.26 Fax (0)231.86.35.14 cl. Sat. lunch; 15/7-6/8

The Dauphin does have rooms and it would be so helpful if I could recommend a central bed with a restaurant attached, but in this case the thumbs down have all been for the hotel part of the deal. Readers have agreed with my impression that they are too expensive for what they offer, somewhat dark and sometimes noisy. So we'll forget that bit and concentrate on the restaurant.

Robert Chabredier never forgets his Norman heritage. That said, his cooking is never dull and predictable. He uses seafood to stuff ravioli, his salt marsh lamb is meltingly tender and he sparks up the traditional apple tart with rhubarb. Go for the 95f menu (not weekends) and you will be delighted. The building was once an old priory in the oldest part of Caen, close to William's castle. In its heavily restored reincarnation the rustic dining room has been retained and the atmosphere there is warm and friendly.

Arrowed as one of the most agreeable places to eat in Caen.

Le Gastronome (R)S-M
43 r. St. Sauveur (0)231.86.57.75 cl. Sat. lunch; Sun. p.m.; 27/7-9/8

NEW A little restaurant in the road bordering the Place St. Sauveur. Excellent value on the 86f. menu.

Le Panier à Salades (R)S-M
24 r. Pierre Girard (0)231.34.22.22

NEW I am always delighted to find a good salad restaurant in France, and this one is good enough to tempt the firmest carnivores. They need not be deprived of their meat because it comes in various guises here along with the greenery. There is a vast range of salads that should please every fancy, and better-than-average desserts, all served in a pleasant atmosphere in an art deco decor. Up to you how much you spend – it could be as little as 40f or as much as a full menu elsewhere.

La Poêle d'Or (R)S
7 r. Laplace (0)231.85.39.86. cl. Sun. p.m.; Sat.; 14/7-15/8. Christmas to New Year

Absolutely nothing to look at, in the boring new section of the city, just off the rue St. Jean near the quai de Juillet. However, the Golden Pan has been retaining its faithful clientele against the new competition by keeping its prices down and giving the customers what they want – simple straightforward Norman cooking. Menus start at 65f and there is a good carafe wine.

La Poterne (R)S
20 r. Porte-Berger (0)231.93.57.46

I like the Poterne for a drink before dinner, either outside on the cobbles of the Vaugueux area, a good vantage point for watching the world go by, or in winter inside by the log fire in the cosy pubby atmosphere. The food has improved recently and the salads and simple meat dishes come in generous portions.

L'Assiette (R)S
2 pl. Fontelle (0)231.85.21.89 cl. Sun.

A cheap and very cheerful restaurant between the Hotel de Ville
and the Palais de Justice, handy after a visit to the Abbaye des
Hommes. I like the fact that they change the menus every day *selon
le marché*. There is a menu *Terre* and a menu *Mer*, starting at 85f.
Good value and well recommended locally.

A late recommendation which I have not yet checked out but which
sounds like the answer to many a prayer is a little hotel in the old
quarter, the **Hotel Cordeliers**, 4 r. des Cordeliers (0)231.86.37.15.
15 rooms a mere 130-350f. Reports particularly welcome.

Map 3E　　**CANAPVILLE** 14800, Calvados. 6 km S of Deauville by N177

Jarrasse (R)M
(0)231.65.21.80 cl. Tues., and Wed. o.o.s.

NEW　　A busy *nationale* is not the place where you might expect to find a
picturesque thatched cottage, but Restaurant Jarrasse is just that. It
used to be called Auberge du Vieux Cour, but now takes its name
from its *patron/chef*, François Jarrasse. Very pretty inside as well as
out, with the dining room painted a sunny yellow. Emphasis is made
on the fact that there is definitely no 'micro' and everything is
cooked *sur commande*, so don't go in a hurry.
　　Food is both smart – fresh *foie gras* and smoked salmon – for
the Parisians who love to drop in here on their way to Deauville, and
simple – farm chicken roasted with mushrooms, and pan-fried bass
for the locals.
　　Pleasant service from the youthful Mme Jarrasse.
　　Menus: 160f with wine included and 200f.

Map 4E　　**CANON** 14270, Calvados. 20 km SE of Caen on the D47. 6 km S
of Mery Corbon off the N13

Deep in the Calvados countryside on the old coach route from
Lisieux to Falaise, the château and, particularly, the gardens of
Canon make a delightful diversion from the main tourist attractions
of the region. Essential, though, to pick a fine day, when a stroll
around the magnificent lakes, following the many streams and

springs and admiring the rose gardens, set out in the 'English' style, can be best appreciated.

Around the 18C château (not open to the public) are the Chartreuses, a succession of flower gardens surrounded by ancient walls, on which apricots, figs and peaches flourish. Wander deep into the woods following the streams (bluebell time especially) and you will stumble upon neo-classical ruins, a Chinese kiosk and a temple.

The house and gardens were designed by an 18C lawyer who instigated the feast of the Bonnes Gens. Once a year the villagers chose from among their numbers a Bonne Mère, a Bon Vieillard (Good Old Man)and a Bon Chef de Famille and rewarded their virtues by a feast in their honour. Bonnes Gens is still the alternative name for Canon.

Open weekends and holidays from Easter to end of June from 2 p.m.- 7 p.m. and every afternoon, except Tues. from 1/7-30/9.

Map 2F   **CANY-BARVILLE** 76450, Seine-Mar. 21 km W of Fécamp by the D925

The Hotel de Ville occupies prime position in the main market square.

Auberge de France (R)M
(0)235.97.80.10 cl. Sun. p.m.; Tues.

NEW   Hard to know where to eat here – the rustic beamed dining room has a warm welcoming air, but I think I would have to choose a table on the terrace overlooking the sparkling little river Durdent. The 120f menu offered a home-made *terrine* left on the table, a *ragout* of mushrooms with garlic, roast duck, a *sorbet*, cheese and dessert. I liked everything about the auberge and its welcoming hostess very much and would welcome some confirmatory reports for an arrow.

Map 2B   **CAP LEVI** 50840 Fermanville, Manche. 15 km E of Cherbourg

---

The D116 out of Cherbourg follows the coast closely until it reaches Fermanville where it carries straight on and ignores the pimple on the map that is Cap Lévi, the coast's northernmost extremity. That is the good news because very few cars bother to deviate. Unless of course their drivers already know about the wonderful coastal walks along the old coastguards' routes, or the uncrowded beaches to lie on or the rocks to scramble over when the tide recedes, or the feeling of being almost out at sea among the passing cargo boats and the lighthouse's warning flashes. There is a tiny harbour here but not much else, except:

➤ **La Lorette** (HR)S
(0)233.44.49.49 Fax (0)233.44.16.15

NEW

Named after the parish of Notre Dame de Lorette in Paris, which founded a children's summer camp here and built a chapel in pink granite. Before that the house was owned by a sea-captain; in the days when Cherbourg was an important port for ocean liners there must have been plenty of interest for him to train his telescope upon.

Nowadays the reincarnation is that of a six-bedroomed hotel, family-run, warm and friendly. They welcome all kinds – ramblers, cyclists, families, weekenders, with equal enthusiasm. The dining room is particularly attractive, with a varnished boat acting as bar. Menus with lots of local seafood are 90f or 140f, but you could settle for a *crêpe* or *galette* with no eyebrows raised.

Breakfast can be taken in bed, looking out onto the sea, or in the garden, with plenty of space for childish exuberance.

Rooms cost 195f or 220f, all with showers and lavs.

'*Pleasant reception, a good place for families, though the soundproofing not perfect. Owner lives in adjoining house with his own family. Simply-cooked seafood dishes very good.*' Lesley Goodden.

This must be the only 'S' hotel so near the sea, so near the ferries, that combines flexible good food, comfortable accommodation and a warm welcome, so an arrow.

Map 2B   **CARENTAN** 50500, Manche. 50 km SE of Cherbourg; 69 km NW of Caen

---

Ⓜ *Mon.*

The centre of the Manche dairy farming industry, a town of many squares too full of cars, a nice old church and some shady arcades, but nothing in the way of lively bar or *brasserie*.

An unsuspected whole new world is to be found if you follow the signs to *Port de Plaisance*. There, dominating the flat marshy landscape of the estuary of the river Douves, rises a forest of masts. The marina here shelters hundreds of boats during the winter. Take the opportunity of a gulp of ozone by taking a walk along the banks of the canal.

Auberge Normande (R)M
bld. Verdun (0)233.42.28.28

The tendency was to shy away from the Auberge Normande when its last patron, the darling of local gastronomes, decamped for Honfleur, but now things have settled down under the new owners, the very rustic, very Normande inn has been smartened up and the buzz is that the cooking, if not still Michelin star-worthy, is very good.

The 130f menu yielded oysters with scrambled eggs, *gigôt* of salt marsh lamb, cheeses and dessert, with a *trou Normand* thrown in halfway through. There is a cheaper 90f version. Worth a new look.

Map 3A   **CARTERET** 50270 Barneville-Carteret, Manche. 37 km SW of Cherbourg

---

Ⓜ *Sat.*

I never thought Carteret could ever change. Its bucket 'n spade, sun 'n fun, easy-going, family-friendly image seemed timeless and immutable. You don't go to Carteret for the latest trends, you go because you fancy an unsophisticated undemanding holiday, gilded with a touch of nostalgia for your own youth spent in similar surroundings.

The surroundings here are still lovely. The little town is built on an estuary whose seaward curves beg for paint-brush or camera. The sandy beach is wide and wonderful especially at low water, with rocks and rivulets to add interest. Sheltering under the cliffs is a row of wooden beach huts where you might expect to see Mum and Dad sitting in deck chairs watching their offspring making sand castles, skirts tucked in knickers, floppy white beach-hats.

So far so little change; the new bit is at the other end of the town, where a new marina has been built and a promenade landscaped. There are new shops, catering mostly for tourists, and the whole place seems to have extricated itself from its time-warp, which may or may not be a good thing. I still like it very much.

One change that is very good news is the arrival of a new hotel:

➤ **Hotel des Ormes** (H)M
quai Barbey d'Aurevilly (0)233.52.23.50 Fax (0)233.52.91.65

NEW   This old house set back from the new road by the marina had only been open seven months when I called, but already it was full, and when I had had a look round I could see why. The owner has cleverly decorated the ten comfortable rooms in light, bright and

*Hotel des Ormes
Carteret*

cheerful fabrics and paint, and they all have pleasant aspects over either the sea or the flowery garden at the rear. There is no restaurant, but the breakfast room and salon are also agreeable places to sit, should the weather rule out the peaceful garden. A visitor's valuable vintage Bentley was securely parked at the bottom. All the rooms have luxurious tiled bathrooms, with bath or shower, and cost from 380f for a double with one bed to 620f for a three-bedded room. Arrowed for the best accommodation in an attractive location.

► **The Marine** (H)M (R)L
(0)233.53.83.31 Fax (0)233.53.39.60 R cl. Sun. p.m. and Mon.; in Feb.; Mar. and Oct. Mon. lunch April-June, and 15/1-15/2

It has been many moons since the Marine was a simple family hotel, and the fifth generation of Cesnes are now in charge. Laurent was not content to take over in the kitchen without some impressive work experience in top kitchens elsewhere – Taillevent to name but one – and a Michelin star was his due reward. The hotel is so near

Carteret

the water that he could stick out a fishing-line from the terrace to provide the ingredients for the next meal.

Fish figures strongly on his menus, in guises to suit both new customers lured by the *macaron* and old faithfuls who might be disappointed to find too many changes. Plaice arrives with an original sauce derived from another Norman staple – Camembert – but *langoustines* are simply roasted to retain their natural flavour and juices. He's good at tripe too. For this standard of cooking the 135f menu (not Sat. p.m. nor Sun. lunch) is a tremendous bargain; otherwise the choices start at 195f. Small wonder that the restaurant is always full.

The 28 rooms likewise – you'll have to be quick off the mark to get one of the best views, overlooking the estuary. None of them is particularly large nor grand, either in the main hotel or in the annexe across the road, but they are comfortable enough, at 290-520f (you pay for that view) and the breakfasts are good.

The Marine has always been a lovely place to stay, with a drink on the west-facing terrace overlooking the estuary as the sun goes down guaranteed to be a holiday highspot, but now with the exceptional cooking of Laurent as a bonus, it is more desirable than ever. The arrow stays of course.

▶ l'Hermitage (HR)M
*Promenade de l'Abbé Lebouteiller (0)233.04.96.29 Fax (0)233.04.78.87 cl.
Sun; 15/11-15/12; 10 days Jan.*

The terrace of this long-established fish restaurant overlooking the water has been admirably smartened up recently, with tubs of manicured bay and window boxes, and immaculately laid tables, served by smart waiters. A game of musical chairs has to be endured to get a table here on a fine summer day, but it will be worth it. Inside is nowhere near so special – modern pine decor and not a lot of atmosphere in the large dining room. But the food in both sections is to be commended, especially the fresh and lavish *plâteaux de fruits de mer*, which have greatly pleased readers. Menus from 95f but a single dish of beautiful fish for the same price is probably a better bet.

The really exciting news concerns the rooms that have been built above the restaurant. You have to climb the hill behind to reach them, and will be rewarded by a superb view from their terraces. They vary in size and price, but all are ultra-modern, and exceptionally well equipped, with kitchenettes apiece (which should keep the cost down somewhat, although it is certainly not excessive at 250-500f).

'*We stayed in a holiday flat behind the restaurant. These are beautifully equipped, bright, comfortable, spacious, wonderful view and would be ideal for a short, self-catering family holiday. The breakfast was walked up the hill on a tray piping hot. Excellent bathroom, bath, hot water, etc. Very quiet. Dinner superb in parts. Huge spider crabs, crunchy fresh and of unparalleled deliciousness and vast assiettes de mer. Vegetables awful, soggy chips, overcooked carrots, but good steak. Choose the fish dishes which are after all their speciality.*' Tim and Alice Renton.

I think that accommodation like this in such an appealing setting, with the option of eating in or at the Marine deserves yet another arrow.

Map 2F	**CAUDEBEC-EN-CAUX** 76490, Seine-Mar. 51 km E of Le Havre, 36 km W of Rouen

 Sat.

Things are looking brighter in Caudebec these days. Nothing can disguise the hideous re-building that took the place of the picturesque town that bordered the Seine pre-war, but pedestrianisation, flowers and fountains certainly help. It's looking less sad and does have some obvious advantages: the site of course, overlooking the river, with pleasant gardens in which to sit and picnic, the wonderful 15C flamboyant church, which Henri IV once described as 'the most beautiful chapel in the kingdom', and which survived the fire that devastated most of the town in 1940, and the Saturday market, which fills the Place du Marché with colour, smells and animation. And that's about it. There are two hotels in prime positions overlooking the river, which have been here for donkeys' years and are still very popular with the Brits. They are the Normandie – (0)235.96.24.11, rooms, from 290-305f, menus from 95f (not weekends) and the Normotel La Marine, (0)235.96.20.11, rooms from 250-420f meals from 98f. They are both clean and efficient, but a bit impersonal for my taste, and often taken over by groups.

Le Manoir de Rétival (HR)L
Rte. St. Clair (0)235.96.11.22 Fax (0)235.96.29.22 cl. Mon.; Tues. lunch; Jan.

NEW

Approaching Caudebec from Rouen you will see a lane winding up the cliff to the right just before you reach the town. It climbs steeply to arrive at the baronial Manoir, which stands proudly at the very edge of the escarpment, offering magnificent views of the loops of the river. The terrace takes advantage of the aspect, and a drink here before an exciting meal makes a very fine start. In fine weather you can lunch out here, but although the sun was doing its stuff on the Sunday we visited, the French customers obviously felt they could concentrate better on the food with no distractions and we were told service was indoors.

The restaurant is very grand and the young chef, Jean-Luc Tartarin, has won a Michelin star by his eclectic cooking. He certainly loves to combine unlikely ingredients – *foie gras* poached with clams, a steak of smoked bacon accompanied with a mini-casserole of hare kidneys – and is clearly going places. 160f for lunch or 190f (upwards) for dinner does not seem excessive in such circumstances. And what essence of luxury afterwards to slip upstairs to one of the two bedrooms (six more imminent) furnished with antiques, exquisite bathrooms and that view over the Seine. They cost 650f.

Map 6B   **CÉAUX** 50220, Manche. 4 km W of Pontaubault by D43

By making a tiny diversion like this from the main road it is often possible to find an unspoiled inexpensive alternative to the parasite hotels and restaurants that prey on tired and hungry tourists in honey pots like Mont St. Michel, just five minutes drive away.

Au p'tit Quinquin (HR)S
(0)233.70.97.20 cl. Sun. p.m. and Mon. o.o.s.

There are rooms here but they are pretty basic and not particularly good value at 208f. That said, they do have all mod cons and there is private parking, But really it is the food that is the attraction. The cooking is imaginative and generous and the dining room is always full of French at weekends. Menus from 70f.

'We wanted to get off along the quiet D275, wanting to stay close to the Mount but away from the ghastly tourist development. It was lucky we did because we landed up in Céaux at Au P'tit Quinquin. What a discovery! The 80f menus were superb in a restaurant which had a decor and service of an incredibly high standard.' Mike Souter.

Map H4   **CHAMBRAY** Eure. 18 km NE of Evreux by D63

The valley of the Eure is exceedingly pretty and this is one of the best stretches, especially towards Pacy, where the Ferme de Cocherel is a possible lodging place (rooms 350f with shower, 400f with bath). It does not get full billing, enchantingly pretty though it is, because the food is overpriced and the *patron* is so often fully booked with Parisians that he has adopted some of their brusque manners.

Le Vol au Vent (R)M
1 pl. de la Mairie. (0)232.36.70.05 cl. Sun. p.m.; Mon.; Tues. lunch; Aug.

The name is appropriate because Christian Dupuis excels at light-as-air *pâtisserie*. His little restaurant, alas, is not down by the river but on a rather busy corner but once inside the elegant interior, all is calm, with a view over a tiny garden.

This used to be a favourite, but perhaps my tastes have changed and M. Dupuis' cooking has not. Personally I now find the traditional dishes he sticks by somewhat heavy, but trenchermen might not agree with me.

Menus from 160f.

CHAMPEAUX 50530, Manche. 14 km S of Granville on the D911

Le plus beau kilometre de France is what the sign says. Well that may be pushing it a bit but the coast road is certainly spectacular with its unique view of Mont St. Michel rising out of the watery mists. On the cliff edge is:

Au Marquis de Tombelaine (R)M
(0)233.50.40.20 Fax (0)233.61.21.52 cl. Tues. p.m. and Wed. o.o.s.

It seems too good to be true to find such an attractive restaurant – low beamed ceilings, flagstones, fresh flowers, romantic setting – that still bothers to give good service and value for money. Menus start at 99f but I counsel going for the next one up to benefit from dishes like grilled *langoustines*. There are six bedrooms, but at the time of going to press they are still pretty basic and not particularly good value at 280f. Any news to the contrary would be welcome indeed.

'A very good restaurant. We had the 145f menu and it took us fully one hour to get through the Assiette de Fruits de Mer, but what a delicious task it was. The waiters were most helpful in coping with our basic French.' Dennis Keen

CHERBOURG 50100, Manche. 124 km NW of Caen

Ⓜ *Tues. and Thurs.*

I'm not sure about Cherbourg these days. The recent changes do not strike me as being advantageous and the trend seems down market. I had high hopes last time I researched the town because of the promising redevelopments around the market and in the Place Général de Gaulle but these seem to have ground to a halt and I could find little new to enthuse about. The little bistros that were blossoming at that time have mostly closed, nearly all my favourite restaurants have moved elsewhere and there is a lacklustre feel to the place. In July the streets were oddly deserted, which I attributed to the Monday blues, (the town is particularly badly affected by the dread 'cl. Mon. p.m.'), except that it was little better on Tuesday. The restaurants that had opened their doors probably wished they hadn't – they were all nearly empty, only the sandwich and pizza bars were doing any trade. Some of the smarter shops have also closed and their replacements are tatty.

The map shows streets of Cherbourg including: Gare Maritime, FERRY TERMINAL, D901, Rue de l'Abbaye, Rue de l'Onglet, Rue H. Dunant, R de l'Union, R de la Paix, Av. Cessart, Rue Grand Vallée, Rue Emmanuel-Liais, Rue Boel Meslin, Place de la Fontaine, Rue au Blé, Rue Grande-Rue, Rue des Fosses, R. de la Marine, Quai de Caligny, Rue Albert Mahieu, Rue des Portes, R. du Château, Rue Gambetta, Rue du M-Foch, Place du Général-de-Gaulle, Rue du Val de Saire, D901, Av. Aristide-Briand, Rue V Grignard, Rue Louis XVI, Quai Alexandre III, Quai de l'Entrepôt, Av. Carnot, D3 (D904), N13

| D901 CAMP SITE NEZ DE JOBURG | N13 CAEN PARIS | St LÔ BAYEUX | D901 MAUPERTUIS AIRPORT |
| D3/D904 CARTERET | | | |

Gare Maritime 50101 — Cherbourg Tel: (0)233 88 65 70

A tale of woe indeed, because this used to be one of my favourite ports. All is not lost though. I considered it a challenge and dug one or two gems from the dross.

Hotels: I suppose that Cherbourg is intrinsically a transit town, with most customers staying only for the odd night (can't say I blame 'em as it stands at present), so we are looking for efficiency rather than character here.

Hotel Mercure (H)M
Gare Maritime (0)233.44.01.11 Fax (0)233.44.51.00

Modern chain hotels are not my all-time favourites, but there's no denying in this case that the Mercure has the best site in town, that is quiet and functional, near the ferry terminal and I would probably rate it as best choice. Avert your eyes from the virulent orange of the bedroom decor and look out of the window at the sailing boats and the sea. 84 rooms cost from 425-495f.

The restaurant used to be a surprising additional bonus, but it's all gone quiet here recently and I have no recent reports of its steadiness or decline.

Le Louvre (H)M
2 r. H. Dunant (0)233.53.02.28 Fax (0)233.53.43.88 cl. 24/12-1/1

As functional as can be but friendly with it. The 42 rooms are spacious and well equipped, all double-glazed against possible noise, but the road outside is semi-pedestrianised these days so a good night's sleep should be assured. Excellent value at 175-360f.

Moderna (H)S
28 r. Marine (0)233.43.05.30 Fax (0)233.43.97.37

NEW Just 25 rooms in this friendly hotel, centrally situated, at a very reasonable price of 170-300f. I cannot do better than quote from a recent experience:

'*Brand-new bathrooms, excellent beds, linen, breakfasts, and cheerful, efficient English speaking service from the manager, all at British b. and b. prices. Three of us warmly recommend this excellent small hotel.*' A. Barker.

→ **La Croix de Malte** (H)S
5 r. des Halles (0)233.43.19.16 Fax (0)233.43.65.66

NEW Another reader's recommendation, without which I would probably not have bothered to look beyond the facade. *Do not* be put off by first impressions, which are of a faded grey shabby building in an uninteresting street. In fact the locality is good – just to the side of the theatre, away from any likely lager-lout activity. Once past the door and inside the lift the picture changes. The hotel has been completely restored and renovated and the decor is light, bright, and in cheerful good taste. There are 24 rooms decorated in pastel shades, all with satellite t.v. and telephone at an astonishingly reasonable price. Even the cheapest, with showers, up in the roof with Mansard windows, are good-sized, at 170f; 205f buys something larger on the next floor down, and the best, at 300f, have a bath. A family of four need spend only 350f for two double beds. M. and Mme Devinante are considerate and welcoming hosts. He even cheerfully deserted his lunch to show me round, which clearly deserves an arrow.

'*Extremely clean and functional, and fine for a short stay. Welcome was friendly, even at 8 a.m., and I was soon installed, for an overnight price, through till 12 next day for 200f (shower, basin, loo in mini bathroom, colour t.v., phone). Mme Devinante kindly stored my case in a locked cupboard until I called for it just before going for the evening ferry.*' John Stock

La Régence (HR)M
42 quai de Caligny (0)233.43.05.16 Fax (0)233.43.98.37

NEW   If you like to eat in your hotel, this recently facelifted Logis de France is probably the best bet. It backs on to a square with good parking and fronts on to the harbour. 17 rooms, recently re-furbed, have all mod cons and range from 280-420f. If you want a view of the port it will be 400f upwards.

The large restaurant is prominent on the main parade and well-known for its seafood on menus from 89f.

'*Excellent Sunday lunch, well patronised by locals and tourists.*' John Stock.

Restaurants: The obvious choice is the string along the quai Caligny, and indeed you could do far worse than drop in at one of these for a platter of *fruits de mer* or a bowl of *moules*. I think I would probably go for the Café de Paris for old times' sake and it is looking quite smart at the moment, all nautically blue and white. My other recommendations, in the back streets, are all new or changed hands since FE9. I hope that their future is not so precarious as that of their predecessors.

➤ **Le Petit Marché** (R)M
59 r. au Blé (0)233.53.67.64 Fax (0)233.94.41.43 cl. Sat. lunch; Sun. (but I have also found it closed on Mon. if there is not sufficient trade)

NEW   That old Cherbourg character Jacky Pain, whose career I eagerly followed ever since I found him cooking divinely in a three-tabled café in a back street, right up to his Michelin star, is a great loss to the Cherbourg culinary scene (he has decamped to open up a restaurant in Nantes). This was the site of his late lamented 'Le Plouc' restaurant.

His departure was the bad news, the good is that Le Petit Marché is carrying on his good work; the new owners have still to establish a reputation and so are trying extra hard, and their prices are way below those that Le Plouc was able to command at the height of Jacky's success. The two pretty little beamed rooms in the quiet street behind the main market have not been greatly changed. There was a big fire burning in the rear, even in July (a cold and blustery one), in order to cook the charcoal grills which are a speciality. It might not be an ideal choice on a brilliant day when the dark and cosy atmosphere is not what one is looking for, but at any other time the warm and welcoming touch is delightful.

Cloths and napkins are wine coloured, curtains are red gingham, and the odds and ends are eclectic to say the least – antique typewriters and gramophone, old barrels, stuffed animals.

The food is excellent both for its value for money and content. On the 79f menu you could choose home-made *terrine* and chicken in a cream and tarragon sauce, plus cheese and pud, or on the 120f version perhaps *frivolite de saumon fumé* (smoked salmon in three guises, fillet of duck with port wine sauce, cheese and a *panaché* of five desserts. Grills are around 58f. In fact I wasn't very hungry on the last visit and could not have been better satisfied than with a dozen oysters for 65f and a generous salad featuring warm wild mushrooms for 30f.

Arrowed for the most interesting food in town.

Le Faitout (R)M
r. de la Tour Carée (0)233.04.25.04 cl. Sun; Mon. lunch and 15 days over Christmas

NEW   Another erstwhile Jacky Pain stronghold, in a quiet street near the market. Wine-coloured paint, even tinier than Le Petit Marché, bistro-style, *cuisine familiale*. That is to say French family style – no burgers n' chips here. A friendly stop with interesting cooking on the 105f menu, or a bargain *plat du jour* at 55f.

Map 5D   **CLÉCY** 14570, Calvados. 37 km S of Caen

Clécy claims to be the 'Capital of the Suisse Normande', and certainly many of that lovely region's activities centre around the village. The whole area is very well organised for tourists; paths and excursions are well advertised and brochures are readily available from shops, tourist offices and cafés. The two most popular outings are south to La Faverie Cross and to Le Pain de Sucre, both of which offer spectacular views of the rocks, river and viaduct. Rock-

Moulin du Vey

climbing, hiking, canoeing, fishing, bicycling, riding – if it makes you tired to think of them the day's activity need be no more taxing than to follow the arrows by car. An impressive example is the road to le Oëtre Rock overlooking the Rouvre gorge. Truth to tell the association with Switzerland is stretching it a bit but certainly it's a particularly attractive area of Normandy with a distinctive landscape of green hills and greener valleys. The river Orne winds peacefully through rich pastureland or dramatically cuts into the rocky escarpment of the Armoricain massif.

1 km east of Clécy on the D133a, at Le Vey, an imposing old bridge crosses the wide fast-flowing river and a scattering of restaurants and cafés on the banks makes the most of the setting. Their balconies overhang the river and the inactive can sit and sup watching the fit get fitter in their pedalos or canoes.

Le Moulin du Vey (HR)M
(0)231.69.71.08 Fax (0)231.69.14.14 cl. Dec.; Jan.

I feel that overworked word idyllic coming on again. Here is the hotel with the most perfect setting. Willows droop into diamanté ripples, water lilies beg to be immortalised by Monet, the river bends obligingly to frame the mellow old bridge and the hotel's flower-filled terrace is the perfect vantage point from which to appreciate the chocolate box scene. If you feel like packing a long muslin dress, straw hat and parasol, this is the place to wear them.

The 25 rooms are in the creeper-covered mill or in one of the annexes, the Manoir du Placy nearby and the Relais de Surosne, 2 km away. Attractive these may be but fight for a room in the Moulin – the setting is what you come here for.

You certainly don't come for the food, which lets the side down. The restaurant is in an adjacent building, and usually full at the weekends, so they don't have to try too hard. Menus from 138f, but you would have to go to 220f for anything interesting. Dover sole, which is my yardstick is a hefty 130f. The rooms on the other hand are very pleasant (but becoming a bit expensive at 530f). I would take a picnic and eat it by the viaduct or slum it a bit in the café La Guinguette à Tartine on the other bank. Or you could try the Châlet de Cantepie in the village, which worked well for me but not always for readers.

| Map 3D | **COLLEVILLE MONTGOMERY** 14880, Calvados. 5 km W of Ouistreham by the D45A |

La Ferme St. Hubert (R)M
3 r. de la Mer (0)231.96.35.41 cl. Sun. p.m.; Mon. o.o.s.

Don't go expecting a farm. Any rustic origins have long since been forgotten. Nowadays it's a modern chalet-like building, set in the middle of nowhere.

Inside is more *rustique* with plenty of beams and an open fire to help make the atmosphere warm and cosy. Cooking is more sophisticated than you might expect and the restaurant attracts local businessmen and ferry passengers who want to remember their last meal in France as something special but do not fancy the stress of parking in Caen.

Menus from 90f (not weekends) then 148f.

| Map 3D | **COLOMBIERS SUR SEULLES** 14480 Creully, Calvados. 8 km SW of Courseulles, 19 km NW of Caen. Signed off the D12 and the D22 |

There is little natural charm (apart from the sea) along the coast here, which is overdeveloped and traffic-jammed in high season. So to drive a mere 8 km inland and find yourself in totally unspoiled countryside is a joy. This is an ideal spot from which to visit the landing beaches, Bayeux and Caen, and so near the ferry.

Château du Baffy (HR)M
(0)231.08.04.57 Fax (0)231.08.08.29 cl. 15/12-15/3

NEW
A lovely 18C château, set in spacious gardens, spattered with daffodils when I visited. The river Seulles flows by.

35 rooms have been restored, retaining their high ceilings and spaciousness but now equipped with mod cons. The furnishings are not as elegant as the château, but the prices have been kept affordable.

There are plenty of leisure activities available on site – tennis, archery, mountain biking, fitness room, horse riding. Or you can just sit under the trees and enjoy that lovely garden.

The food is surprisingly good and breakfast is included in the price of the rooms.

Rooms from 380-560f.
Menus from 95-198f.

Map C3   **COMMES** 14520, Manche. 2 km SE of Port en Bessin by D514

La Chenevière (HR)L
(0)231.21.47.96 Fax (0)231.21.47.98

> A truly lovely dignified 19C manor house set amongst ancient trees
> in a spacious *parc*. Everything about it is elegant and pleasing to
> the eye – the pastel colours of the bedrooms, the luxurious
> bathrooms and the light and airy dining room. The only snag is that
> it has now become well-known and popular with incentive groups
> and business meetings and the prices will put it in the 'special-
> occasion' bracket for most of us.
> 17 rooms from 700-1,000f, two apartments 900f or 1500f.
> Menus from 130f (lunch) then 180f-350f.

Map 5D   **CONDÉ-SUR-NOIREAU** 14110, Calvados. 13 km N of Flers

Ⓜ *Thurs.*

> Not a very interesting town, almost completely post-war.

➤ **Le Cerf** (R)M
18 r. de Chêne (0)231.69.40.55 cl. Sun. p.m.; Fri. o.o.s. and school holidays.

NEW

> Tucked away in an unpromising side street, but signed from the
> main road, flush on the narrow pavement, difficult parking.
> That's the bad news, the rest is all very good indeed.
> Just seven tables were squeezed into the front room on the out-
> of-season day of our visit. There is another larger, smarter dining
> room at the rear, but we were very happy where we were, looked
> after so cheerfully by nice Madame Malgrey. With great daring I had
> poked my head round the door, announced that we were *tres
> pressés* (What's new?), and looking for a quick light lunch. And this
> was the sacred Sunday mid-day! No problem said Madame and no
> problem it was, even when we ordered just a glass of wine each to
> go with our snack.
> Other diners were tucking into the admirable four course 90f
> *Logis de France* menu' – a duo of homemade terrines, fillet of
> salmon with cucumber sauce, cheeses and *crème brûlée*. During
> the week the price reduces to 67f at lunchtime, with the admirable
> formula of an *entrée du jour*, a *plat du jour* and cheese/pud, but
> Patrice Malgrey can rise to the heights of homemade *foie gras*,
> sautéed lobster and a fondant cappuccino for those prepared to
> pay 170f on the special menu for the 10th anniversary of Le Cerf.

Us? I had just the terrines – wonderfully juicy and flavoursome, one boar, one chicken liver-based, while Husband enjoyed pan-fried fillets of hake.

There are nine rooms here, which I hadn't the heart to ask to see at this busy, under-staffed time, but if they are as clean and wholesome as the rest of Le Cerf, with kind Madame Malgrey officiating, they must be very good news. 204f or 240f.

Arrowed for excellent cooking, good value.

Map 3G   **CONNELLES** 27430, Eure. 13 km W of Les Andelys, 37 km SE of Rouen

---

To follow the D313, which hugs the river from Les Andelys, is a charming way to see the Seine at its most beguiling. As far as Muids the chalk cliffs provide a charming background to the river's contortions. The road then turns inland but the scenery through the valley is no less pretty, peaceful and unspoiled. Ideal picnicking territory.

Moulin de Connelles (HR)L
(0)232.59.53.33 Fax (0)232.59.21.83 cl. Sun. p.m., and Mon. from Sept to May; Jan.

NEW   When I am very rich, or on my second honeymoon, or both, I shall stay at the Moulin. I shall recline on the island in the river and listen to the gurgle of the water; having bathed in the circular tub I shall eat a delectable dinner seated at one of the four tables on the verandah overlooking the river, then retire to sleep in the room in the tower. Breakfast will be on the terrace of my beautiful room of course, with another view of the encircling arms of the river. Pure bliss.

All the rooms are attractive, as you might expect: with a price tag of 600-900f, but one with a view of the river is essential here (you can look out over a parking lot elsewhere).

The brochure photo does not do justice to the reality of the mill. What looks like an eccentric gabled Norman folly turns out to be truly lovely with the bonus of a swimming pool. Arrowed for its site and comfort.

Some consolation for leaving the Moulin might be to enjoy the drive along the D19, which continues to be extremely attractive, chalk cliffs on one side, river on the other.

Le moulin de Connelles
Connelles

Map 3F **CONTEVILLE** 27210 Beuzeville, Eure. 13 km NW of Pont Audemer

Ⓜ *Thurs.*

The coast road from Honfleur to the Pont de Tancarville, the D312, is even quieter now that much traffic has been diverted over the new bridge. It's very rural, very green, with glimpses of the river along the way, and a famous restaurant that well merits a diversion.

➤ **Auberge du Vieux Logis** (R)L
(0)232.57.60.16 cl. Tues. p.m.; Wed., and 25/1-25/2.

If you wanted to end a Norman holiday with a meal to remember you should head here before catching the ferry. What very good news it is to know that the family succession is assured and that the good work originated by the renowned M. Louet is continuing in the capable hands of his son Guillaume.

Fresh from *stages* in some of France's most prestigious restaurants (Robuchon to name but one), he brings with him a freshness and lightness that is a most welcome complement to the richness of the traditional Norman cuisine, but never forgets his origins. Fresh cod is partnered with Vire *andouille*, sweetbreads are combined with local lobster in a shellfish *coulis*, delicate *millefeuilles* are layered with chocolate and served with bitter cherries. The 145f menu is a bargain – just two choices in each course. For us it was oysters, a *galette* of salmon with mushrooms and that wonderful *feuilleté*, this time with apples. Next price up is 245f.

The decor has not changed – call it *soigné* Norman – and service and welcome are the best – family-orientated but professional.

The arrow stays, for even better cooking.

Auberge du Vieux Logis

Map 3B   **COSQUEVILLE** 50330, Manche. 15 km E of Cherbourg

The stretch of coast between Cap Lévy and Gatteville offers good walks but not a lot else. The beaches are deserted and desolate for ten months of the year; the Plage du Vicq is probably one of the better choices, with fine sand and a handful of fishing boats in a little natural harbour, but the best reason for visiting here lies five minutes walk inland:

➤ **Au Bouquet de Cosqueville** (H)S (R)M
(0)233.54.32.81 cl. Tues. p.m.; and Wed. o.o.s.; 10/1-10/2; 20/6-30/6

What a transformation since I first discovered this unassuming little restaurant and included it for position and potential rather than for charm and cuisine.

The youthful Pouhiers, Mylène and Eric, have conjured up from very modest beginnings an elegant restaurant, with some of the best cooking, especially seafood, in the region. Their enthusiasm and dedication has not been exhausted and I forecast the rise and rise of Le Bouquet.

Wisely, perhaps, they have concentrated on the restaurant side of their venture and left the rooms pretty much as they were, i.e. extremely simple. At the moment their standard bears no relation to the sophisticated cooking downstairs.

Menus start at 108f; one the next one up at 140f I greatly enjoyed nine oysters, a *gigôt* of lamb, cheeses in perfect nick and a flaky tarte. *Langoustines*, crab and lobster figure prominently on the *carte*.

A bouquet and an arrow for deserved success.

Map 6B   **COURTILS** 50220, Manche. 8 km E of Mont St. Michel. On the D75 from Pontaubault to Mont St. Michel

Manoir de la Roche Torin (HR)M-L
(0)233.70.96.55 Fax (0)233.48.35.20 cl. 15/11-20/12 and 3/1-15/2

Well-signposted down a lane off the main road, with the Mount well within view across the marshes. It's a 19C gothic-style building covered in creeper and set in well-tended grounds. Its peaceful situation has earned it a place in the Relais de Silence group. Perhaps the stone walls inside are not strictly original but they give a warm and cosy feeling to the dining room, enhanced by a big log fire, when justified, and polished copper. A new conservatory extension is a welcome addition. The rooms are all different, good-sized, well equipped and tastefully furnished. I believe that anyone wanting a luxurious, relaxing stop near the Mount could do no better but I do have a vague question mark over the food, so all reports particularly welcome.

Rooms from 440-680f or 790f for one with spa bath.
Demi-pension obligatory in high season 420-650f per person.
Menus from 150f.

Map 4B **COUTANCES** 50200, Manche. 75 km S. of Cherbourg

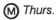 *Thurs.*

The largest cathedral in the Cotentin, Notre Dame de Coutances, dominates the town, as it has done for over seven centuries, miraculously surviving the 1944 bombardment. The towers of its facade have stood there, in the market place on the hill, for even longer; they were salvaged from the Romanesque original when it was burned in 1218. In complete contrast is the Renaissance St. Pierre, with its striking lantern tower, just a step down the rue Geoffroy de Montbray.

Otherwise the best thing about the town are the public gardens, with Son et Lumière three nights a week in summer.

For a sizeable town, it is bizarre that Coutances has no recommendable hotel nor restaurant. It was not trying very hard to please last time I was there. An unseasonable July drizzle made its inhabitants scuttle in and out of the traffic, and deprived me of the chance to sit outside a bar and sum the place up. The parking lots were all full, the cathedral was closed and sale notices obscured the windows of the shops, but worst of all inescapable pop was blaring out of speakers on every corner. I gulped down my indoor coffee and left, pausing only at the Tourist Information Bureau to make sure I had not missed a winner; all the loyal employee could come up with was The Normandie (pleasant owners but old-fashioned, on a busy corner) and the Cositel (modern cube on the outskirts). She was floundering over restaurants when a local interrupted: 'Forget the town, make for La Voisinière at Savigny' (33.07.60.32). Unfortunately I was heading in the opposite direction, so all reports particularly welcome.

Map 3D	**CREULLY** 14480, Calvados. 19 km NW of Caen, 13 km E of Bayeux. From Arromanches take the D 465, then the D22

Ⓜ *Wed.*

The little town of Creully, high on its escarpment above the valley of the Seulles, is dominated by the 15C château. This is an area where defence has always mattered. Castles and fortresses abound. At the Château of Creully General Montgomery set up his caravan headquarters in June 1944.

➤ Hostellerie St. Martin (RH)M
pl. Ed. Paillaud (0)231.80.10.11 Fax (0)231.08.17.65 cl. Sun. p.m.; Mon. lunch o.o.s.; Christmas, Easter

NEW

I was particularly delighted to discover the St. Martin (prompted by a reader) because I fear this kind of small family- run hotel, maintaining exceptionally high standards, is a dying breed. This one scores on all counts.

Standing in the main square, backing on to the château, it was originally part of the market *halles*, and provided storage space for the victuals destined for the château residents. The restaurant is a delightful room, with vaulted ceilings, rough stone walls and big fire in big chimney. Flagged floor, pink cloths, soft lights, cane chairs and gleaming copper are all just right. There are tables too outside on the terrace for summer sipping.

M. and Madame Legrand are the proprietors and he naturally, as in all good family-run affairs, is *chef de cuisine*. His specialities, naturally again, are regional, and his *feuilletés* and desserts show what a fine pastry chef he is.

The 12 comfortable rooms (wise perhaps to ask for one away from the square) cost from 220-250f.

Menus from 60f.

A winner I'm sure and arrowed accordingly.

Map 3E	**CRICQUEBOEUF** 14600, Honfleur. 6 km SW of Honfleur, well signed off the coast road, the D513

➤ Romantica (HR)M
Chemin du Petit Paris (0)231.81.14.00 Fax (0)231.81.54.89 cl. Wed. lunch; Thurs. o.o.s.; 15/11-20/12

NEW

The last day of the last tour of reconnaissance for this book revealed one of its best discoveries – an exciting but affordable hotel near Honfleur.

In fact the Romantica was built six years ago, so I am amazed that it has remained such a well kept secret until now. It is built in the Anglo Normand style beloved by architects a generation ago, with full complement of fake beams, turrets and balconies, and although it is set some distance back from the sea, its height enables many of the rooms to enjoy really lovely views over the unspoiled countryside to the water.

The front rooms are super – large and light, same with balconies. I would bag the one on the corner, with an extra large balcony, going for 400f, but there are 350f versions available too. Nineteen rooms at present and 16 more being built, with more salons.

With a swimming pool, peace and quiet and proximity to Honfleur this has to be an arrow, but I should welcome first hand reports about the food.

Map 2G   **CROIXMARE** 76190, Seine-Mar. 8 km SE of Yvetot by N15

Auberge de la Forge (R)M
On the N15 (0)235.91.25.94 cl. Tues. p.m.; Wed.

I am puzzled why there has been absolutely no feedback on this charming little restaurant, conveniently situated on the main road, in an area short of alternatives, and open on the dreaded Sun. p.m and Mon. moreover. I re-assessed it and liked it as much as ever so the recommendation not only stays but could be an arrow with a few confirmations.

There are several small beamed rooms inside, busy with French families at the weekends. *Chef/patron* Christian Truttmann is a truly imaginative cook. He likes to experiment with dishes like a *terrine* of pork trotters, he stuffs raviolis with a *purée* made from pike and serves it with a chervil cream. The cheapest menu is 97f but the 158f version includes good wine so could be a better deal.

Map 1G   **DIEPPE** 76200, Seine-Mar. 58 km NE of Rouen, 103 km E of Le Havre, 185 km from Paris

Ⓜ *Sat.*

So many changes. Those who have not visited for a few years will hardly recognise the place without the ferries dominating the old harbour. The new port means less dependence on the state of the tides but a certain loss of bustle and salty character to the town centre.

The newly-liberated quays could have been put to better use, one feels. Sit at one of the restaurants along them now and the view is of a busy car park, not of marine activity. However, it has to be admitted that the parking situation in the town is dire, so perhaps the extra places were essential. So, I suppose, are the exasperating one-way systems. It is usually quicker to walk within the town, so confusing are the limitations.

Walking is best anyway, either along the quays checking out the menus, or for an ozony blow along the seashore, with the the backdrop of the great castle, or in the pedestrianised heart of the town, the Grande Rue.

An hour can be passed quite happily here, up one side, down the other, with an obligatory pause at the Café des Tribuneaux. Perhaps there is less atmosphere than in the days when Oscar Wilde used to linger here and revolutionary young artists – Pissaro, Renoir, Monet, Sickert, Whistler – fascinated by the challenge of portraying the clarity of the coastal light, would sit and argue over a glass of wine or *absinthe*; the lingering now is by the old ladies sitting on the wall for their evening gossip; *les jeunes* take over the fussy interior, while tourists like me prefer to put in some serious people-watching on the terrace.

Shopping along the Grande Rue is interesting; no big chain stores apart from a modest Monoprix but individual boutiques, particularly strong on household goods and gifts. The specialist food shops seem to be disappearing but Claude Olivier's establishment in the nearby rue St. Jacques, still sells only the best cheeses, *charcuterie*, oils, and a selection of good value wines.

But best of all for food shopping is the Saturday market, one of the biggest in Normandy, which spills over from the Place Nationale into the neighbouring streets. Farmers and their families arrive from miles around to display their wares. Cheeses are particularly mouthwatering, especially the unpasteurised varieties that are becoming victims of bureaucracy. Discuss with the vendor the day on which you want to eat the cheese and he will pick out one that will be in the pink of perfection for the show-off dinner back home. For hypermarket devotees (or anyone with a wet hour to kill) the Belvedere Mammouth shopping centre on the Rouen road has 55 shops.

Dieppe's two most famous monuments are her church and her castle. St. Jacques has been built and re-built over many centuries. The 14C central doorway, looking a little shabby alas, is surmounted by a fine rose window, particularly impressive in the evening when the sun spills the colours on to the floor. The nave is 13C, ornamented a century later and there are chapels donated by wealthy ship-builders from the 15C onwards. Look above the sacristy door for the frieze which depicts a file of Brazilian Indians, recalling the travels of Dieppois explorers. It comes from the palace of Dieppe's most revered son, Jean Ango.

You can't stay in Dieppe for long without being reminded, by road and café names, of this 16C maritime counsellor to Francis I. He took on the Portuguese fleet off the coast of African with notable success and became Governor of Dieppe. He is buried in the chapel which he donated to St. Jacques.

The 15C castle dominates the promenade, with its wide stretches of grass dotted with picnickers and joggers. Inside is a maritime museum displaying not only all things nautical but a fine array of ivory. In the castle's shadow is a plaque commemorating the controversial Operation Jubilee, the costly Anglo-Canadian raid on Dieppe in 1942.

Hotels: It does seem strange that in a town like Dieppe with so many advantages, scenic and practical, there are not better hotels. The obvious ones to choose are those facing the sea, but I cannot get excited about any of them. Readers' first choice is the **Plage**, (H)M 20 bd. Verdun (0)235.84.18.28 Fax (0)235.82.36.82, where 40 rooms cost between 250-330f. I liked the look of the **Epsom**, 11 bvd. Verdun (0)235.84.10.10 Fax (0)235.40.03.00, which at least has been refurbished and is bright and cheerful. The arrival of a new hotel on the sea front was an event to which I looked forward enthusiastically, but the l'Europe proved a disappointment. The breakfast room is more canteen than restaurant and the prices for the 60 plastic two-star rooms are ridiculously high. I still have high hopes for the **Présidence** (0)235.84.31.31 Fax (0)235.84.86.70, whose new Manager tells me that re-decoration of the 88 bedrooms is in progress, and that the restaurant, Le Panoramic, already blessed with the best view in Dieppe, will be upgraded. It has a lot going for it, since the rooms are spacious and look over the sea, but with so many changes in the offing there is not a lot of point in writing about my recent stay there. Current prices are 270-515f, but expect increases.

There is one good deed in this wicked hotel world, not on the sea front but in a side street near the church:

Au Grand Duquesne (HR)M-S
15 r. St. Jacques (0)235.84.21.51 Fax (0)235.84.29.83

NEW   When I called in to see the rooms and asked the jovial patron which were his closing days, he replied 'Never'. They're a hard-working team here, who never like to turn away good custom. Sunday night is a problem in Dieppe. Parisians are homeward bound and the restaurateurs put their feet up after a prolonged lunch session. Those restaurants that are open seem to attract few customers and the atmosphere is not a cheerful one. On a dark and dirty September night, having had one unfortunate experience (see below) we trudged round the corner to the Duquesne, in a *faute de mieux* mood, only to find the place buzzing with customers and busy waiters. There was not a table left in the first, more attractive, dining room, but we were happy to grab the last in the rear alternative, rubbing our hands, already convinced that we had found a winner

The food was all that I would wish food to be in an unpretentious family- run hotel, and better. Generous portions, fresh produce, cheerful service. The 72f menu is a real bargain, probably the best in Dieppe, but there are other more ambitious alternatives, up to 220f. On the 115f version the *croquante de moules* surprised us by its sophisticated presentation. It arrived in a Chinese money-bag of filo pastry containing juicy mussels surrounded by a garlic sauce. Excellent. The *terrines* are home-made and particularly good, and the presentation is that of a far more expensive restaurant, with attractive china and linen. Just one word of warning – anyone with a sensitive palate should avoid the carafe wine!

This is predominately a restaurant with rooms, but the 12 bedrooms are comfortable, if simple, and cost a modest 185-212f.

An arrow for good unpretentious value.

Le Saint Jacques (R)M
12 r. de l'Oranger (0)235.84.52.04 cl. Thurs. lunch; Mon.

NEW

It's not often I have to say 'We hated it but do go', but such is the case with the St. Jacques. I'll get the story out of the way: one of the virtues of this chic little maroon-painted bistro in the shadow of St. Jacques is that it is open on Sunday evening. I had heard some good reports and a menu-check looked highly promising; after a week of fishy indulgence we both fancied meat and on every menu and the *carte* beef was prominent. Admittedly the welcome was less than warm and the wait to order inordinately long considering there was only one other table taken (by a French couple who got precedence over our earlier arrival) but we liked the look of the place – a tiny yellow and green room, and the smells were wonderful, so were still in good spirits when we ordered our beef from two different menus. 'Beef is off,' was the curt rejoinder. 'Pity,' we said, 'what other meat do you suggest?'. 'No meat. Duck.' 'No lamb, no veal, no offal?' 'Just duck. This is Dieppe you know. We eat fish here.'

Well we would have been very happy to eat fish there too – the speciality of *saumon chinoiserie* arrived on the next table and looked very good, but not in an atmosphere that suggested we should never have ordered an item that appeared on the menu and that did not offer an apology when it was not. So sadly we left, to find the wonderful Duquesne pleased to see us.

But... I am sure the cooking here is of a very high order and good value, with the lunchtime Menu Duquesne at 65f offering *terrine aux crêpes*, *escalope de saumon* and *tarte chaude*, and the 115f Menu Viking suggesting *assiette de pecheur*, duck casserole, cheese and *poires au coulis*. With a top price menu at 195f, Benoist Carteret is trying to please with his prices if not with his manners. So do go and trust that he is too busy in the kitchen to be offensive in the restaurant.

La Musardière (R)M
61 quai Henri IV (0)235.82.94.14 cl. Mon. o.o.s.

There is a string of tiny restaurants along the main quay, all with tables outside, all strongly fishy. This is one of the newer recruits, long and narrow, pink cloths, trellised walls, mock windows. The service was a bit stretched the night we ate there, with just one girl and a young *patronne* heavily encumbered by a small baby but the food was o.k. We ate marinated salmon, *coquilles St. Jacques au jus de l'ail*, very tender filet *à la Bordelaise*, a salad and strawberries – all on the 128f menu. The cheese board looked a bit tired for Normandy. There is a rather limited 85f menu too.

Les Arcades (H)S (R)M
1 Arcades de la Bourse (0)235.84.14.12 Fax (0)235.40.22.29

The tourists all make for the south-facing quai Henri IV, to sit outside the restaurants and snack bars in the sunshine. At right angles are the arcades, which keep the sun off the tables on the pavement there. That doesn't worry the French, who only choose to eat outside if it is very hot, when the arches provide pleasant shade; they otherwise prefer a comforting fug indoors, but the tourists like to snatch every minute of al fresco refreshment and so give the restaurants along here a miss. Their loss because Les Arcades is probably the best of the restaurants overlooking the harbour and the one that the locals recommend first.

Inside is a *brasserie*-like atmosphere, with benches and bustle, and a very professional approach. One feels that other restaurant upstarts might come and go but Les Arcades is here to stay. Seafood is very good. On the 79f menu we ate mussels *à la crème* and brill with a *langoustine* sauce.

They were so busy at lunchtime that I didn't have the nerve to ask to see the rooms, so all I can report is that there are 21 of them, from 260-350f.

Comptoir Deep (R)M
Place Camille St. Saens (0)235.06.09.11 cl. Mon. and Jan.

NEW
An attractive newcomer to the Dieppe restaurant scene, housed in an antique shop in a quiet square behind the promenade. You can make up your mind about making a purchase while eating lunch, dinner, or even tea, for which this is a particularly welcome find. Management is young and enthusiastic, ingredients impeccably fresh, cooking precise, tending towards the classical with dishes like home-made *foie gras* and scallops in a shellfish sauce based on the prickly sea urchin. Menus from 78f (lunch) then 198f.

Marmite Dieppoise (R)M
8 r. St. Jean (0)235.84.24.26 cl. Sun. p.m.; Mon.; Thurs. p.m. o.o.s.; 20/11-10/12

Another old favourite that soldiers on amongst the flashier newcomers, dishing up reliable traditional fare at prices that please the regulars. Dark and cosy, tucked away in a side street near the arcades, it is perhaps not first choice for a sunny lunch, but it's the food not the view that is important here. Menus from 83f., including lots of fish and the eponymous dish of *marmite dieppoise* of course.

➤ **MéliMélo** (R)S
55 quai Henri IV (0)235.06.15.12

NEW
'*We are greatly appreciated by the British*,' said the *patronne* of this just opened salad bar on the quay. I'm not surprised. It was certainly greatly appreciated by me. I sat outside at one of the pretty white and green tables, enjoying 'La Mistral' – blue cheese, cucumber, nuts, *crudités*, ham and salad, all for 46f chosen from a menu of dozens of alternatives, imaginatively combining meat, fish, eggs, cheese, with greenery. There were warm ciabatta sandwiches too for 39f and hot *quiches*, *raclettes* and toasted cheeses for chillier days, when the equally attractive interior with yellow flowers on the walls might be more appropriate. The *Formule* at 60f offered any of the menu dishes and a dessert like *le crumble aux pommes et framboises*. Perhaps the rice pudding is a concession for the Brits. All the dishes can be taken away to eat as a picnic. A good choice too at teatime for a cuppa with interesting pastries to accompany. Bienvenu and an arrow for this enterprising newcomer.

Just outside Dieppe in the suburb of Rouxmesnil, on the Arques road, is a little hotel I would never have found without local help:

L'Eolienne (HR)S
30 r. de la Croix de Pierre (0)235.84.53.75 Fax (0)235.82.19.50
Open every day

NEW　　In a restored stone barn Régine Levasseur, the very pleasant
owner, has contrived seventeen bedrooms and a rustic restaurant.
Five of the rooms are equipped with jacuzzis, all are comfortable,
with their own bathrooms, and cost from 220-280f.

　　The restaurant prides itself on Norman specialities like *canards
de Rouen*, *tripes au calvados*, and *boudin noir grillé aux pommes*,
plus lots of open fire grills. Friendly atmosphere. Although only 2 km
from the town it is surprisingly quiet and peaceful here. I think this
would make a very satisfactory base.

Map 3E　　**DIVES SUR MER** 14160, Calvados. 2 km SE of Cabourg, 24 km
　　　　　NE of Caen

Ⓜ *Sat.*

　　If, as many tourists do, you take the coast road, exploring the
seaside resorts from Deauville to Cabourg, you will probably miss
the heart of Dives altogether and might be forgiven for thinking it is
just an undistinguished harbour and marina, facing Cabourg across
the mouth of the river from which the town takes its name. The fact
is that the most interesting part of Dives is no longer 'sur-mer', since
its port, important in the Middle Ages, silted up. Nowadays its heart
is several km inland, centring on the magnificent 15C market halls.
Their massive oak frames still look impressively sturdy, easily
capable of supporting the old tiled roof. Look inside to find the
wrought iron signs that designated the various merchants who used
to ply their wares there. On Saturdays this is still the site of the
colourful weekly market. The *halles* stand on the Place de la
République, on the other side of which is the 16C Manoir de Bois-
Hibou.

　　Five centuries before the market halls were built, Dives acquired
another distinction. It was here that William the Conqueror
assembled 3,000 vessels, the backbone of the fleet that would
make the historic attack on England. On the 12th September 1066
they set sail to St. Valery sur-Somme where further reinforcements
were waiting and 16 days later began their epic Channel crossing.

　　The town acknowledges its association with frequent references
to Guillaume. Most obvious is the *Village Guillaume le Conquérant*,
an arts and crafts enclave within the precincts of the old inn of the
same name. The folksy little boutiques and cafes, though
undeniably very pretty (and worth a visit) didn't appear to be

prospering when I was last there, but that was in March; I hope that in the holiday season they do better.

Guillaume-le-Conquérant (R)M
2 r. Hastings (0)231.91.07.26 cl. Mon. p.m.; Tues. o.o.s.

NEW

I am incurably sceptical that anywhere as attractive as this cannot fail to capitalise on its assets and take short cuts. However, readers assure me that it is not so, so I went along to recce. This is the very old inn set in the *village*; the dining room has massive wormy old beams, a good log fire, striped tapestry chairs, chandeliers and is a very 'serious' restaurant – the absolute opposite of my other Dives entry. Its menus feature expensive delicacies like home prepared *foie gras* flavoured with *morilles*, grilled lobster, braised turbot, and if you want sole you must pay 300f for two people (never come across that one before).

I never actually ate there, so all I can report is that the decor is worth sticking your head inside the door. Readers who know better please write.

Menus start at 102f, but go for the 150f to get something more interesting.

The rest of the town is nothing special, apart from one enormous bonus that would merit a detour from me whenever I was anywhere near:

➤ **Chez le Bougnat** (R)S
27 r. Gaston Manneville (0)231.91.06.13 In winter open for lunch only, plus Fri. and Sat. p.m.; in season. Cl. Tues.

NEW

I had only to push open the door of this mildly insalubrious building in the main street to know I'd hit a winner. The buzz and bustle were the first indication, Fred was the next. *Patron* Fred (no-one seems to know or bother about any other name) is a butcher/*charcutier* by trade and looks exactly as a butcher should – portly, mustachioed, beetle-browed, flashing eyes, white-aproned. He approached us, rubbing his hands and miraculously cleared a space for a table in what appeared to be a packed house. In no time we were provided with a menu and our third evidence that this was going to be good. The problem was that, having eaten well the night before and planning another gourmet exercise later that same day, I knew that I could not do justice to the mouth-watering selection on the carte. Tentatively I explained the situation to Fred, who sorted me out: 'Have just the *terrine* and a salad.' He added, 'And share it with your husband,' which I thought was a bit odd until

I saw the kilo of chicken liver *terrine* he dumped before me and the family size bowl of salad. But nothing was wasted – that *terrine* was so juicy and flavoursome (and easily the best I've ever tasted) that I somehow found an appetite.

Everything Chez le Bougnat comes family-sized. Everything but the bill. Here were the cheapest oysters I found in a Normandy restaurant – 55f for a dozen of the best St. Vaast – mussel dishes at 35f, six salads at 18f and huge portions of beef, pork lamb and veal at 68f, all served with good fresh veg. and *frites*. Meat is obviously a speciality but all the fish is prime-fresh; *feuilletés* are another house favourite, I insulted Fred by asking him if he had made the *terrine* himself. '*Bien sur,*' he replied, '*et aussi les persillades, les rillettes, les boudins et toute la charcuterie.*' I should have known.

Most of the locals were taking advantage of the admirable 79f menu, but there was no way we were up to its hefty four courses. Husband compromised with an order for 'just a pork chop'. It came butterfied Barnsley-style, two massive chops complete with crispy crackling, just like pork used to taste before they eliminated all the fat.

If you imagine that by ordering fruit for a dessert here you can accommodate a small appetite, forget it. 'Pineapple' means a pineapple – a whole one, peeled but otherwise *au natural*. The cheese board would put many a gourmet restaurant to shame, the wine list is fabulous and inexpensive, and you get a complimentary Calva when you ask for the (excellent) coffee.

The food here may be the main reason for a visit, but the decor is something else. While you are digesting, look around. The room is galleried, with some more tables up above. Decor is vaguely art deco, eclectic to say the least, every inch of wall and ceiling space occupied. Helmets, cartoons, an old lift, jugs on ledges, three wooden propellers suspended from on high, a stuffed Charolais head, huge papier maché heads – a chef, a sailor, a clown – a weighing machine. Table cloths are paper, floor is tiled.

I wouldn't choose le Bougnat on a summer's day – it is at its best when a cosy fug is to be preferred to fresh air; I wouldn't choose it for a romantic occasion – too cheek by jowl; I wouldn't choose it if I had a headache – the crescendo of happy eaters, Fred booming away, the coffee machine grinding, is prodigious, but in every other circumstance I can't think of anywhere I like more. So an arrow.

N.B. No credit cards accepted.

Map 6C   **DOMFRONT** 61700, Orne. 40 km SE of Vire; 98 km S of Caen

Ⓜ *Fri., Sun.*

The main road through the town gives no indication of any character whatsoever, being lined with post-war buildings. In order to gain an idea of how it must have been before the destruction it is necessary to park the car and climb the narrow cobbled Grande Rue to its mediaeval heart. Immediately the traffic fret is left behind and all is calm. The ruins of a castle keep are strategically sited to command a view of the surrounding countryside and the ramparts no doubt once helped to keep early invaders at bay.

Unfortunately there are no hotels up here to profit from the noise-free zone, but there are signs of new interest, like the Auberge du Grand Gousier. The food is pretty standard on printed-ahead menus (76f menu) but the restaurant is very pretty and comfortable, with check cloths, rough stone walls, and a light and fresh feeling about it that would remedy car fatigue. Alternatives are snack bars and a *crêperie*.

Map 6D   **DOMPIERRE** 61700, Orne. 9 km NE of Domfront

Just a crossroads on the D21.

Restaurant du Bon Laboureur (R)S
(0)233.30.44.90 No closing except one week in Feb.

The closing times are an indication of how hard Madame Humbert works. I hardly recognised the place after a five year gap. It used to be an extremely basic bar/*tabac* that dished up extremely basic nosh when they were not flat out with 'banquets'. It still is a bar/*tabac* but now the dining room is quite smart with peach flowery drapes. The son has joined Madame H. as chef and cooks a four course meal for 55f midweek and 78f at weekends. The *plat du jour* is a good bet at 38f – that's what the locals order.

Map 2F   **DOUDEVILLE** 76560, Seine-Mar. 13 km N. of Yvetot on the D20

Totally unspoiled countryside around here, in the heart of the pays Caux, only 38 km from Dieppe.

Le Relais du Puits St. Jean (HR)S
(0)235.96.50.99 cl. 15/2-15/3

NEW

Here's one that's definitely different, with loads of character and atmosphere. In the unlikely setting of a rather grim large 19C house M. Lemonnier presides over a kitchen whose speciality, pressed duck, is famous far and wide. If you've never tried it, you don't need to spend a fortune in Paris at the Tour d'Argent; just order it here, where it's every bit as good at a fraction of the price. Home produced *foie gras* is another calorific house speciality. Don't think of eating here without a robust appetite.

The dining room is redolent of leisurely hearty meals enjoyed over the years by leisurely hearty Frenchmen. Nothing distracts from the food; cloths are white, decor minimal. This is old-fashioned bourgeois tucking-in as it used to be. If you don't fancy the duck there is a menu at 50f and the carafe wine keeps the bill down even further.

A brief stagger up to bed might be a good idea here and there are four rooms, simple but with bath, at 230f. Half-pension is 280f but you'd need a stay in a health farm afterwards if you stayed here long.

Map 6B   **DUCEY** 50220, Manche. 11 km of Avranches

Take the pleasant little D78 rather than the main roads to find the village of Ducey.

Auberge de la Sélune (HR)M
(0)233.48.53.62 Fax (0)233.48.90.30

It was with some misgiving that I re-visited the Auberge. It has had such success since I first found it, now featuring in the brochures of several British tour companies, that I feared the worst. I need not have worried. If anything it is even nicer than I remembered it, and the hardworking owners, Jean-Pierre and Madame Girres, are not at all spoiled by easy custom. On the contrary, they are still looking for ways to improve on what was already delightful.

The entrance hall has been enlarged and smartened up, there is a new dining room, a bigger terrace, the bedrooms have been re-decorated, the garden running down to the river from which the auberge takes its name is even more flowery and agreeable and the food is said to be better than ever. Bookings may be good (don't go on spec), but prices have not soared. 200f for a double with shower and 290f with bath is excellent value, as is the 80f menu.

Arrowed for pleasant situation, good food, kind owners, and value.

Auberge de la Sélune, Ducey

Erqueurdreville-Hainneville
50100, Manche. 4 km W of Cherbourg.

Don't be tempted to follow the signs to 'Le Bourg'. Just stick to the coast road and you will find the little restaurant easily.

La Gourmandine (R)M
24 r. Surcouf (0)233.93.41.26 cl. Sun. p.m.; Mon. 14/7-5/8

NEW   The entrance is in the main road but there is a garden at the rear, with a view out to sea, something that is not easily found in Cherbourg. It makes a change from the port restaurants that often are too tourist-orientated. M. Lebas is a brave man in offering a

vegetarian menu in carnivorous France. It looked a good one –
three courses for 70f. Otherwise there is the *Menu de la Saline* for
70f or (preferable) a 135 version with some interesting options like
hot oysters in Beaumes de Venise.

Give it a try and let me know.

Map 2E   **ÉTRETAT** 76790, Seine-Mar. 28 km NE of Le Havre

 Thurs.

The scene along the beach will be instantly familiar because of the
much-painted, much-photographed distinctive arched white rocks.
Take a stroll towards them along the prom, lined with cafés and
souvenir shops, fishing boats pulled up on the cobbles providing
the colour. For a longer walk continue up the steep hill past the golf
course to look down upon the monumental arch of the Porte d'Aval;
serious walkers can continue to follow the marked route and make
a circuit of three hours. Alternatively at the other end of the beach
there is a 180-step ascent cut out of the chalk cliffs to the Falaise
d'Amont, where the little seamen's chapel, Notre Dame de la
Garde, has a magnificent view of Étretat, its surroundings, the long
single beach to the Porte d'Aval and the solitary island-rock,
l'Aiguille.

Another church, Notre Dame, is a good reason for a less taxing
walk past typically French holiday villas, rose-covered, white-
shuttered. It's a wonderfully simple Romanesque church, nine
centuries away from the 20C 'amusements' on the prom.

In summer Étretat is a lively little resort, full of happily squealing
children, precarious wind surfers and ice cream bars. In winter it
gets forgotten and dies. The architecture generally is eccentric
Norman, beamed and turreted, and there are reconstructed
covered market halls, now used for craft shops.

Not my favourite town, apart from the walks, partly because the
hoteliers are almost without exception so unpleasant. Their season
is short, so that they have to grab every franc while they can. It was
high season when I was there last, the hotels were full and their
staff weren't wasting any time in being agreeable. The best-known
hotels in the main street are the Normandie (17 rooms at 220-
350f)and the Falaises (24 rooms at 250-380f), both with adequate
rooms and food, but no more.

I did find two exceptions to the general couldn't-care-less attitude:

Hotel Residence (H)M
bvd. Rene Coty (0)235.27.02.87

NEW   Probably the oldest building in the town, with worm-eaten old
beams and impressive staircase. It does not have a standard hotel
classification because the rooms and their prices vary so wildly,
from 170 to 640f.

   The owner broke all the rules – he was young, well-dressed,
helpful, polite and ready to show me all the rooms, although he was
fully booked for that night. The antiquity of the building has not
resulted in a gloomy interior. On the contrary, all is bright and
cheerful, with contemporary furnishings, fabrics and bathroom
fittings. Breakfast is served on a kind of landing lounge. I liked the
atmosphere very much here, but as the set-up is so unusual I do
need first hand reports.

Hotel St. Christophe (H)M-S
Le Tilleul, 3 km S of Étretat on the D940 (0)235.28.84.19 Fax (0)235.28.84.30

NEW   A little modern chalet-like hotel set back from the Le Havre road,
with tables outside for repose and drinks.

   All is bright, clean, efficient; 21 rooms, including one for the
handicapped, with all mod cons. cost from 280f, to 330f. A useful
overnight stop on the way to the ferry.

Le Galion (R)M
bvd. Réné Coty (0)235.29.48.74 cl. Thurs. lunch; Wed; Dec.

NEW   An old timbered building in the main street, with lots of character
from old beams and pillars; it offers the only serious cooking in the
town. The cheapest menu is now 115f, traditional fare, with lots of
seafood.

Map 1H   **EU** 76260, Seine-Mar. 31 km N of Dieppe

Ⓜ *Fri.*

   5 km inland from Le Tréport, a town steeped in history but often
ignored by tourists hurrying to catch the ferry or beach-bound.
Normandy obligingly bulges its border to the north to accommodate
Eu, where its most famous son, William the Conqueror, married
Mathilda of Flanders in 1050. The castle where the ceremony took
place was destroyed on the orders of Louis XI in 1475. The
replacement château, begun in 1578, was one of the favourite
residences of Louis Philippe. Queen Victoria liked it too and stayed

there on two occasions. It is now used as the Town Hall and houses the Louis-Philippe museum.

The heart of the town is the beautiful collegiate church dedicated to Our Lady and St. Lawrence O'Toole, Primate of Ireland who died in Eu in the 12C. It was erected in the 12th and 13th centuries in the Gothic style. Don't miss the haunting 15C entombment in the St. Sepulchre chapel (second on the right).

The vibrant Friday morning market takes over the area around the church and is the biggest and best in the area. On other days the food shops are particularly good here, in the agreeably pedestrianised area. Mouthwatering *charcuteries, chocolateries* and *pâtisseries*, all of high quality, emphasise that this is a town where the locals shop, not one dedicated merely to tourist fast food. I recommend it not only on this count but for its situation in the valley of the Bresle (lovely walks), surrounded by the forest from which it takes its name, conveniently between the two ferry ports.

Hotel de la Gare(HR)M
20 pl. de la Gare (0)235.86.16.64 Fax (0)235.50.86.25 cl. Sun. p.m.; 18/8-2/9

NEW   A delightfully old-fashioned hotel whose decor can hardly have changed for a century, and all the better for that. M. and Madame Maine are the kindly hosts. The cooking is exactly what one would wish for in this setting – traditional, copious, good value, especially on the 90f menu and the restaurant is appreciated by locals as well as house-guests.

The 22 rooms are simple, nothing special but comfortable enough, with bath or shower, at 300-370f; demi-pension is obligatory in high season at 380f per person.

Map 4G   **EVREUX** 27000, Eure. 120km SE of Le Havre

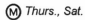 *Thurs., Sat.*

For a Norman town, a situation near the provincial border has always meant a history of sack and pillage. Evreux from its earliest days has faced hordes of destructive enemies – Romans, Goths, Vandals, Normans, English, French and finally Germans, whose 1940 attack left the town burning for a week. After each devastation the townsfolk have picked themselves up, dusted themselves down and started all over again.

It's truly a miracle that any part of Notre Dame, Evreux's cathedral, has survived, but there it is, rising up above the rivulets of the river Iton, still the focus of the town, an assembly of every phase of Gothic to Renaissance architecture, with astounding 15C glass, miraculously intact after being removed to safety during the war.

Evreux is a university town and university towns invariably acquire some of the liveliness of their students. This certainly applies to Evreux, with tables on pavements, bars and cafés patronised by an animated clientele.

Hotel de France (HR)M
29 r. St. Thomas. (0)232.39.09.25 Fax (0)232.38.38.56 cl. Sun. p.m.; Mon.

I can never work out how the rear rooms and lovely dining room of the France have views over the river Iton, yet I can never find it when I look behind the hotel. It does have a habit of going underground and popping out again at various points around the town. When it does, there are invariably grassy borders and a waters- edge path, which makes for good picnicking, The Hôtel de France has for long been the town's principal hotel, which can sometimes lead to complacency, but this time I sensed an air of renewal, and freshness. The restaurant overlooking the water is one of the prettiest I know, supervised by *chef* Mario Mathoux and *patron* Bernard Meyruey.

His clientele, especially at lunchtime, tends to be businessmen and businessmen like substantial meals, so don't chance this one for something light. Menus start at 148f.

The 15 rooms are nothing special but reasonably priced at 255-350f.

Vieille Gabelle (R)M
3 r. de la Vieille Gabelle (0)232.39.77.13 cl. Sun. p.m.; Mon.

NEW An exceedingly ancient building in central Evreux. Pretty beamed dining room and a 69f menu, *Le Rétour du Marché*, which offers a *terrine* of quail with grapes, cod steak with leek purée and Brie on a salad bed. Next menu up, with more choice, is a four courser 110f.

Le Bretagne (R)S
3 r. St. Louis (0)232.39.27.38 cl. Mon.; Wed. p.m.

NEW Behind the Mairie, a short step from the Tourist Office.
Very popular with locals at lunchtime. No wonder, with the 56f *menu formule* including a *pichet* of wine. Reliable cooking from the *chef-patron* and generous helpings on the four-course 72f menu.

I also liked the **Brasserie des Arts** in the main Mairie square. *Fin-de-siècle* decor, solid brasserie dishes enjoyed by local businessmen, but no problem about just a sandwich or salad. Excellent *frites*.

Map 5D **FALAISE** 14700, Calvados. 34 km S of Caen

Ⓜ *Sat.*

Mercifully, the 12C keep of the castle survived the 1944 destruction of the rest of the town, and continues to dominate the town as it always has. It was from here that Robert, younger son of Richard II, Duke of Normandy, watched the lovely seventeen-year old Arlette as she washed her clothes in the nearby river, and fell instantly in love. The proud Arlette declined a clandestine affair and rode defiantly over the drawbridge to meet her lover, a liaison that resulted in William the Bastard (the Conqueror). His magnificent statue rears below the castle ruins.

Things to do in Falaise? Take an interesting walk along the riverside path or drive northwards via the N158 to the Devil's Breach, a gorge hollowed out in the typical sandstone crests of the Falaise countryside. The hotels are nondescript, built post-war in the yellow Caen stone but without much character. The Poste in the main street is probably the best, with 21 rooms from 200-390f. The restaurant scene however is distinctly more promising.

➤ **La Fine Fourchette** (R)M
52 r. Clemenceau (0)231.90.08.59 cl. Tues. p.m. and Wed. p.m. o.o.s.

An old favourite that never lets me down, and actually welcomes customers on the dead Sun. p.m.; Mon. In the main street, decor typical *bourgeois* French – cane chairs, mock beams, orange drapes – food top quality ingredients lovingly prepared by *patron chef* Gilbert Costil. His specialities are sophisticated dishes like a *gaspatcho* (sic) of salmon and tuna with grapes, home-made *foie gras* in a hazelnut cream, and sweetbreads cooked in dessert wine, but you don't have to spend a fortune on the *carte* to sample really interesting dishes. On the 83f menu you could dine on a *terrine* of salmon and pike, then the *suggestion du chef* (always a good idea), salad and a dessert like a wicked *Dôme de chocolate*.

Arrowed for consistent high standards.

➤ **L'Attache** (R)M
1 km out of town on the N158, direction Caen, at the l'Attache roundabout. cl. Wed. o.o.s.; 23/4-30/4

Such a pretty little restaurant (just a few tables so be sure to book) with rough stone walls and a strong feel of Normandy about the decor and the cooking. Chef Alain Hastain believes in using plenty of herbs and spices in his inspired cooking but his basis is Norman ingredients, like using camembert in a kind of *quenelle* and flavouring it with chives, or roasting *langoustines* with cardamom. Leave room for desserts, which are particularly good.

Menus from 85f at present but this one is going places, so get there and enjoy a bargain while you can.

An arrow for encouragement.

Map 2F   **FÉCAMP** 76400, Seine-Mar. 40 km N of Le Havre

Ⓜ *Sat.*

No doubt that the heart of the town is its harbour; Fécamp is France's most important cod-fishing port and nowadays there is a large marina for pleasure boats too. The biggest tourist attraction however is the Benedictine distillery a few blocks back. In the 16C a monk, Vincelli, found on the chalky cliffs the herbs that gave the liqueur its distinctive flavour. The exact recipe is a closely-guarded secret but visitors are welcome to inspect the 27 plants and spices that are used today in the distillation. A tour round the *salle des plantes* in the museum is a feast for the nose as well as the eye. The building is a bizarre, Disney-esque piece of fantasy, whose courtyard is heaving with tourists at peak periods. Go early or late in the day.

Above the harbour is Richard I's church, La Trinité, rebuilt in the 12C after being struck by lightning. Subsequent re-building and additions mean that it is now a hotchpotch of architectural styles up to the 18C.

Its well worth arranging a schedule around the Saturday market that takes place in the square and streets around the church. It is one of the best in the area and brings animation and custom to the shops and bars in this area, usually neglected in favour of those along the quays.

Hotel de la Plage (H)S
87 r. de la Plage (0)235.29.76.51 Fax (0)235.28.66.30

NEW   In a quiet street one block back from the port. No sea view, but 22 comfortable, bright and clean rooms costing 320f. Nothing special but the best that the town can offer.

Auberge de la Rouge (HR)M
St. Leonard, (2 km S on D925) (0)235.28.07.59 Fax (0)235.28.70.55 cl. Sun.
p.m; Mon.

Renowned locally for its cooking and always fully booked for
Sunday lunch.

Unwise to bank on a table on Saturday evening either. There are
two biggish *rustique* dining rooms and a pretty little garden. I
thought the cheapest menu (105f, not Sundays) somewhat
uninspired and the next one up is 190f, so I'm not quite so excited
about the place as when I first found it, but readers have been well
pleased with the quality and quantity of the fairly traditional cooking.
If you're tired of fish, this is a good place to sample duckling cooked
the *rouennais* way, on the silver press.

The eight rooms cost from 300-370f, but they are really
accessories to the highly successful restaurant.

➤ La Marée (R)M
75 quai Bérigny (0)235.29.39.15 cl. Sun. p.m.; Mon.

NEW

On the quayside is a busy fish shop selling fish straight from the
boats. Even if you are not thinking of eating you should take a look
to learn the names and varieties of the specimens and also to see
what pristinely fresh fish looks like. They also sell takeaway
delicacies like various fish *terrines* and *pâtés*, *soupe de poissons*,
and home-smoked salmon, herrings, cooked lobsters and crabs,
etc. so you could cater for a special picnic here.

Upstairs is a large, surprisingly smart restaurant, not aggressively
nautical, more sage green and cream than the expected navy and
white, with only a few token burgees, knots and boaty pictures
hung haphazardly on the walls. Bag a table at the panoramic
windows, La Marée's answer to the other restaurants' quay side
tables, and you are on to an undoubtedly good thing.

I could not resist a huge simply grilled sole which was worth every
franc of 110f, but the 98f menu produced a good creamy crab
bisque, a perfectly cooked and herb-crusted cod steak and a
dessert. Arrowed for fishy perfection.

La Plaisance (R)M
quai Vicomte (0)235.29.38.14 cl. Tues. p.m.; Wed. p.m. 15/11-30/11

NEW

The fish and nothing but the fish. Here you can eat it on the quay
side terrace if you wish. Fish from the *carte* is the most popular
choice, but there is a menu at 130f, which offers an *assiette de*
fruits de mer, fish of the day, cheese and desserts that are better

than in most fish restaurants (i.e. a trilogy of home-made sorbets with a cassis *coulis*).

→ **Le Grand Banc** (R)S
63 quai Bérigny (0)235.28.28.68 cl. Thurs.

Ask local gourmands about Fécampois restaurants and they will almost certainly quote the Marée first, then the Plaisance, both for irreproachable fresh fish (not so common as you might think in a fishing port) and then Le Grand Banc for *qualité-prix*. I was pleased to have this confirmation of the unlikely discovery I made a few years ago of a really humble bistro run by an enthusiastic young couple. I recommended it with several reservations (it really was *very* humble), readers flocked, and reported back that the value was every bit as good as I had found. Now I need have no qualms about the decor. The little restaurant has been smartened up and freshly painted in blue and white, the tables are set further apart, and the menu extended.

Inevitably all this means an increase in prices, but not much. The menu is 68f, which in this town is still a tremendous bargain, and fresh sole, that yardstick of value, is 100f. There are other items like wild boar *terrine*, to relieve the fishy diet.

I wish the owners well in their obvious success but hope that they don't get any smarter than this. The arrow stays.

La Ferme de la Chapelle (H)M
Cote De la Vierge (0)235.29.12.19

NEW I write about this one more in sorrow than in anger. I am not recommending it but, because of its marvellous position and the shortage of other hotels in Fécamp, I think readers might like to know exactly what to expect if they do decide to stay here.

First the good news:

Look up at the cliff high above the northern side of the port and you will see a tiny mariners' chapel. Behind it lie the old farm buildings around a courtyard, which someone had the brilliant idea of converting into a hotel. The view from the chapel (though not from the farm) is magnificent, the air is clear and the traffic noise minimal. A large swimming pool is available for the guests' use.

Now for the less-good: Whoever was responsible for the conversion got away with murder. The flintstone wall of the chapel ends abruptly in a hideous concrete and slate erection, used for *seminaires*. The gilt Madonna on the spire looks down bemused at the folly of man. Her chapel survived the Hundred Years War, the Wars of the Religion, the destruction of 1944, with pillaging and rot in between, only to suffer this desecration.

The conversion of the farm into bedrooms built two-storeys high around the courtyard is very basic. Ground floor rooms have French windows but those upstairs are very dark with tiny Mansard windows. The great courtyard is grassed but entirely bereft of any flowers; the swimming pool is only used in high summer because it is always windy up here and it is unheated.

Furnishings are basic/modern. Blonde wood bed and drawers, white walls, no pictures, apart from a photo of the Fécampois fishing boat after which each room is named (the only nice personal touch)

Breakfast is eaten at tables of six in the barn-like breakfast room. Evening meals have to be reserved ahead on a no-choice, demi-pension basis. Cars have to be left outside the gates and, believe me, with a damaged knee and an upstairs room, it's a long painful hump of the baggage across the courtyard. No help offered.

I found this a great opportunity missed. The situation, the chapel, the courtyard all could have been turned to such advantage with more sympathetic handling.

Rooms 300-450f.

Map 5D   **LA FERRIÈRE AUX ÉTANGS** 61450, Orne. 13 km from Domfront on the D21

A grim little town, dominated by mines and chimneys. All the more surprise then to find:

➤ **Auberge de la Mine** (R)M
Le Gué-Plat (0)233.66.91.10 cl. Tues. p.m.; Wed.; 1/9-17/9

NEW   A very smart little restaurant, run by an enthusiastic young couple, Catherine and Hubert Nobis, who have made up for the greyness outside by furnishing the dining room with bright flowery curtains and dividing it with trellis.

The weekday menu, at 90f, is commendably *Selon le marché*. In other words you get whatever Hubert thinks is the best buy in the market that morning. Otherwise, on the 125f version you could sample a *bavarois* of asparagus, a chicken breast *roulé* studded with fresh herbs, cheese, and a chocolate and almond 'pudding' with an orange *coulis*.

A real find, good value, highly recommended, and a new arrow.

Map 6D   **LA FERTÉ MACÉ** 61600, Orne. 6 km N of Bagnoles de l'Orne

(M) *Thurs.*

If Bagnoles is too ordered, too contrived, head for La Ferté Macé, a pleasant little French town. Except that the parking is a nightmare if you wish to get to the pedestrianised centre.

Le Celeste (HR)S
6 r. Victoire (0)233.37.22.33 Fax (0)222.38.12.25 cl. Sun. p.m; Mon. o.o.s.; mid Oct-mid Nov.

NEW   Hopeless to achieve by car, except perhaps by ignoring No Entrance signs, which the French are better at than the Brits. Stop near the cathedral, dive into the hotel and ask for guidance.

It's tucked away in a pedestrianised street but easily spottable because of its colour – Barbara Cartland pink. This lapse of taste does not extend inside. And there's a surprising terrace at the back.

Cheapest menu is 90f, and the fourteen rooms run from 90-300f, the divergence reflecting their state of refurbishment, the cheapest having only a *lavabo*.

Auberge du Clouet (HR)M
at Clouet, on the outskirts of the town. (0)233.37.18.22 cl. Sun. p.m.; Mon. o.o.s. mid Oct to mid Nov.

NEW   If you do not wish to get involved in the traffic tangle, this is a good bet, well signed from all directions. Peaceful too. It's a long stone building, with a covered terrace. Six rooms cost from 320-400f and meals start at 90f so it's not exactly a bargain.

Map 2A   **FLAMANVILLE** 50340, Manche. 21 km SW of Cherbourg by D 904, to Lesieux, then D23 and D408

Very peaceful, very rural, near the coast, not too far from the port.

Hotel Bel Air (H)M
(0)233.04.48.00 Fax (0)233.04.49.56 cl. 1/1-15/1

NEW   A pretty old stone building, full of character, once an outbuilding to the Château de Flamanville. Dany and Serge Morel have furnished it with flowery curtains and unpretentious furniture and the ten rooms are cosy and comfortable, with every mod con. At 215-268f they represent good value. I peeked at the visitors book and found it full of glowing commendations from satisfied customers from all over the world. Alas, no restaurant, but the breakfast buffet could carry you through the day, and Dany is happy to recommend local alternatives for the evening. I think this one could well become an FE favourite. More reports would win an arrow.

Le Semaphore (HR)S
(0)233.52.18.98 Fax (0)233.52.36.39

NEW
I missed this one, but here is a report from someone who didn't:
'*Wonderful isolated position, pleasant dining room and accueil. Excellent lunch at 69f*'. Lesley Goodden.

Map 5D   **FLERS** 61000, Orne. 43 km E of Argentan

Ⓜ *Wed., Sat.*

Not a particularly attractive town, but one well served with hotels and restaurants, so perhaps a good stopover. Unfortunately both the hotels I was hoping to inspect were closed (contrary to their published times) so all I can report is that the locals recommended Le Galion, 5 r. Victor Hugo (0)233.64.47.47 Fax (0)233.65.10.10. 30 rooms from 200-260f.
I was luckier with restaurants and found two winners:

Auberge Relais Fleuri (R)M
115 r. Schnetz (0)233.65.23.89 cl. Mon.

NEW
On an unattractive street corner on the edge of the town, in the quartier St. Michel direction, comes a delightful surprise:
A lovely dining room with rough stone walls, elegantly decorated, and nice young Véronique Louvel welcoming and taking orders for the food skilfully prepared by her husband Vincent. His style is modern – light and imaginative – without being showy. Dishes like scallops with a mild curry butter or a lasagne layered with *langoustines* illustrate his flair. The cheapest 95f menu (Sundays too N.B.) offers less extravagant ingredients, e.g. mussels, roast rabbit, cheese, dessert, but no less caringly prepared.
A highly recommended place for an enjoyable evening, particularly in winter when the log fire glows so invitingly.
Arrowed.

Au Bout de la Rue (R)M
60 r. de la Gare (0)233.65.31 53 cl. Sun.

NEW   A surprise to find in this unsophisticated country town a stylish, *fin-de-siècle*-themed bistro/brasserie. The paint is dark green outside, dark red within, the atmosphere is cosy and convivial. Find it, as its name suggests, at the end of the road leading to the station.

Patron is Jacky Lebouleux, who cooks variations on old brasserie favourites, like *andouille* encased in flaky pastry, roast lamb in a rosemary sauce, apricots baked in orange juice. There is a wide choice of dishes on the *carte*, plus popular *plats du jour*, for a set price of 150f, and an equally eclectic and reasonable wine list.

A potential arrow after more reports.

Auberge des Vieilles Pierre (R)M
(0)233.65.06.96; 2 km S of Flers on the Briouze road, the D924.

NEW   A really pretty little restaurant, all trellised, light and airy, with a warm welcome from Madame Cesbron and easy parking for those who do not wish to get involved in town traffic.

The four course Tues.- Sat. lunch costs 78f; otherwise it's two courses for 102f (terrine of wild boar with pistachios, pork *noisette* with endives and hazelnuts), or 112f for three courses.

Map 2H   **FORGES-LES-EAUX** 76440, Seine-Mar. 42 km NE of Rouen by A28, D919 and D915

Louis XIII, his Queen and Richelieu used to take the waters in this spa town, whose name derives both from the metalwork that used to be its main occupation until the 15C and from its waters. You can still drink the ferruginous, clear liquid that gushes from a *buvette* in the Spa Park – it is said to be very stimulating. Overlooking the park is the lovely facade of a hunting pavilion, formerly belonging to Louis XV and brought here from Versailles. There are several half-timbered 17C buildings in the rue de la République but the central square I find bleak and unattractive in spite of the wealth of flowers lavished upon it.

It was big excitement in Forges when Club Med decided to open their premises in the grounds of the casino, but in fact the inhabitants keep themselves to themselves, contained in their camp and grounds.

La Paix (HR)S-M
*15 r. de Neufchatel (0)235.90.51.22 Fax (0)235.09.83.62 cl. Sun. p.m. o.o.s.;
Mon.; 16/12-8/1*

NEW

Michelin gives the 78f menu a red R for good value and they are right to do so. This is an example of not expecting too much from a simple restaurant. I deviated from the rule and chose the 125f version, which gave me an unappealing artichoke salad with a few chilly prawns and no dressing on the chopped lettuce, then a small skate wing, dry and disastrously over-cooked in an unsubtle cream sauce. The cheaper menu on the other hand was well within the chef's capabilities and yielded a perfectly good chicken *terrine* and grilled trout.

Madame, described by the next table as *formidable*, trudged unsmilingly around, and offered no comment on my uneaten fish. A disappointing experience because my first inspection of the hotel and menus had promised an arrow. I thought it had all the virtues of being unpretentious, family-run and inexpensive. The rooms are new, well-equipped, peacefully sited behind the hotel, well off the main road, and good value at 230-280f, and there is safe private parking.

The hotel is very popular with the British, including many readers. If you stick to the cheap menu and ignore Madame's gloom it could be good news. Perhaps my experience was unfortunate, but no arrow I'm afraid.

Auberge du Beau-Lieu (HR)M
at Le Fosse, 2 km SE on the D915 cl. Tues. o.o.s.

NEW

Local opinion is highly in favour of the Beau-Lieu, the newish *restaurant gastronomique* just outside Forges. It's a very pretty Norman-style restaurant with smart service and presentation, usefully open on the dread dead Sun. p.m. and Mon. Cooking is based on regional dishes, with a personal touch. Cheapest menu (a very good one) is 105f, then 158 and 255f, with an interesting, wide-ranging wine list.

The style of the five bedrooms is simpler than that of the restaurant, but they are comfortable and have excellent bathrooms. Good value at 300f.

Map 4H   **FOURGES** 27630, Eure. 15 km E of Vernon

The Epte is a particularly appealing river – big enough to be interesting, small enough to be unspoiled. Here it is shallow but fast flowing over rushes and between willow-hung banks. I heartily recommend a picnic, or:

→ **Le Moulin de Fourges** (HR)M
(0)232.52.12.12 Fax (0)232.52.92.56 cl. Sun. p.m.; Mon. o.o.s.

NEW

I discovered the Moulin a while aback but had to write 'What a pity that somewhere so utterly charming should be too run-down for a mention'. Not so now. Very good news indeed here. A new enthusiastic team have taken it over, smartened it up and are realising its very considerable potential. It always was ridiculously pretty; so pretty that one thinks Disney-fabricated, but here the wavy roof, huge rustic water wheel, rustic galleries and balconies, faded salmon pink paint, gardens running down to the river's edge are for real. And now the interior has been re-thought, and tastefully restored. The first floor dining room has high arched beams, tables discreetly wide apart, and sunny yellow decor. The welcome is warm and the service friendly and efficient.

Menus from 95f during the week, which is the time to aim for because with a setting like this it's all going to be packed out at weekends, when the menu price goes up to 150f. Cooking is traditional with occasional innovations – *tête de veau*, turbot with vanilla – interesting wine list. I ration the word 'idyllic', but it is totally justified here, and if you pick a fine day and eat outside on the lawn, I have no doubt you will agree with me.

Arrowed for setting and *accueil*.

Map 4H   **GIVERNY** 27620, Eure. 3km E of Vernon

On the opposite bank of the river from Vernon.

Giverny and Monet are practically synonymous. Here is the house in which he lived from 1883 until 1926, enjoying the proximity of the river Epte and the quality of Norman light. He grew to become as passionate a gardener as a painter and his garden is a continuing memorial to his talents as a composer of living pictures. In his old age he was so fascinated by the water lilies that crowded the lake that he painted the scene more than fifty times, working away in the newer of the two studios here. So many visitors want to see the spot that a tunnel had to be built under the busy D5 to the Japanese water garden, where the wisteria-festooned green bridge over the water and the lilies feature in many a souvenir photograph.

The garden in front of the house, Le Clos Normand, is packed with shimmering colour and sensuous scents. The rectangular beds bisected by straight paths are full of cottage flowers – tulips, forget-me-nots, wallflowers and daisies. Nasturtiums scramble freely, as do roses and clematis over formal arches and pyramid frames. In autumn the hectic colours of the season – orange, flame, gold and fuchsia – can seem altogether too much to our sensitive English eye.

The garden has become a victim of its own popularity. It was never intended as a popular showpiece; the scale is domestic and intimate and shuffling round in a line does not add to its attractions. Much of the magic will be lost unless you contrive a visit early or late.

The house itself is surprisingly simple, with painted furniture in the sunshine yellow dining room; the blue-tiled kitchen has gingham curtains and rows of gleaming copper pans.

In 1992 the Musée d'Art Americain Giverny was opened nearby, as the centre of American Impressionism in France. Among the American painters represented are John Singer Sargent, Whistler and Theodore Robinson, who in 1892 painted "The Wedding March" depicting the wedding procession of Monet's stepdaughter Suzanne. There is a 200 seat theatre here for lectures and films, a restaurant and shops and the gardens are beginning to look mature and interesting.

Les Jardins de Giverny (R)M
Chemin du Roy (0)232.21.60.80 cl. Sun. p.m.; Mon; Tues. p.m.

An appropriate house for a restaurant devoted to Monet garden visitors. It's Norman, and rambling, and slightly faded, and set in a pleasant garden of its own. Not a place to snatch a quick lunch, but to linger awhile. The menu at 130f is surprisingly interesting for an establishment that doesn't have to look too far for its clients – a salad of hot Vexin goats cheese, a *fricassée de poulet Normand*, more Norman cheese and a good *tarte aux pommes*. Don't even think of trying to get in for lunch on busy weekends.

Map 4D   **GOUPILLIÈRES** Halte de Grimbosq 14210, Calvados. 8.5 km N. of Thury Harcourt, 50 km S of Caen

---

All very peaceful, very serene, with the wooded hills of the Forêt de Grimbosq rising from the river Orne to provide the perfect backcloth to the rural scene. One reader actually witnessed a train on the single track that crosses the D171 at the Halte, but I don't think the noise from passing traffic, road or rail, would be too serious a problem here.

Auberge de Pont de Brie (HR)S
(0)231.79.84 cl. Mon. p.m.; Tues. o.o.s. Open every day between 1/5 and 30/9

The Auberge was one of those happily-remembered spots that one hesitates to re-visit in case all has changed. Here indeed it has. The bad news was that the family who had run this simple little hotel have sold up. The good news is that it has been bought by the young M. and Mme Cottarel and it is better than ever. Tastes change and 'simplicity' is going out of fashion if it means leaky showers and bare boards. The 8 rooms have been upgraded; there are now six with a shower – 220f, one with a bath – 250f and one family room with mezzanine – 350f for four.

There have been even bigger changes in the restaurant, now considerably smarter and enhanced by M. Cottarel's cooking. 90f for three courses, or 120f for four courses on the *Menu du Terroir*. A drink on the terrace overlooking the rural scene or in the little bar would make a wise preamble.

There aren't many recommendable little hotels within easy reach of the port and the coast, and this would make an admirable cheap break, as many Britons seem to have found out. The arrow stays for the new management.

Auberge du Pont de Brie
Goupillière

Map 5A   **GRANVILLE** 50400, Manche. 26 km SW of Avranches; 104 km S of Cherbourg; 107 km SW of Caen

Ⓜ *Sat.*

No. 1 choice for me on the Manche coast. Granville is a lively town, big enough to maintain interest beyond the overnighter and with something for everyone – a wide sandy beach (when the precipitous tide allows), plenty of rocks to provide shrimping interest, a prom along which to take the ozone, more interesting shopping than anywhere else in the peninsula, excursion options to the Iles de Chausey or Jersey, a sizeable working fishing port and market for piscine connoisseurs, a plethora of bars, *crêperies* and restaurants, and the interest of the Haute Ville.

The Haute Ville is another world from the bustling commercial town below. Cross over the ancient drawbridge and within the ramparts a sense of serenity is immediately evident. Even in high summer the narrow streets seem unnaturally quiet, footsteps echo, the windows of the tall dignified houses remain shuttered and no children play. It's a good spot for a picnic on a bench in the small

Granville

park at either extremity, both with sensational views of the harbour, the Brittany coast as far as Mont St. Michel and the Iles de Chausey. Otherwise there are a couple of *crêperies*, a bar, a *tabac*, a church and a restaurant.

Hotels: Not a great choice for such a tourist-worthy town, and nothing in the Haute Ville. The old Hotel des Bains has been considerably smartened up and blessed with a good restaurant, but you're talking 600f if you want a sea view. Fortunately an old favourite at a fraction of the price is back on form:

➤ **Hotel Michelet** (H)S
5 r. Michelet (0)233.50.06.55 Fax (0)233.50.12.25

The new owners have not changed the character (or the prices) of this erstwhile villa set sideways on to the road on the hill beside the casino. The wallpapers and decor are firmly two-star and the furniture of the plastic persuasion, but the rooms are good-sized and so are most of the bathrooms, the situation is central but quiet and there is a parking lot. Bag a room with a balcony if you can and then you can have breakfast with a view over the rooftops to the sea and St. Malo. 19 rooms from 150-290f, excellent value and arrowed accordingly.

Restaurants: Here the scene is much more encouraging. Here are a few of my favourites:

➤ **Le Phare** (R)M
11 r. du Port (0)233.50.12.94 cl. Tues. p.m.; Wed. o.o.s.

The first floor dining room has the best *vue panoramique* in town, so try and book a table in the window to get your money's worth of fishing boats, private yachts and shabby cargo ships. The owners, Valerie and Philippe Vercella, bank on you looking out of the window rather than at the decor inside, which runs to flashy chandeliers. But it's the fish and nothing but the fish that you come here for. A dozen oysters costs 68f, a *sole meunière* 90f – about par for the course; if you come across 'fresh' fish for much less you should view it with scepticism. Menus from 90f and mammouth platters of f. de m.
  Arrowed as the best fish restaurant in the port.

The Phare is a long-term favourite and I always head directly there, but amongst the numerous fish restaurants that line the port two others have been specially recommended, Le Cabestan, 70 rue du Port (0)233.61.61.58, which has more tables outside so if the sun is

too good to miss, make for here, and Le Guépratte at 34 rue du
Port (0)233.50.00.85, which has been specially commended by a
reader. With these three to choose from you can juggle with
opening days.

La Citadelle (R)M
*10 r. Cambernon (0)233.50.34.10 cl. Sat. lunch; and Mon. o.o.s.; 20-30/9;
20/1-10/2*

NEW   A pretty little restaurant just inside the drawbridge of the Haute Ville.
Four tables on the terrace outside shelter beneath dramatically-
striped blue and white canvas canopies. Inside is stone-walled,
elegantly rustic, with imaginative food, both fish and meat,
represented on the 145f menu. There is a also a token 100f
version, but it would be a shame to skimp here. Arrowed as the
most interesting cooking in town.

La Gentilhommière (R)M
152 r. Couraye (0)233.50.17.99 cl. Sun. p.m.; Mon. o.o.s.; 1-15/2

NEW   This is Granville's *restaurant gastronomique*, well respected by
local gourmets. I haven't tried it yet, because it's in the opposite
direction to the port and when by the seaside I like to see the sea.
It's small and very popular, so you should certainly book. More
reports particularly welcome. Menus from 95f.

➤ Le Pierrot (R)S-M
16 r. Clement-Desmaisons (0)233.50.09.29 cl. Wed.

Probably the most popular small restaurant in town, thanks to its
central position, pleasant owners, M. & Mme Pelissie.
Predominately fishy, but with plenty of other options. Menus from
98f. All readers reports have been enthusiastic, especially about the
generous *fruits de mer*, so an arrow is justified.

La Poste (R)S
8 r. de l'Abreuvoir (0)233.50.02.25

Popular with locals, always crowded, good honest value for both
food and wine. Menus from 65f.

➤ l'Enchauguette (R)S
24 r. St. Jean (0)233.50.51.87 cl. Thurs. o.o.s.

An excellent choice for a cheap meal in the Haute Ville, this rustic little *crêperie*/restaurant offers charcoal grilled meat and fish as well as a range of *crêpes* and *galettes*. Everything freshly cooked. The arrow stays as the best *crêperie* in the Manche (if you know better please tell me).

Map 4B   **GRÂTOT** 50200, Manche. 4 km NW of Coutances by D244

On the left-hand side of the road (coming from Coutances)

Le Tourne-Bride (R)M
(0)233.45.11.00 cl. Sun. p.m.; Mon.

An attractive old house standing sideways on to the road, run by Martine and Denis Poisson. Inside the character comes from dark beams, olde-worlde, particularly welcoming if the weather is not kind. The food is easily the best in the Coutances area, and local families and businessmen make up the clientele.

Menus start at 98f (then 135 and 185f) and include interesting house specialities like *fricassée de lapin aux girolles à l'ail doux*.

Map 4B   **HAMBYE** 50650, Manche. 23 km SE of Coutances; 26 km SW of St. Lô

The village of Hambye is just a wide sloping square of old stone houses and a few shops selling basic necessities. The abbey of Hambye is actually 3½ km to the south, nearer to Sourdeval in fact, but you won't resent the journey; the road, the D13, runs through delightfully green countryside, following the valley of the river Sienne. You'll know you've arrived when you come to a bridge, with picnic tables thoughtfully provided at the side of the gurgling stream. The abbey is down a track to the left, backed by a steep escarpment. The ruins, approached through a gateway thick with iris, glowing with golden lichen, are open to the public. On weekend summer evenings flaming torches dramatically illuminate the scene and piped Gregorian chant floats up to the Auberge nearby.

➤ **l'Auberge de l'Abbaye** (HR)M
(0)233.61.42.19 Fax (0)233.61.00.85 cl. Sun. p.m.; Mon.

I can't resist a little boast about the Auberge – it is one of the most rewarding stories. I was so impressed with it twelve years ago that it became the Hotel of the Year in the first Normandy book. Hard to know exactly why I liked it so much – it's not a particularly attractive building – a post-war slab of grey stone at the side of the road, but certainly its kind owners, Micheline and Jean Allain, had a lot to do with it. Jean was and still is a cook far superior to those in most little country hotels and for Micheline nothing is too much trouble to make her guests feel welcome and cosseted.

The rooms were very simple then, without much in the way of mod cons, and were really intended as accessories to Jean's cooking. They still are – this is a restaurant-with-rooms rather than a hotel-with-a-restaurant – but recently their space has been re-allocated to provide bathrooms with bath or shower, and pastel colours make them bright and light and cheerful.

Pastels again in the large dining room, full at weekends with local gourmets who know how lucky they are to have Jean cook for them. Curtains and walls are pale peachy pink, effective new lighting is by dozens of tiny bulbs, flowers are fresh from the garden.

AUBERGE DE L'ABBAYE   HAMBYE

On the cheapest 95f menu I enjoyed every mouthful of *fruits de mer*, *brochettes* of local lamb charcoal-grilled, Norman cheeses and fresh strawberries, but it hardly matters what you choose here – it is bound to be good. Every night there are two *plats du jour*, one fish, one meat or poultry, but always plenty of seafood and fresh vegetables. All excellent value.

There have been many changes over the Allain's tenure here, all of them for the better (you can't often say that), with the friendly atmosphere preserved throughout the Auberge's growing popularity. Not least has been the addition of Emilie, now aged five, who arrived after twenty years of childless marriage, first dumbfounding then delighting the Allains (and their guests). The only snag is that now Michelin has at last cottoned on it is not so easy to get a room or meal. Otherwise a good deed in an increasingly wickedly expensive restaurant/hotel world, and still 101% arrow-worthy.

Map 4F   **HARCOURT** 27800, Eure. 6 km SE of Brionne by D137

A village dominated by its famous château, previous home of the celebrated Harcourt family.

l'Auberge de l'Abbaye (R)S-M
cl. Wed. o.o.s.; Thurs.; Feb.

NEW   In the village square by the ancient wooden market hall, now the Mairie. Simple but good food in simple but good surroundings. More reports please.
Menus 89-175f. Good house wine.

Map E2&3   **LE HAVRE** 76600, Seine Mar. 86km W of Rouen

Ⓜ *All day every day except Sun. (2 p.m.-6 p.m.)*

They say that Le Havre lost its heart in 1944, when it won the doubtful distinction of being the most bombed port in France, and never replaced it. Architect Auguste Perret tried. He devised two hearts – the Place de l'Hôtel de Ville and the Place Gambetta, amid a grid system of wide roads, among them the avenue Foch, intended to outdo the Champs Elysees. Then he lined the streets with identikit concrete apartment blocks, which give the town its distinctive grey and uniform character. It helps when the sun shines, the waters of the *bassin* sparkle and the flower beds in the Place de l'Hôtel de Ville provide a vivid contrast to the bleakness, but there is no warmth to any heart any more.

Sadly the only part of the town that tourists generally see is the most boring bit – the triangle between the rue Royale, ave Foch and the bvd. François 1er. (It was François who ordered the original Le Havre to be built in 1517, to replace the ancient silted-up port of Harfleur.) The scale of the town deters exploration beyond the pl. Gambetta, where the concrete igloos of the cultural centre effectively block off the only interesting view of the town, towards the *bassin* and swooping white bridge.

| N40 FÉCAMP | N15 HARFLEUR ROUEN | N182 TANCARVILLE BRIDGE |
| ÉTRETAT | YVETOT PARIS | LILLEBONNE |

Terminal de la Citadel 76600 — Le Havre Tel: (0)235 19 78 50

The real Le Havre begins behind the Town Hall, where the department stores and small shops begin. I cannot claim that the noisy r. Réné Coty is Normandy's finest but at least there is animation here, even in winter, when the reconstructed Havre dies.

To paint an even gloomier picture, the town is suffering badly from the competition enduced by the wonderful new Pont de Normandie. Why stay in a characterless port when in no time at all you could be strolling round the colourful Honfleur? A further nail in Havre's coffin was the exit system from the new ferry port, which means that most cars now head directly away from the town. Many of the shops in the rue Royale and the bars along the old ferry quays are shuttered, many restaurants have gone under.

However, needs must. There are times, perhaps with an early ferry departure or late arrival, when a stay here seems strategic. With time to kill, make for the Musée de Beaux Arts, one modern building that is a great success.

Built entirely of metal and glass, it looks out to sea on the point before the road swings back to Ste. Adresse. You proceed up and down ramps in this model of intelligent display to view the collection of Dufy, a native of Havre, Impressionists and Post Impressionists, and of Boudin, born in Honfleur but attracted to Havre. (What would he make of it now?)

Downstairs is a colourful exhibition of marine excitements – beautifully modelled boats, from fishing to steamer, and more paintings.

Shopping? Make for the area around and behind the Hôtel de Ville to find Monoprix, Le Printemps and Les Nouvelles Galeries. Best for food shopping, particularly if the weather is bad, is the Halles Centrales. Find them a street or two behind the pl. Gambetta by walking along the rue Voltaire. Cheap wine here in the Nicolas outlet and easy parking outside.

Two hypermarkets serve the town, Mammouth is at Montivilliers, signposted from the Tancarville road and Auchan in the Haute Ville (take the Cours de la Republique past the station through the tunnel and follow the signs to the vast Centre Commerciale).

Hotels: The uniformity of the blocks makes many of the hotels look alike and I have difficulty in remembering which is which, so dull a bunch are they. However, the following have been endorsed by readers as fulfilling their function of providing a clean, inexpensive night's sleep not too far from ferry and restaurants:

Hotel Foch (H)M
4 r. de Caligny (0)235.42.50.69 Fax (0)235.43.40.17

33 rooms from 300-335f.

Celtic (H)S
106 r. Voltaire (0)235.42.39.77 Fax (0)235.21.67.65

14 rooms 190-265f

Richelieu (H)S
132 r. Paris (0)235.42.38.71 Fax (0)235.21.07.28

19 rooms 160-265f.

Restaurants: The Quartier St. François, near the new ferry terminal, is thick with eateries to suit most tastes and pockets. If you are looking for something more interesting, the following should provide it:

La Petite Auberge (R)M
32 r. de Ste. Adresse (0)235.46.37.42 cl. Sun. p.m.; Mon. 4/8-25/8

Well worth making the short journey out of the immediate town centre, via the place de l'Hotel de Ville, rue Braque, and the rue d'Étretat (which becomes the rue Ste. Adresse) but make sure you have a reservation first – this is a long-term favourite of the Havrais, and of FE readers too. It's small, dark and cosy, serving more or less traditional food of high quality. No fireworks, just the kind of cooking you came to France for.
Menus from 118f (not Sat. p.m.), then 130f.

Petit Bedon (R)M
37 r. Louis Brindeau (0)235.41.36.81 cl. Sat. lunch; Sun.

Another long-established Havrais institution, with *chef-patron* Guy Poyer established here for twenty years. More sophisticated classic French cooking, like chunks of monkfish served with rice enriched with inkfish juice (go for it!). Menus from 155f.

➤ **Le Bistro des Halles** (R)S-M
7 pl. des Halles-Centrales (0)235.22.50.52

NEW   A welcome newcomer, and first choice for lunch. The market square is always a good place to look for bars and restaurants, and this is no exception. The 78f *formule* was obviously popular with the youngish office workers when I last ate there. Husband volunteered to guinea-pig and enjoyed his roast duck, three sorbets and glass of Côteaux de Lyonnais, compliments of the house. I just had a medley of home-made *terrines* (42f) with a salad, but would have been equally happy with a cheese platter for 35f. If you eat *à la carte*, starters are around 35f and mains 70f with a fillet of sole in sorrel sauce costing 75f.

The Bistro is unusual in that it is also a wine bar, and you can get a decent glass of wine without necessarily eating here. The burgundy coloured paint outside emphasises its vinous connections and wine cases decorate the walls along with the usual bistro baggage of Byrrh, St. Raphael and Suze tin signs, lace curtains, blackboard menus, and iron-based tables.

There is pop music but so subdued that even my over-sensitive ear was not offended.

A Kir costs 18f and I was delighted to see an unusual old favourite of mine, a Lillet. If you're looking for a fresh apéritif, try it here for 20f.

An arrow for a little bit of character and good value.

The young owners have recently opened up a new restaurant in Ste. Adresse, which might merit a visit. It is **Coboco**, 6 pl Frederic Sauvage, with menus at 139f and open for Sun. p.m. Reports please.

Ste. Adresse, along the coast to the north of Le Havre, is a pleasant residential area and beach resort, with wooden huts on the cobbles, and a bay full of windsurfers and infant sail-training boats following their mother-duck instructor. Some of its fading turreted houses give a faint taste of pre-war character. I used to recommend it for an overnight stop in one of the faded houses, but tastes have changed and it is now *too* faded, too primitive to be popular. I also used to recommend Yves Page because it was the only restaurant intelligent enough to work out that weekends end on Sun. p.m. and that there would be many a British ferry-passenger looking for a meal then before catching the night boat, so staying open should be popular. It was, the restaurant was packed. But now the hours have changed and it is as shuttered as the rest of the town. However, if you fancy a meal overlooking the sea, this is still the only option. The details are:

Yves Page (R)M
7 pl Clemenceau (0)235.46.06.09 cl Sun. p.m; Mon.

Menus from 130f.

Le Winch (R)S
1 Quai Southampton (0)235.41.75.18

> A flourishing little restaurant, with nautical decor and easy parking,
> is only five minutes from the ferry terminal – ideal for a last meal in
> France.
>
> The small close-together tables, with pretty tablecloths, are busy
> from 7 p.m. onwards. Service is swift, with menus specialising in
> *fruits de mer* starting at 58f (not after 8.30 p.m.). Otherwise it's 75
> or 90f. Good-value wines in pichet or bottle (we paid 52f for 50 ml
> of Beaujolais Villages) and aperitifs from 10f.

Map 4B   **HÉBÉCREVON** 50180, Manche. 5 km NW of St. Lô

> Take the D972 direction Coutances to St. Gilles. In the village
> centre take the D77 Periers road, direction Pont-Hébert. The
> château is 3 km further on.

➤ **Château de La Roque** (HR)M
(0)233.57.33.20 Fax (0)233.57.51.20 open all year

NEW
> There is sometimes a fine line between *chambres d'hôtes* and
> small hotels. Because the owners of the Château eat with their
> guests we decided in favour of the former and included it in *Bed
> and Breakfast in France*, but now Mireille Delisle has given me the
> excuse to enter it here too – she now terms her establishment
> *Auberge de Campagne*. In truth it does not come precisely into any
> category – there are fifteen bedrooms which would tend towards a
> hotel, as would the fact that it is open year round and meals are
> available, but then the owners are so involved with their guests that
> the atmosphere is decidedly more *chambre d'*. Let's say we have
> the best of several very pleasant worlds here.
>
> It's a collection of mellow old stone buildings, 16 and 17C, set
> round a wide courtyard with well-tended flower beds and a massive
> *pressoir* in the centre of the lawn which slopes down to a big lake.
> The view is to the verdant valley of the little river Terrette and all is
> very rural and very peaceful.
>
> The bedrooms are in the two buildings which flank the lawn and
> are all different, all newly decorated, all very attractive. I liked the one
> in red plaid with twin beds and a kitchenette, but then that had a
> shower and I prefer a bath, so perhaps another would be first
> choice, with a stylish bathroom. It hardly matters, they are all so
> delightful. 330f for a double bed or 380f for twins. Dinner is eaten at
> a long table in the big dining room – 95f with wine or home-brewed

cider; home-made bread and jams feature at breakfast and their own chickens often appear on the dinner menu. I like this one very much indeed – definitely an arrow for comfortable accommodation, in delightful surroundings, good value and friendly owners.

Map 2F   **HERICOURT-EN-CAUX** 76560, Seine-Mar. 10 km N of Yvetot by D131

This is one of the prettiest parts of the Caux country, with picturesque villages tucked away in countryside of the deepest green, threaded through by the river Durdent.

Restaurant St. Denis (R)S
(0)235.96.55.23 cl. Wed. and Tues. p.m.

NEW   A pretty little restaurant, coral-coloured within, beamed without, where the 82f (not weekend) menu offers good value. We ate avocado mousse, trout from the nearby river, cheese and a refreshing homemade rhubarb sorbet, prepared by *chef/patron* M. Touze, and considered ourselves extremely well off.

Map 3A   **HONFLEUR** 14600, Calvados. 20 km S of Le Havre. 60 km E of Caen

---

Ⓜ *Sat. a.m.*

Last time I wrote about Honfleur it was 57 km from Le Havre, via the Tancarville Bridge; now it is within half an hour of the port, thanks to the Pont de Normandie, which is as beautiful as it is practical. I do not know of a lovelier structure; cobweb-fine, supported by a wishbone either side, it is a pleasure to drive over it, even with the stiff tolls.

Whether or not it is attributable to the new bridge I do not know, but I sense an air of prosperity and enthusiasm in Honfleur, which was previously lacking. The town looks spruced up, freshly painted; there are numerous building projects in progress and lots of new restaurants prepared to claim a stake for the regular tourist trade. Always a fan, I like it better than ever.

Not everyone shares my taste. Those who visit in August or at busy weekends deplore the crowds and the short tempers of overstretched waiters. I have to admit that I have no similar experience because on dozens of visits I have always been lucky enough to see the town out of peak period, when it never ceases to delight. Nor do I find the grumbles that it is expensive justified. Sure, there are plenty of restaurants here that cater for rich Parisians who drive out for a Sunday lunch treat expense regardless. I have reluctantly dropped even a mention of the famous Ferme St. Simeon because I think any Brit who is prepared to pay 2300f for a room and 550f for a meal (a) wants his head read and (b) will probably let his secretary do the booking rather than read *French Entrée* for himself. But there is tremendous competition in the town amongst the smaller less-well-known restaurants and I found no shortage of these to recommend as good value.

The hotel front, I have to admit, is not rosy. It is surprising that in a town with the tourist potential of Honfleur that there are so few. I have been disappointed in even old favourites and two arrows have gone. I am almost (but not quite) driven to say try the chains here; the Mercure group always choose good sites, and Honfleur representative is no exception. No need for further description – seen one, seen them all.

The town is blessed with two centres, both highly photogenic, both ancient, both pullers. The Vieux Bassin (harbour) and the Place Ste. Cathérine, the site of the colourful weekly market. The harbour is a gem; years of familiarity have not yet spoiled the impact of the framework of lanky old grey houses, some seven storeys high, reflected in the water, where yachts are bobbing and gulls screech overhead. The historic Lieutenant's house, recognisable from many a postcard, guards the entrance. Hard to think of a more pleasant exercise than to join the strollers round the quays, observing the artists at work, peering down on the boats below, watching it all happen from one of the cafés on the edge. The main fishing harbour, full of brightly painted boats, is on the other side of the lock and part of Honfleur's enduring charm is that it is still a working fishing port, not just a tourist facade. When the summer parasols are folded away it still has its living to earn.

Tearing oneself away from the harbour is made easier by the fact that there is more, much more to see. In Honfleur's alternative heart, the Place Ste. Cathérine, is a most unusual church, which gave the square its name. The Eglise Ste. Cathérine is built by local shipbuilders in the material and style which they knew best – wood and boat hulls, of which the roof of the nave is constructed. This was their thanksgiving that the English had at last departed after the Hundred Years War. It's not the oldest church in the town – St. Etienne on the quay side was built during the English occupation from 1419-50 – but it is undoubtedly the most popular.

Little snippets of historical interest like this keep cropping up in this multi-faceted town. Throughout the eight centuries of its existence it seems to have bred a particularly forceful band of men. Intrepid sons of Honfleur, mariners, explorers, scientists, were forever taking to sea in search of new horizons. One discovered

Brazil, one opened up the mouth of the St. Lawrence river, and one, Samuel de Champlain, enlisted local seafarers to sail to Canada and start a colony there.

In the 17C, Colbert ordered the demolition of most of the town's old fortifications designed to thwart the English, and constructed the Vieux Bassin. He built three salt warehouses to store the salt necessary for preserving, the fishermen's catch. Two of these still remain behind the Mairie (look for the *greniers de sel* signs). There has been some sensitive restoration of this area recently and it is now a pleasant place to stroll, between the stone and timbered houses, checking the menus of the bistros and *crêperies* there.

The 19C saw the beginning of a new role for Honfleur – that of an artistic focus. Painters like Boudin and Jongkind, musicians like Erik Satie, writers like Baudelaire were born or lived there. The town art gallery is named after Boudin; it is in the rue Albert 1er, an interesting building, half-modern, half-chapel, though I can't claim that the examples of Boudin's work there do him justice, the museum, which is primarily devoted to the Honfleur school of painting in and around the Seine estuary, has recently been much improved, so it might be worth another look.

Boudin was the centre of the group of young artists fascinated by the effects of the opalescent northern light on the estuary waters, who attempted to capture their impressions on canvas and later became known as the Impressionists and Post-Impressionists.

It is ironic that the meeting place of this group of impoverished Bohemians is the very same Ferme St. Simeon that I now find too expensive to consider. It was once an inn owned by Mère Toutain; Monet, Sisley, Cezanne, Pisarro, all knew it well; Courbet portrayed it on canvas in 'Le Jardin de la Mère Toutain'.

Drive past the old grey stone building now so pristine and manicured, along the steep and winding coast road, the D513, known as the Côte de Grace, and you will come across the charming 17C chapel of Notre Dame de Grace, the Mariners' Chapel. The walls and nave inside are crammed with thanksgivings for lives saved at sea – very moving. Whit Monday is dedicated to a special pilgrimage here for all manner of seafarers.

Le Castel Albertine (H)M-L
19 cours Albert-Manuel (0)231.98.85.56 Fax (0)231.98.85.56

Conflict of reports here. I gave it an arrow for accessibililty, comfortable elegant rooms, but one reader was most unhappy:
'*There were no rooms available on the garden side so we ended up in a cramped bedroom with a rather ancient bathroom overlooking the main road.*'

I don't feel too guilty; the hotel has changed hands, which is a pity because it now lacks the personal warm welcome of the previous owner, but otherwise I think what I wrote still gives a fair picture of what to expect:

'A 19C manor-house set back from the main approach road, with the bonus, unusual in Honfleur, of an extensive leafy garden, with a little lake, bridge and rowing boat. As for rooms, you get what you pay for: my favourite, No. 3, all green and cream and Laura Ashley, with long windows opening onto the garden, now costs 600f, (worth every sou) while a comparatively small doubled-bedded room overlooking the road (but with little traffic noise at night) costs 450f (not such good value). In between is a variety of combinations of double/twin/bath/ shower, so state your preference when you book.'

The reception area has been smartened up and a sauna room added but the atmosphere is much the same, and it would remain my first choice in the town.

I still find the rooms overlooking the garden serene and dignified and so did another reader:

'We found Le Castel Albertine fully lived up to your description.' Ivan McCracken.

l'Ecrin (H)L
119 r. Eugene Boudin (0)231.14.43.45 Fax (0)231.89.24.41

An impressive 18C town house, set back in its courtyard from a quiet street between the town centre and the Côte de Grace.

Its restoration has been extravagant and the lavishness of its furnishings cannot fail to impress and astonish; sometimes it feels more like a museum than a hotel. Four posters, drapes, swags, gilt, crimson plush, tropical plants, are combined with mod cons: film-star bathrooms and big colour TVs. There are some new rooms in the Annexe which are somewhat less fussy and still include an excellent bathroom, but these involve climbing a winding narrow staircase. Breakfast is served in an airy conservatory overlooking the garden.

Rooms in the house cost 800f, those in the Annexe 550f.

'We had the most marvellous stay there in one of the bedrooms on the top floor and were beautifully looked after. We simply could not understand how Le Castel Albertine got a thumbs up and l'Ecrin did not. We also felt very secure leaving our car parked in the private forecourt which was locked by 9 p.m.' Christina Bentley.

Motel Monet H(S-M)
Cherrière du Puits (0)231.89.00.90 cl. Jan.

> To find a base in Honfleur that is both practical and inexpensive
> takes some doing, but le Motel Monet would seem to fulfil both
> criteria. Readers' reports were all positive but suddenly it's all gone
> quiet, so there may be some new doubts here. Therefore the
> recommendation is a qualified one, based on previous experience. I
> should very much like to hear about any new visits, but meanwhile it
> seems a pity to omit an establishment that is unique in this area.
>
> The word Motel can be off putting, with associations of
> impersonality, but the Monet's proprietor is welcoming and helpful
> and the only similarity between this and the general motel
> stereotype is that of easy parking and access. It is particularly
> recommended for the disabled driver or passenger. The rooms are
> modern, clean and functional at 250f. It is a little way from the town,
> on one of the routes to the Côte de Grace but still within walking
> distance.

➤ l'Assiette Gourmande (R)M-L
2 quai des Passsagers (0)231.89.24.88 Fax (0)231.89.90.17 cl. Mon.
PREMISES

NEW PREMISES
> I can hardly keep pace with the Bonnefoy's shooting-star career.
> Now they have moved again, taking Gérard's Michelin star with
> them to what must be their dream premises in the old Cheval Blanc
> building along the quay, but retain their previous restaurant
> premises in the Place Ste. Cathérine as a more modest
> establishment (see below). May good fortune continue to shower
> down on their well-deserving heads. Honfleur has many goodish
> restaurants but anyone interested in seriously talented cooking
> should not miss this one, especially the 160f menu, which must be
> the town's best bargain. I drooled over *tartare* of salmon with
> caviare cream, *langoustine* risotto and the kind of *crême brulée* that
> makes me want to give up ever preparing one again. Arrowed for
> excellence.

l'Absinthe (HR)L
*10 quai de la Quarantaine (0)231.89.39.00 Fax (0)231.89.53.60 cl. 12/11-
30/11*

NEW ROOMS
> A candidate for Honfleur's most attractive restaurant. In a 16C
> presbytery on the quay, with a plethora of low beams and gleaming
> copper. The food is classy and pricey, better for an out-of-season
> dinner than for a sunny carefree lunch. You will eat very well on the

159f menu. There are now seven luxury bedrooms appended, whose bathrooms boast hydrotherapy jacuzzis. 500-700f.

Au P'tit Mareyeur (R)M
4 r. Haute (0)231.98.84.23 cl. Mon. p.m.; Tues.

NEW MANAGE- MENT News of a change of management here had me worried – I liked the Mareyeur just the way it was – but so far so good. Nothing has changed decor-wise, the service is even better than erstwhile and the cooking still some of the best in town at this level, with no concessions to easy tourist trade. It is minute, so booking advisable.

Menus start at 120f with extensive *à la carte*. The arrow will have to be held in abeyance until we see how things have settled down but I would certainly recommend taking the risk.

'Now being run by a couple who are renting (with option in a year's time to buy) from the owners. We went twice and enjoyed a good meal on both occasions. The only reservation was that there was only one 120f menu, with good choice and a very limited plat du jour variation. A choice of different-priced menus would have been helpful. Nevertheless Madame was warm and friendly and speaks English, having trained in London.' David Rasten.

Terrasse de l'Assiette (R)M
8 pl. Ste. Catherine (0)231.89.31.33 cl. Sun. p.m.; Wed. o.o.s.; 15/12-15/1

NEW There is a whole row of restaurants spilling their tables attractively out on to the Place Ste. Cathérine. By all means walk up and down and check out the menus, but, if you take my advice, put this one top of the list. It is under the skilful direction of Gérard Bonnefoy (he of the Michelin star at l'Assiette Gourmande), and his expertise and judgment shows. The menus may be more limited than at the parent establishment, the ingredients less exotic, but the standard is still high. A probable arrow after a few more reports. Menus from 129f.

Le Bistro du Port (R)S
14 quai Quarantaine (0)231.89.21.84 cl. Mon. p.m.; Tues. from Jan to April.; 20/11-20/12

I don't know whether to be pleased (I've been recommending it for years) or fed up (prices could go up, tables become hard to come by) that le Bistro has now made Michelin. We have always used it because it was such honest good value in an expensive town, accommodating all tastes. It is the place we turn to if one of us fancies a bowl of *moules*, another a full menu, another a ham sandwich and another a steak. The exterior may not inspire confidence, over-folksy among other more up market restaurants, but inside is better; it's a very old timbered building, with cross-beams and mind-your-heads dividing the upstairs restaurant (bag a table overlooking the water). Downstairs there are a few more tables and in chilly times a welcome log fire. If the sun shines there is the terrace alternative. It does already seem to be on the up and up, prices included, and menus now start at 90f. Reports have varied from 'the worst meal ever' to the 'best meal ever' so the arrow will have to go until a more reliable standard is reached.

➤ Auberge du Vieux Clocher (R)M
9 r. de l'Homme de Bois (0)231.89.12.06 cl. Sun. p.m.; Wed. except July and Aug. 2/1-25/1; 24/2-1/3

Here's another one from way back that has climbed steadily up the ladder from S to M. and a place in the Michelin. I have now run out of really cheap, really fun, really small, really exciting bistros in Honfleur. However, the dining room is less cramped, the plumbing is more reliable and the service smoother. The food is pretty good too, but I preferred paying peanuts to the current 125f cheapest menu.

'*The best meal of our entire stay. On the 150f menu my husband started with a delicious fish soup served with lot of lovely croutons and crispy things. I had a mousseline of salmon and asparagus with a tomato coulis which was gorgeous. Wonderful home-made bread. Then lamb chops so tender they just melted in our mouths then a selection of local cheeses (goats cheese just amazing). Husband ordered an apple tart to die for, soaked in calvados. A churn of double cream with ladle was placed on the table for him to help himself. We cannot recommend it more highly*' Christina Bentley.

Perhaps I can accept the increased prices after all. The arrow stays.

Ascot (R)M-S
76 quai Ste. Catherine (0)231.98.87.91 cl. Wed. p.m.; Thurs. o.o.s.; mid Nov.-mid Dec.

NEW
I haven't tried this one personally, but I hear only good reports:
'*Our favourite. A charming small restaurant, friendly service and a very interesting good menu. Opens late also.*' Beryl Brown.
Menus from 99f-189f.

La Tortue (R)M-S
36 r. de l'Homme de Bois (0)231.89.04.93 cl. Wed.

Tiny, beamed, very pretty indeed, tucked away along the picturesque rue de l'Homme du Bois, beyond the average tourist tread, readers have given consistent thumbs-up to this one for interesting cooking and fair prices. Menus from 90f.

Château de Prêtreville (H)M
Gonneville sur Honfleur (0)231.89.37.06 Fax (0)231.89.28.39

I'm not sure if this should be included here amongst the hotels, or in *Bed and Breakfast in France* amongst the *chambres d'hotes*, since it is neither, but self catering accommodation. Since it is so good, I shall bend the rules and put it in both. It's a 19C 'château' set in 3 hectares, with a variety of studios and apartments for from two to six people, perfectly equipped, and run by the charming M. and Mme Rémi Bodet, who speak perfect English. The tariff is very complicated, with prices from 775f for two nights, so do ring and check.

Map 1F   **INGOUVILLE** 76460, Seine-Mar. 3 km SW of St. Valery-en-Caux

Look for 'le Bourg' of Ingouville and les Hêtres is signed from there

➤ **Les Hêtres** (HR)L
(0)235.57.09.30 Fax (0)235.57.09.31

NEW   To turn up at lunchtime on a sunny Sunday at one of the smartest restaurants in the *département*, without a reservation (and without any intention of eating or staying) is asking for trouble. Passing all the expensive cars (French) in the car park I hardly dared to push open the restaurant door but there in a flash was a welcoming Eric Liberge, regretting that they were fully booked but if he could be of service otherwise? Would that there were more Erics around.

After that I admit he had me eating out of his hand but even with a less courteous reception I could not but have helped falling in love with les Hêtres. Set in a tastefully colourful garden, the building is thatched, beamed and very very pretty, both inside and out. The four luxurious bedrooms (and yes, Eric actually took time off to show me these too) are in a separate building, priced (reasonably for the quality on offer) at 580-650f.

I remember Bertrand Warin, the chef, with the fondest of recollections, at his former eponymous restaurant in Rouen (now les Nymphéas) and missed him, the best cook in the city, when he decamped, so it is good news that he has re-surfaced here and is cooking as divinely as ever. His 160f menu must be the bargain of the year. Items on the day I visited were Breton *langoustines* cooked with Chinese-style cabbage, and *brochettes* of quail served with a beetroot and Parmesan gâteau.

Ingouville
des Hêtres

I am going to break a rule here and award an arrow to an establishment I have not actually sampled personally. The rooms looked so comfortable, I know that Warin cooks like an angel and local opinion was so glowing that it seems a pity not to point readers in this direction. And I hope to make up for my shortcoming very soon.

Map 3B	**ISIGNY-SUR-MER** 14230, Calvados. 11 km E of Carentan. 61 km SE of Cherbourg

Ⓜ *Wed.*

Not really sur-mer but near the mouth of the Vire, which means oysters and all manner of other shellfish. There is a little quay, with green and red fishing boats tied up and sheds full of baskets of assorted crustaceans. The heart of the dairy industry and *pré salé* country, where the tastiest sheep graze.

France (HR)S
17 r. E Demagny (0)231.22.00.33 Fax (0)231.22.79.19 cl. Fri p.m.; and Sat. o.o.s.; 1/12-15/1

NEW
An old-fashioned very French hotel in the main road (so could be noisy). The 19 rooms cost from 180-310f, but it is the food that I am recommending .

The 58f menu is a remarkable bargain – three courses of substantial well-cooked fare, with plenty of local seafood. The restaurant is full week-long but at weekends it's bulging and the cheapest menu price goes up to 170f.

Popular with readers for a cheap en-route meal – grills, kebabs, etc – was the Flambée right on the quay, but I hear that there has been a change of management, so new reports would be welcome.

Map 5H   **IVRY LA BATAILLE** 27540, Eure. 17 km S of Pacé-sur-Eure

---

(M) *Wed.*

Following the little D143 along the meandering course of the Eure makes a soothing alternative to the parallel north-south main roads. It's all very green, very relaxing, passing through flower-strewn villages, like Ivry, with glimpses of water and good picnicking possibilities.

Le Moulin d'Ivry (R)M
(0)232.36.40.51 cl. Mon. p.m.; Tues.

Many changes here in this old watermill straddling two strands of the river. Inside all is much as was – lovely red Toile de Jouy fabrics in the ancient, low-beamed dining room, even if perhaps it's all a bit smarter, a bit less rustic, a bit livelier than of yore. But outside there have been unthinkable additions. Tacked on to the side of the mill is a completely new building, pink and green, aggressive and unapologetically out of sync with its neighbour. It was not quite finished when I was there and I assumed it was new bedrooms for the restaurant, but, no, I was told it would be apartments. Best avert the eyes and enjoy the lovely setting, with wide terrace running along the river, for summer *dégustation*. Not surprisingly, one hour from Paris, the mill is very popular on sunny weekends, so be sure to book. The *Menu du Marché* 150f.

Map 5A   **JULLOUVILLE-LES-PINS** 50610, Manche. 8.5 km S. of Granville

---

The bay sweeps all the way round from Granville to Carolles, sand all the way and That View (Mont St. Michel) dominating the seascape. Jullouville used to be a sleepy little family resort but it's growing all the time and so is the number of souvenir shops and fast food outlets. For bucket n' spaders though it would still be a good choice.

Hotel Equinoxe (H)S-M
28 ave. de la Libération (0)233.50.60.82 cl. 1/11-1/4

NEW   A spruced-up villa, one row back from the sea, which means the prices are much more reasonable than those for hotels with sea views. There is a bar, a terrace in the garden for breakfast and drinks, and private parking, which I think makes this really good value at 150-340f. It is on the main road but the traffic noise is minimal. A good twin-bedded room with bathroom would set you back no more than 260f, which in a seaside town in high season is not bad. Good atmosphere too.

Map 3G   **JUMIÈGES** 76480, Seine-Mar. 28 km W of Rouen

The village of Jumièges is dominated by the ruins of the great Benedictine abbey, founded in the 7C, razed by the Vikings, rebuilt in 1067 and consecrated with William, the great Duke of Normandy, in attendance. The monks were forcibly evicted during the Revolution and an auction was held to dispose of the building. A builder and timber merchant made the successful bid and used his new acquisition as a stone quarry. 130 years ago it was rescued and now belongs to the state.

You get a lot of ruin for your money. The entire nave, roofless, soars 90f high to the sky and some of the chancel and transept remain. But it is the twin towers either side of the main door that will be familiar from posters. A most rewarding hour could be spent here wondering and wandering through the history-steeped grounds.

From here to Duclair the river makes a spectacular loop; the road, that follows it, the D65, is known as the *Route de Fruits*, lined with

Abbaye de Jumièges

fruit stalls neath umbrellas. Sheltered by chalk escarpments this is perfect picnicking ground and alongside the river numerous families set up their parasols and unpack their copious lunches. There are one or two small restaurants, like La Pommeraie for snacks, and a *salon de thé*, Le Parc, with a nice terraced garden. Not to be missed.

Auberge des Ruines (R)M
pl. de la Maire 02.35.37.24.05 cl. Sun. p.m.; Mon. cl. for dinner o.o.s.; exc. Fri. and Sat.

Big improvements here. An enthusiastic young couple, Agnes and Loïc Henry, have rescued what used to be a dusty and decrepit old inn, only viable because of its superb position opposite the abbey walls, and turned it into an excellent restaurant. I do not know what their plans are for the bedrooms (which were in a disgraceful state when I saw them last), but never mind. For the moment they do well to concentrate on Loïc's cooking.

Given his talent and the site it is not surprising that the auberge is usually full, so plans to eat here should be made in advance. The dining room is not at all plush, but has plenty of atmosphere and bulges with noisy enjoyment at the weekend.

Menus from 92f (weekdays and Sat. lunch only), otherwise 164f.

Map 3H   **LYONS-LA-FORÊT** 27480, Eure. 35 km E of Rouen

 Thurs.

... by N14 and then the leafy D321 through the forest from which the little town takes its name. In other words a comfortable distance from the city and an attractive drive. No wonder that at the first glimmer of sunshine all the tables (and there are many) in the square are taken and the café and restaurant owners have so much custom that they do not have to be pleasant to anyone.

It's a picturebook-pretty town, with some enchanting black and white houses. One of them, on the hill leading off the square was occupied by Maurice Ravel and it was here that he composed Le Tombeau de Couperin. The focal point of the town are the market halls sheltered by a fine 18C timber roof.

I recommend a visit to Lyons but not an overnight stay or even a meal. There are plenty of eating opportunities, but they are becoming more and more of the fast-food persuasion, with the exception of the famous La Licorne hotel and restaurant which occupies prime position overlooking the square. It is a lovely old building, with a delightful shaded courtyard, but since other serious competition has faded away it has become far too expensive and far too arrogant. Readers have *not* been happy here. The dragon-*patronne* (I suppose it was she; otherwise she should be sacked instantly) was one of the rudest I have met for a long time. Her hotel was full so why should she bother until it was empty again? The twelve rooms are from 400–480f and meals start at 190f.

Map 6D   **MACÉ** 61500 Sées, Orne. 4.5 km NW of Sées on the D238

Clearly marked, via various narrow roads in rather dull countryside.

Île de Sées (HR)M
(0)233.27.98.65 Fax (0)233.28.41.22 cl. Sun. p.m.; Mon.; 15/1-15/3

Very imposing gates for such a little hotel. It's modern, but softened by creeper. Nice garden, tables outside, utter quiet. Inside the decor is a bit plush for the countryside, but the lounge is comfy and the dining room pretty in pink and yellow with cane chairs. Menus here start at 78f for lunch – salad, steak and dessert – or 98f – terrine, steak, cheese and dessert. Everything well prepared, and good carafe wine. The 19 bedrooms are on the small side, but again comfortable and well equipped.

The Île is featured by several tour companies and very popular with the British, who like its position away (but not too far away) from the town and traffic, and its reliability.

Map 4B   **MARIGNY** 50570, Manche. 14 km NE of Coutances, 14 km SW of St. Lô

Ⓜ *Wed.*

A little market town unremarkable apart from being the surprising site of a very well-respected restaurant.

Restaurant de la Poste (R)M
pl. Westport (0)233.55.11.08 Fax (0)233.55.25.57. cl. Sun. p.m. 1st fortnight in Jan and 23/9-7/10.

I have found readers very perverse in the past in not, as far as I can tell, heeding my strong advice to eat here. Ne'er a letter about La Poste, good or bad. Well, this is your last chance. I hear rumours that Joel Meslin might be deserting his restaurant to spend yet more time as Chairman of a gathering of local restaurateurs. Meanwhile catch him in his kitchen if you can.

Certainly his amiable plump wife Liliane will be there to greet and serve. The cooking is Norman with imagination. Oysters are the house speciality, served in more ways than you can think of.

Generous menus start at 110f (not weekends), then 145f upwards.

Map 1G   **MARTIN-ÉGLISE** 76370, Seine-Mar. 7 km SE of Dieppe

---

So near the port yet so far in mood. Take the D1 out of Dieppe and the suburbs stretch almost all the way to Martin-Église, where they suddenly come to an abrupt halt. One minute it's factories and lorries and then, all the more welcome for the surprise, rolling fields and cows. In the centre of the village is:

Auberge du Clos Normand.

Auberge du Clos Normand (HR)M
22 r. Henri VI (0)235.04.40.34 cl. Mon., Tues., 15/11-15/12 and 1st week in April

They don't come more *rustique* than this, a weathered 15C inn with large leafy garden running down to the river Eaulne. Nine simple bedrooms (and more to come) are in a converted stable block, creeper-covered, faded timbers. The only disturbance is an occasional quack.

The *chef-patron* M. Hauchecorne cooks on an open range at one end of a dining room almost too pretty to be true. Dark beams, shining copper, red ceiling, white napery, high-backed cane chairs and lots of flowers contribute to a warm and cosy atmosphere that is textbook Norman.

Because of its ideal position and attractiveness, the auberge has a core of faithful customers and it is not easy to get a room. I think perhaps this might be the reason that the prices are on the high side for the amenities – 380f for a double with bath, and menus from 160f – but if you want a guaranteed peaceful night near Dieppe, with only a step across the garden towards a good dinner, this one takes some beating. Arrowed for accessibility to Dieppe and Norman charm.

Map 2B   **MAUPERTUS-SUR MER** 50840, Manche. 10 km E of Cherbourg

---

The *Route Touristique de Val de Saire* east of Cherbourg, starts off badly through shabby suburbs. Persevere and reward is at hand. Surprisingly soon the road begins to climb, buildings fade away and the view is of rolling countryside to the right and the Channel far below to the left. At Anse du Brick is a good sandy beach set in a sheltered bay, with a cluster of snack bars. High above is:

La Maison Rouge (HR)M
(0)233.54.33.50 cl. Mon.

Readers have been delighted to discover this comfortable restaurant, with *panoramique* view so near to the port. It's a bar and *salon de thé* as well, so a drive out in this direction might well be enhanced by a drink with a view, but don't think of arriving straight from the beach with damp cozzies – it's not that kind of situation at all. Cathérine and Philippe Delsaut have smartened the place up and the decor is blue and yellow rather than the old red that gave the restaurant its name. Lots of seafood of course; the French clientele were busy demolishing expensive lobsters purported to have been trapped in the rocks below. Menus start at 90f. There are three new rooms, but you have to crane a little for a sea view. 200f without a loo, 330f with bath.

Map 3H   **MENESQUEVILLE** 27850, Eure. 28 km SE of Rouen by N14

Relais de la Lieure (HR)S-M
(0)232.49.06.21 Fax (0)232.49.58.87 cl. Sun. p.m.; and Mon. o.o.s.

NEW

M. Trapagny caught me snooping round the back of his roadside hotel, having looked in at the bar and thinking perhaps it was not worth wasting too much time here. I was very glad he did, because the Relais is much better inside than out.

The 16 rooms in the annexe at the rear, well away from traffic noise, are surprisingly large and well-equipped – good value at 255-320f. Meals are served in the rusticated dining room next to the bar and menus start at 80f.

Map 4E   **MÉRY CORBON** 14370, Calvados. 26 km SE of Caen

(M) *Wed.*

Actually in the hamlet of Lion d'Or, on the main Caen-Lisieux road the N13, in the commune of Méry-Corbon.

Le Relais du Lion d'Or (R)M-S
Tel and Fax (0)231.23.65.30 cl. Sun. p.m.; Mon. o.o.s.

An old favourite and an arrow under the previous management. I was sorry to hear that it had been sold but all reports of the new regime are favourable. Virginie and Christophe Dabout are said to be carrying on the good work and changing very little the winning formula of imaginative but simple food served in the charming wayside restaurant.

It is much prettier inside than out, with two small stone-walled dining rooms. Floors are flagged, chairs are cane, fires are log and the death-defying spiral staircase still has to be navigated in order to get to the loo. I look forward to more reports to reinstate the arrow.

Menus from 98-208.

Map 2H   **MESNIÈRES-EN-BRAY**, Seine-Mar. 5.5 km NW of Neufchatel via the D1

A sleepy flowery village dominated by the great Renaissance château, now housing a private institution.

Auberge du Bec Fin (R)M
(0)235.94.15.15 cl. Mon.; 1/3-15/3; 1/11-15/11

NEW   Extremely pretty, black and white, on the corner next to the château, with a nice garden and tables outside on a terrace hung with (plastic) wisteria.

Inside is equally delightful, all dark beams, copper, lots of flowers, smart covers, smart service, lots more room than one might imagine from the cottagey exterior.

This is the only *gastronomique* restaurant in the region and understandably popular, but they have not loaded the prices accordingly. There were really interesting items on the cheapest menu, at 88f, and the 138f would be a feast.

A few more reports please for an arrow.

Map 1H   **MESNIL-VAL** 76910, Seine-Mar. 5 km SW of Le Tréport

A peaceful village, nestling in a gap in the characteristic chalk cliffs that only stirs and comes to life in the season. Nearby Le Tréport provides the buzz.

La Vieille Ferme (HR)M
(0)235.86.72.18 Fax (0)235.86.12.67 cl. 3/1-21/1

A very popular, long-established hotel, distinctively black and white in the style designated Anglo-Norman. Very pretty garden to sit in and geraniummed window boxes at every aperture. An old grape press lends further character. The tiny beach is 200 metres away.

The 34 rooms, for the most part in two detached houses in the grounds of the hotel, are calm and agreeable, though not large and not luxurious. Some of them involve climbing steep steps, so the infirm should check before booking.

And book you will have to, well in advance, since the biggest disappointment expressed by readers has been failing to get in.

The best deal is demi-pension (obligatory in high season), since the food is said to be good, 305-370f per person. Otherwise it's 280-450f for the room.

Royal Albion Hotel (H)M-L
1 r. de la Mer (0)235.86.21.42 Fax (0)235.86.78.51

NEW
One of the few establishments approaching L grade along the coast and particularly welcome because although the ambiance is de luxe the prices are not. Still new and trying hard.

The building is said to be an old manor-house, but the conversion has been total and stylish and now it is more reminiscent of New England than Normandy. Very attractive are the white clapboard porches and rocking chairs on the balconies.

The rooms are set around a wide courtyard at the rear; although there is admirable architectural cohesion, they are all different in size, decoration, facilities and outlook. Choose any combination of four poster, double/twin, modern and bright/pretty-pastel, courtyard/garden/seawards

Royal Albion Hotel, Mesnil-Val-Plage

It's all very peaceful and away from the traffic fret, with extensive *parc* at the rear, dotted with recliners. No restaurant but the Vieille Ferme is nearby and all the fishy options of Le Tréport are a ten minute drive. The gentlemanly, English-speaking owner will be pleased to advise.

Prices range from 280f for a standard double with bath overlooking the patio to a king-size room with four-poster overlooking the sea at 490f and buffet breakfast is 40f.

A promising new find. Reports please for an arrow.

Map 4F   **MONTREUIL L'ARGILLÉ** 27390, Eure. 22 km SW of Bernay on
          the N138

Ⓜ *Tues.*

In the verdant valley of the Charentonne.

➤ **L'Auberge de la Truite (Chez Jacky)** (R)S
(0)232.44.50.47 cl. Tues. p.m.; Wed. 15/1-15/2

NEW   The arrow is not a suggestion, it's a command. No-one passing
           through this area should fail at least to drop in at Jacky's, even, as
           in our case, it was far too early for lunch. I really wanted to snoop
           and a *café crème* at the bar and a visit to the loo provided the
           opportunity to view two of the remarkable collection of fairground
           organs for which Jacky's is famous. I needn't have been tentative.
           Madame left her ironing and set the huge 1930 Orgue Mortier into
           action. The volume was overwhelming, with drums, accordions,
           cymbals, bells, all taking their turn, sometimes solo, sometimes all
           together. Entrancing. In the room upstairs reserved for functions
           there are others, all highly colourful, and in deafening working
           order. Parked outside the restaurant is a green vintage car, so that
           brides can ride back from the church to the function all in the same
           time-scale.
               The restaurant is pretty enough in its own right, even without its
           unique decoration. Rustic-simple, with blue checked cloths, brass
           implements on the walls and friendly service. Menus from 85f, as
           yet untested by me but obviously approved of locally judging by the
           numbers starting to arrive by mid-day when we left. Reports
           welcome for food – the arrow is for the decor!
               P.S. An item for a pieces of useless information collection. The
           organs are known as Orgues de Barbarie. But why? After much
           questioning I elicited eventually that they were originally built by a M.
           Barbarie.

Map 6B   **MONT ST. MICHEL** 50116, Manche. 22 km SW of Avranches

           I have admired the Mount in winter, grey like the sea and the sky,
           remote, eerie; in the spring, when its colours change like those of
           nature from sullenness to sparkle; in autumn, when it swims in early
           mists and catches fire from late sun – but never before has there
           been an occasion to visit in summer. This was part-deliberate – I am
           naturally crowd-allergic and this miraculous place has particular
           claim to be experienced in peace – and part-accident; I simply
           hadn't been in the vicinity in high season and was happy to glory in

the prospect dominating the bay from afar across the glittering water.

Until this year. July was the time allocated and July it had to be, and I am in a way glad that it was because now I can urge with every possible emphasis that no *French Entrée* reader should ever contemplate a visit then. They say this is the most-visited monument in Europe and it qualified for the title on that one afternoon alone.

Husband took one look at the thousands of cars parked as far as the eye could see and flatly refused to be involved. I, dear readers, am made of sterner stuff and trudged the half-mile queue to the entrance, muttering about sheep. I meant the tourist variety, but the other kind were out there too, munching away at the salty vegetation that would lend them such fatal flavour. I really needed to check up on all the foodie options on that one steep drag, but on this occasion duty called in vain. The procession of pilgrims was solid and hardly moving. Even my well-campaigned elbows would have made little impression. So all I can reliably report is that there are dozens of possibilities for everything from a pizza to a Mère Poularde omelette, currently selling at an iniquitous 95f (and the main secret ingredient is air!). In fact there are so many eager outlets that the customer does get the benefit of the competition: the prices looked very reasonable and you can hardly go wrong on a plateful of mussels for 45f, particularly if you choose one of the restaurants on the right-hand side and bag a table near the window for that fantastic view.

Enough of summer – just don't do it. For the rest of the year the Mount lives up to its appellation *Le Merveille*. From a northern approach particularly it dominates every landscape, glimpsed from little seaside resorts around the bay, to Avranche's heights, to surrounding marshlands, and the magnetism is undeniable. The Archangel Michael, whom it honours, is said to have become irritated with the tardiness of Hubert, Bishop of Avranches, who failed to build the customary hilltop shrine in his honour on Mont St. Tombe, as the mount rising from the forest was then called. A few preliminary dream visitations failed to spur Aubert into action, so Michael tapped him so forcibly on the forehead that he dented his skull – there for all sceptics to see for themselves in St. Gervais in Avranches.

Left in no doubt about his boss's wishes, Aubert built the first oratory in 907, replaced by a Carolingian abbey on which successive generations piled more and more elaborate edifices in Romanesque and Gothic styles. Each one demanded formidable dedication of skill and industry, with granite blocks having to be imported from the Chausey Islands and Brittany and hauled up to the crest of the Mount. The many sections are too complex to describe here but those of the 14C Merveille to the north of the

Mount are certainly not to be missed. Allow more time than you might think necessary. Ideally a circumference on foot (tides permitting!) is the way to assess the scale. You may have to paddle.

The combination of this man-made miracle, set in the natural miracle of the racing water, which leaves only a causeway for the pilgrims across the water meadows and at new and full moons surrounds the Mount completely, has always drawn admirers, so perhaps one should not carp that it still does. Just make sure you have space, time and peace to make your pilgrimage a blessing not a penance.

Mont Saint-Michel.

St. Pierre (HR)M
Grande Rue (0)233.60.14.03 Fax (0)233.48.519.82 cl. 15/12-10/2

NEW   Rather like Disneyworld, the way to get this big tourist attraction to yourself, before or after the hordes have left, is to stay on site. This little hotel built into the ramparts, is a surprisingly good bet. The 15C building, classed as a *Monument historique,* has attractive well-equipped rooms and probably the best restaurant on the Mont.

Food is admirably simple – *gigôts*, grilled lobster, good *fruits de mer* – menus starting at 90f.
21 rooms from 330-630f.

New hotels are springing up on the *digue* – the approach road to the Mount. Personally I wouldn't choose them because they lack character and are purely functional for Mount tourists. If all you care about is somewhere to put your aching feet up you could look at the Relais du Roy and the Digue. Otherwise consider Beauvoir, p 57.

Map 3G   **MONTIGNY** 76380, Seine-Mar. 4 km W of Rouen by D982

Most of Rouen is contained in a huge loop of the Seine. Cross the river into the forest of Roumare and immediately you are in deep greenery, far away from the stress of the city. Nearby at St. Martin de-Boscherville is the glorious 12C abbey of St. Georges, which I urge you not to miss. It has recently been cleaned and the white stone is now gleamingly pristine. It was the last abbey to be build in the Norman style and has survived through the centuries intact, with only one addition – the vaulted nave built on intersecting ribs, which itself is no parvenu – it was built in the 13C.

➤ **Le Relais de Montigny** (HR)M
(0)235.36.05.97 Fax (0)235.36.19.60 cl. 26/1-5/2; R cl. Sat. lunch

NEW   My heart sank when we pulled up outside the Relais. I had imagined that a *relais* in the forest would have some character and here was a great ugly modern building of the kind I usually avoid. Thank goodness I had a reservation and it was getting too late to move on. As I ought to know by now, outward appearances in France are not always to be trusted and I nearly missed a gem.

First the location – to be this near to Rouen, in a quiet village, is a huge bonus. Second the staff, and management – M. and Madame Lenoble are the most friendly, helpful, and professional of owners. There was a wedding party in the large and leafy rear garden at the time we arrived and all the staff were fully occupied, but they made absolutely sure that we were welcomed and shown to our rooms with attendant baggage-carrier (increasingly rare). The 22 rooms are large and exceptionally well-equipped, as are the bathrooms. Most of them have balconies overlooking the garden. Ours was huge – ideal for breakfast, as an alternative to the general terrace. The prices are bargains – 280-395f. We ate in Rouen so I cannot vouch for the food served in the pleasant dining room (menus from

100f and good carafe wine) but the arrow is a certainty for the accommodation, location and management.

Map 6F   **MORTAGNE AU PERCHE** 61400, Orne. 38 km NE of Alençon

---

Ⓜ *Sat.*

My favourite town in the area. Perhaps I would not go along with the proudly proclaimed *Le plus beau bourg de France*, but I'm pleased that someone thinks so, because it is not a town appreciated enough by the Brits. It deserves better – here is an unusually animated town centre, several squares, several bars, with a wealth of old houses and monuments in intriguing narrow mediaeval lanes, having survived many a war and hostility. Affluent townhouses like the Hôtel du Receveur des Tailles (the tax collector's house), which was built by a Parisian banker in the time of Louis XV, are pleasures to behold, as is the Hôtel Ste. Croix with a pleasing 18C curved façade. Behind the Town Hall is a small public garden with a *vue panoramique*, a gentle panorama of venerable trees and the softly rolling countryside of the Perche. Good for picnicking (or take an excursion to the La Trappe and Perche forests, divided by the river Avre to the north-east of the town, where you can snack by one of the many lakes).

Amongst all its many attributes, there is one of which the Mortagnais are particularly proud. Their town is the home of the black sausage. Every year at the Black Sausage Fair no less than five *kilometres* of sausage are consumed! The competition to produce the No.1. black sausage is predictably keen and every year the heat is on to name the proud butcher who is judged to have succeeded. What used to be a local contest has spread and our North Country entrants have several times had the temerity to win. You might like to consider becoming a new member of the Knights of the Black Sausage. You would be welcomed at the spring meeting so long as you are prepared to swear to eat black sausage once a week, to vaunt its qualities and to promote its consumption.

A super little town deserves a super little hotel and, belatedly, there is one such:

➤ **Hotel du Tribunal** (HR)S
4 pl. du Palais (0)233.25.04.77 Fax (0)233.83.60.83 Open every day

NEW   A charming old stone building, both 13C and 18C, set in a strikingly quiet leafy square just behind Notre Dame. It always had great potential and now, praise be, that has been realised by M. and Mme Le Boucher, who took over the faded hotel in 1993 and have

Hotel du Tribunal
Montagne - au - Perche

completed their refurbishment. The interior courtyard, flowery and quiet, is a joy, particularly for summer breakfasts, and in winter the dining room looks out onto the greenery. Make sure you ask for a room with this aspect.

The bedrooms are good value at 220-320f, with choice of bath or shower, and the menus too won't break the bank. The *Menu Terroir*, featuring a *Salade Percheronne* (with meltingly hot local cheese), the famous black sausage and a *tarte aux pommes* flamed in brandy, costs 100f, but there is a cheaper *Menu Formule*, good for a quickie lunch, at 68f, for one main dish and one dessert.

I really like the atmosphere here, with friendly Madame Le Boucher officiating. An arrow for good position, good value.

Genty Home (HR)M
4 r. Notre Dame (0)233.25.11.53 Fax (0)233.25.41.38

Very compact, an ancient stone house squeezed into a side street leading into the main square. The eight bedrooms are compact too, but furnished in the same style as the restaurant below, i.e. in the elaborate mock Louis XV decor so beloved by French restaurateurs. Each has a shower, loo and basin and costs a modest 230-295f.

The dining room is intimate and best by candle-light, when the chandeliers and boudoir atmosphere seem more appropriate than for a summer's lunch. The French would not agree with me – there is no shortage of businessmen tucking into substantial tucker, especially on a Monday when Madame de Gournay obligingly stays open. Trust them to cotton on to a good thing – the 89f menu is very good value, and the carafe wine too, served in such elegant surroundings.

The enterprising Madame de Gournay never lets grass grow under feet. Her second venture was the Château des Carreaux, a lovely 18C château five minutes drive from the town, set back from the RN12. This, described as an annexe to the Genty Home, would suit those who prefer to stay in the country (the *nationale* does not intrude) in somewhat grand style at a not very grand price. The rooms are furnished in the same Louis XV style but here it looks exactly right in the dignified and high-ceilinged salon and four spacious and gracious bedrooms. They cost a very reasonable 355-480f. Throw in tranquil grounds in which to stroll and it all looks a very good deal, but you would have to drive into Mortagne for dinner.

The enterprise does not stop here. Next door to the Genty Home is a cheaper establishment known as La Grillade; that too is now under Madame's auspices. It's all very light and cheerful, with plenty of tables outside commanding the best view of the square. Just the kind of place to know about if you're looking for a quick inexpensive meal or a coffee stop. 55f menus, and an omelette costs 25f.

This will be a joint arrow – for inexpensive accommodation both in the town and in the country, for good food in the restaurant and ditto in the Grillade, serving a wide range of tastes, appetites and budgets.

Map 3A   **NÈGREVILLE** 50260 Bricquebec, Manche. 22 km SE of Cherbourg; 8 km W of Valognes

---

We are talking seriously deep countryside here. If you look up Nègreville on the maps (always supposing you succeed in finding it) you are in the wrong place. Rocheville would be nearer and if you asked there, someone might just know. Far easier though to give up and turn off the RN 13 at the St. Joseph exit to follow the spasmodic signs that James Boekees has been allowed to erect to guide his would-be guests. Five were the maximum allocated to him and he has decided to use them all in this direction.

➤ **Le Mesnil Grand** (HR)M
(0)233.95.09.54 cl. Sun. p.m.; Mon.

It's worth persevering. The almost tangible peace and quiet that awaits you makes even the most tortuous journey worthwhile. I came across it six years ago when it had only been opened a few months, but even then I sensed a winner and winner it has proved to be. James is English, married to Pascale, who is French. He used to teach in a hotel school, so is now able to pick the most promising graduates and prevail upon them to come and cook here. At heart he considers this a restaurant-with-rooms, rather than a hotel-with-a-restaurant, and as the rooms are very nice indeed that's fine by me. He and Pascale and the bank dedicated much time, thought and money in restoring a derelict old farm (ask to see the photos to see what they have achieved). Money may have been tight but he was determined not to take short cuts and the result is tasteful and efficient. A bar was top priority – a rare hotel accessory in France. A carpenter relation carved the one behind which James presides. Drinks can spill out into the pleasant garden whenever the weather is kind. Pascale is at present out of the picture, coping with a second baby, but it was she who chose all the Laura Ashley fabrics and wallpapers in the bedrooms. If one were super-critical perhaps it could be said that the time has come when these could be renewed, but as bedrooms go these are still among the best in the region, with good bathrooms apiece. Highly significant is the fact that the dining room is always full at weekends (and often mid-week too) with French, who clearly consider it worthwhile to drive into the country to eat as well as this. The cooking is imaginative and uses prime ingredients. Demi-pension is the answer to anywhere as remote as this, and in this case it is no hardship. 620f for two people covers a double room, breakfast and a four-course dinner. There is no choice unless you particularly don't fancy any item on the menu, but personally I rather like being forced to try something that someone else has chosen for me. Certainly I would not have picked fillet of pork from the menu but was very happy with the tenderness and creamy sauce of the version that was offered. Equally good was starter of warm spinach and mushroom salad and the raspberry tartlet. Only the cheeses were less than first-rate. Menus are 135f and 200f. The friendly relaxed atmosphere is what wins most praise of all. James has proved a friend in need several times during his tenancy, in cases of illness and loss. At the Mesnil Grand you will feel secure, comfortable, cosseted and well-fed. I think that adds up to another arrow.

Le Mesnil Grand
Négreville

'Superb! The Boekees are a delightful welcoming couple and the converted farmhouse is just my cup of tea — solid and rustic but luxurious too. The food was excellent. Could not be faulted.' Sue Robinson

'This place really is a treasure. We certainly would not have discovered the Mesnil Grand without your book but now we shall certainly return.' Diana Holmes

Note from James: *'The French Minister for Tourism awarded the Mesnil Grand with a bronze medal for its contribution to tourism within the area. I bet they had to bite hard giving that to a Brit!'*

Map 2H   **NEUFCHATEL EN BRAY** 76270, Seine-Mar. 36 km SE of Dieppe

Ⓜ *Wed. and Sat.*

A prosperous farming town, whose wide central street is the scene of an important market, where you will be able to buy in various shapes and sizes the Neufchatel cheese which has own *appellation d'origine*, insisting that it can only be produced locally.

To the south-west of the town is the forest of Eawy (pronounced Eehvee), the most extensive beech forest (16,500 acres) in Normandy. Cut through by an arrow-straight divide, the Allée des Limousins, it covers a jagged crest, bordered by the Varenne and Bethune valleys, and makes a delightful change from the surrounding predominantly flat country.

Les Airelles (HR)M
2 Passage Michu (0)235.93.14.60 Fax (0)235.93.89.03 cl. 15/12-5/1

NEW   A dignified creeper-clad white house, grey-roofed, set well from the main road behind a lawn, and surprisingly peaceful. It is well-known and appreciated locally and banking on a table at weekends would be bound to lead to disappointment.

The 89f menu is particularly good value — copious and traditional food of high quality.

There are 14 simple but comfortable rooms, from 208-260f.

Map 6F   **NOCÉ** 61340, Orne. 8 km E of Bellême on the D203

Deep in the heart of the lush Perche countryside, near the forest of Bellême.

➤ L'Auberge des Trois J.(R)M
1 pl. du Docteur-Gireaux (0)233.73.41.03 cl. Sun. p.m; Mon.

Everyone who knew I was compiling a restaurant guide
recommended the Auberge as being No.1. in the *département*, let
alone the Perche region. It is surprising to find such a renowned
restaurant in a small sleepy village, not very near anywhere. It's in
an old Percheronne farmhouse in the main village street, with an
unpretentious bar for the locals. Once inside the dining room the
story changes – rustic elegance is the theme, with blue
predominating.

The three Js. are M. Joly, père, and his two sons. The younger,
Stéphan, is a chef of outstanding talent. Catch him while he's
young and you can afford his prices.

The 142f *Menu du Perche* suggested a salad of shrimps,
salmon and avocado in a spicy sauce, then an old farmhouse dish,
poule au pot, enriched with local farm sausages, then cheeses and
a pudding that might well be a version of English crumble with
apples and pears, served with honey ice cream and poached figs.
For imaginatively cooked freshest fish it is necessary to go up one
to the 192f version, presenting roast scallops with a *confit* of endive
and lime, or bass in a pastry case.

One caveat – the wines can push up what looks like a bargain
alarmingly. You can, however, rely on the carafe here.

A real treat and arrowed for good food.

Map 2A	**OMONVILLE LA PETITE** 50440, Manche. 24 km NW of Cherbourg, 6.5 km NE of Nez de Jobourg

---

So near to the port in miles, so far in character. This part of the
Cotentin is quite different from anywhere else, more Cornwall than
France, with deep green valleys and time-warped hamlets inland,
and magnificent cliffs at the western extremity You are almost
certain to lose your way and then you have a problem because
there is never anyone about to consult. The sleepiness is so evident
that not a cat stirs let alone a human being. It's all very delightful
and well worth the effort even if you do not intend to stay here. Even
better if you do, so I tried hard to find somewhere congenial. Not
easy.

La Fossardière (H)S-M
(0)233.52.19.83 cl. 15/11-14/3

NEW

In the hamlet of La Fosse. cl. 15/11-14/3. Look for Digulleville and you're not far away.

It will have to be that word again. Idyllic is the only one that will do for the setting of this little stone cottage, set in a garden blazing with old-fashioned flowers, stream trickling through towards the old bakery, a tiny stone building where breakfasts are now served. Giles Fossard has contrived ten rooms out of this building, and two other modern purpose-built constructions just across the road. All is very tasteful, pretty, efficient and not expensive at 250-360f for a well equipped room with bathroom. No restaurant could be a bore in bad weather, but there is a bar and the splendid Moulin à Vent nearby at St. Germain des Vaux. If I hesitate it is because I sensed a lack of welcome, a reluctance to do more than absolutely necessary for the guests. I hope I am wrong. Certainly I am not the only one to have found it difficult to be shown round the premises before booking a room (I decided against), and the impression one reader gained was that M. Fossard did not like to be disturbed from his private quarters opposite. This is all very vague and I look forward to reading that my woman's intuition is quite wrong, and that everything in La Fossardière's garden is as lovely as it seems.

Map 4F   **ORBEC** 14290, Calvados. 20 km SE of Lisieux

 Wed.

Orbec how can I ever forgive you? You used to be one of my favourite little towns, peaceful, historic, full of interest, to be gently savoured. And now you lose all affection by introducing my *bête noire* – compulsory pop music. Yes, those unspeakable loudspeakers have been rivetted to every corner, to assault every eardrum.

We had ear-marked a table outside in the main street for a people-watching elevenses break, but soon realised our mistake and fled. What can the authorities hope to gain by such an incongruous introduction? I can only hope that we were unlucky and that the punishment is not continuous, but those instruments of torture looked pretty permanent.

Assuming that either (a) the din is not perpetuated or (b) that you are hard of hearing and therefore immune, I can still recommend Orbec. It lies in one of the most attractive of the valleys of the Auge, and would make a good base from which to explore the region, rich with châteaux and manor-houses. Some are open to the public, some offer only tempting glimpses down long avenues, some are well-maintained, many are shabby by our houseproud standards. Bellou, Grandchamp, St. Germain-de-Livet and the moated Compesarte are within an easy drive. A pleasing diversion is the source of the Orbiquet; take the Vimoutiers road, then turn left onto the D130 and D130A to La Follètiere-Abernon on the right bank of the river. Park just before the bridge and follow the path to the spring. Take a picnic.

The town is steeped in picturesque antiquity. The rue Grande has ancient wooden gabled houses and glimpses of courtyards and gardens. Debussy wrote Jardins sous la Pluie in one of them. Typical is:

Au Caneton (R)M
32 r. Grande (0)231.32.73.32 Fax (0)231.62.48.91 cl. Sun p.m.; Mon.; 2/1-16/1

I am assured that this is a favourite restaurant of our royal family, but failed to discover which members. Enlightenment please. Certainly the Queen has a penchant for small typically Norman country establishments (see Breuil-en-Auge), which serve exceptionally good food. Au Caneton fits the bill – 17C, heavily beamed, warm and cosy, with Didier Tricot performing superbly in the kitchen, and Chantal offers an encouraging welcome. The eponymous duck does not feature as prominently as of yore but you can sample *sauvageon grillé* at 260f for two people, or an *escalope de canard au vin de cidre* for 90f. It doesn't show at all on the cheapest 95f *Menu d'Affaires* but on the 140f *Normand* (and this is the one I would recommend) you can kick off with *pâté de canard*, followed by *aiguillette de canard*. Lots of other options of course, including grills on open fire.

All very agreeable. Arrowed for good food in an exceptionally attractive town, muffled from the blast outside.

Menus from 95f. (not Sat. p.m.) 145f, 220f, 320f.

l'Orbecquois (R)M-S
60 r. Grande (0)231.62.44.99 cl. Wed. p.m.; Thurs.

NEW

Lacking the seal of royal approval perhaps but still a worthy contender for Orbecquoise culinary honours. What's more, it is usefully open on the two dead days, Sun. p.m.; Mon.

It's smaller and much less imposing than its rival, with almost a bistro feeling about it, but pleasantly furnished and with a good atmosphere, generated by its young owners, Hervé Doual and Karine. There is a no-choice three-course menu at 78f, which looked perfectly adequate, but you get an extra course for 98f, with some interesting dishes – leek soup with cockles, cheese, *tarte Tatin*, alongside the old traditionals like *boeuf bourgignon*.

I liked it very much and I already have one reader's approval. One more for Orbec's second arrow.

Menus at 78f, 98f, 143f and 180f.

Espace Normand (R)S
101 r. Grande (0)231.32.32.08 cl. Sun. p.m.; Mon.

NEW Something different, good for a light lunch. It's an antique shop/*salon de thé*, where red gingham cloths cover the tables set for anything from coffee to omelettes. *Crêpes* particularly good.

Map 4E **OUILLY DU HOULEY** 14590, Calvados. 11 km NE of Lisieux by N13 and D137

A picture-postcard rustic Norman inn, set in picture-postcard rustic Norman countryside, complete with river Paquine flowing by. Don't even try and pronounce the name of the village – we settled for Ooly du Hooly.

Auberge de la Paquine (R)M
31.63.63.80 cl. Tues. p.m.; Wed. 11/11-1/1

In summer you can eat in the flowery garden which must be very pleasant indeed. For us it was a chilly March night and the log fire was most welcome. The auberge at first sight appears to be as simple as can be – just six tables, tiled floor, red roof between the beams, and the necessity to brave the dark and dirty night in order to visit the loo, with a mad dog going frantic behind his wire. But the cooking is something more than simple Norman fare. The 160f menu yielded a *terrine* of skate and scallops, breast of duck with cherry sauce, cheese and a *tarte aux pommes* that indicated a skilled pastry chef. This would certainly be an arrow, since readers have approved, were it not for lack of welcome. I wondered if we had been unlucky, but local opinion agreed that it was the one thing lacking. Pity.

Map 3D   **OUISTREHAM RIVA BELLA** 14150, Calvados. 14 km N of Caen

Ⓜ *Tues. at Ouistreham, daily at Riva from 15/6-31/8, then Fri.*

Ouistreham nowadays is associated for the most part with Brittany Ferries, and no longer as merely a little fishing port at the mouth of the Caen canal. However it still manages to retain a good deal of character and to avoid the concrete and commerce of a big port. If we arrive early for the ferry (after a long drive), a walk over the lock and along the canal or out towards the sea over the sand dunes is something to look forward to, as is the busy Friday market when local seafood stalls offer the possibility of taking home some caught-today fish.

Riva Bella to the west is totally different in character, more geared to the French bucket and spade customers than to the Brits in transit. The sands are splendid but the gaudy funfair and casino perhaps less so. One street back and it all becomes sedately residential with rows of *maisons secondaires* shuttered out of season. The hub is the bvd. de la Mer, on which are concentrated all the shops. Recently pedestrianised, this has become a lively, cheerful space to while away an hour or so. Better, certainly, than sitting in the car in the ferry car park.

Yet another aspect, which few tourists bother to explore, is the bourg of Ouistreham, a few km inland, where the locals shop and worship in the interesting 12C fortress church, a survivor of the wartime destruction that removed so much of interest in the surrounding countryside. Well worth a visit to observe its ancient buttressed belfry and Gothic chancel.

Around the main square in Ouistreham are grouped a variety of cafés, restaurants and hotels, almost entirely devoted to ferry passengers. I would choose from this bunch:

Normandie (HR)M

71 ave. M. Cabieu (0)231.97.19.57 Fax (0)231.97.20.07 cl. Sun. p.m. and Mon. from 1/11-31/3

A little Norman-styled building set back a little from the main square. Ouistreham's prosperity has been reflected here in the glossy increasingly ambitious menus, upgrading of the dining room and the prices. Menus (not weekends) start at 88f. The 22 smallish rooms cost 320f. without bathrooms.

At Riva Bella an old budget entry has got new management:

Le Chalet (H)S
74 ave. de la Mer (0)231.97.13.05 Fax (0)231.96.31.47 cl. Dec.; Jan.

> This central hotel established a loyal following under the previous ownership and the current incumbents seem likely to build on that. The 18 rooms are simple but clean, modern and efficient. The best one, with new bathroom, costs 260f, so you can see that this would make a very reasonable overnight stop (or longer for a seaside holiday base). There is a useful bar which serves snacks as well as drinks. Plenty of restaurants nearby.

Le Metropolitain (R)M
1 Rte. de Lion (0)231.97.18.61 cl. Sun. p.m., Tues. o.o.s. and one week late Nov-Dec.

NEW
> The theme is that of the art deco entrances to the Paris metro. Tables are in carriage-like compartments, lamps are low and swinging. The seafood is particularly recommended on menus from 90f.

Map 3E   **PENNEDEPIE** 14600 Honfleur, Calvados. 1 km W of Honfleur

---

> Take the winding dipping coast road, the D513, along the surprisingly unspoiled Côte de Grace.

Moulin St. Georges (R)S
(0)231.81.48.48 cl. Tues. p.m.; Wed.

> There are two beamed rooms in this unsophisticated bar/restaurant at the road side. It has remained resolutely unsmartened up over many years, and the bar is still popular with the locals – both unusual attributes in this area. 78f buys *moules, poulet Vallée d'Auge* and dessert. 139f produces an *assiette de fruit de mer*, hare cooked in cider, salad and cheese and a *tarte maison*. Carafe wine helps to keep the bill down.
> Readers have approved of the no-frills value for money here.

Map 2B   **LA PERNELLE** 50630, Manche. 32 km E of Cherbourg; 10 km S of Barfleur

---

> One of those surprising mounds that rear up unexpectedly through the flat Norman landscape, as though some divine landscape

designer has thought, 'This view is too good to miss – better give 'em a vantage point.' On the St. Vaast to Barfleur road it is signed on the left. Drive up past the weird grotto carved out of the rock to the ancient church, inspiringly simple inside; take a photograph of what must be the smallest Mairie in the land and get your bearings from the *table d'orientation*. Straight ahead is the point at Réville, that island is Tatitou, to the right on the promontory is the fort of La Hougue and the bay curves round the landing beaches all the way to Le Havre at its extremity.

Le Panoramique (R)S
33.54.13.79 cl. Sun. p.m.; Mon.

An up-market *crêperie*, surprisingly large inside; so many tables suggest it might get very busy at peak periods. I use it for elevenses or at teatime, when you get the view thrown in with the cuppa. They do seafood and a variety of snacks, but don't invest a lot of money here.

Map 3E   **PIERREFITTE EN AUGE**, 14130 Pont l'Evêque, Calvados. 5 km S of Pont l'Evêque

---

Turn west off the D48 south of Pont l'Evêque, on the D280A, following the sign *La Route des Douets*.

Douets are the streams that flow into the river Touques and add even more character to this picture-postcard region of Normandy, to be found, amazingly enough, only a few km either side of the autoroute. They tumble into mini-cascades, as at Clarbec, or fill the mediaeval *lavoirs*, as at St. Hymer, adding their sparkling, gurgling contribution to the intensely rural scene. In an area of exceptionally pretty villages, Pierrefitte, set on its hill above all this natural artistry, must qualify as one of the prettiest, so it is fitting that its auberge should be special.

Les Deux Tonneaux (R)S
(0)231.64.09.31 cl. Mon.

My, how things have changed here! It used to describe itself as *Café-collation, tabac-épicerie*, in other words the centre of the village and provider of all its necessities, but on my most recent visit my request for a *café crème* at 11 a.m. was turned down – they were too busy setting up the dozen or so tables that now furnish the ancient beamed room for the party they were expecting for lunch.

The bad news is that I can no longer write that les Deux Tonneaux is 'undiscovered', nor 'totally unspoiled' judging from the cool reception. But I suppose this is inevitable. I heard that it had featured on a BBC cookery programme,. and I even saw a glowing report on its rustic charms in a glossy Italian magazine. Tourist offices recommend it as *typique*, so I suppose it's going to be less *typique* every year. The good news is that the basic character of the restaurant, as I suppose I must now call, it hasn't changed. Admittedly whereas you used to sit round the edge of the room on upturned barrels, there are now chairs and tables, but the red and white gingham cloths are in keeping and apart from adding a larger bar and service area, they haven't tarted up the place. The two barrels from which the name is derived are still there, dispensing good farm cider.

As for the food – well, the menu hasn't changed much. The farm chicken still figures prominently (book ahead), with bright yellow omelettes, home-made *terrine* and local cheese. And when the lady of the house, Jacqueline Rayer, is around, the welcome is more evident. Reports differ widely: '*Having sampled their basic menus, we booked ahead to enjoy the "farm chicken". We were served with what can only be described as two legs of supermarket chicken in plenty of fat. Chips were extra! The chicken cost 69f.*' Alternatively: '*It was marvellous to find this real gem, so friendly and the pre-ordered roast chicken came freshly cooked all crackly hot. We loved it.*' Ann Soames, and: '*We enjoyed our "collation" – a glass of Pommeau, pâté and cornichons, omelette and locally made cheese – as much as our chat with the lady of the house.*' H. J. Brooks.

Hmm – I leave you to make up your own minds on this one, but with such conflicting evidence the arrow will have to go.

Map 3F   **PONT AUDEMER** 27500, Eure. 41 km SE of Le Havre via the Pont de Normandie, 24 km SE of Honfleur

Ⓜ *Mon. and Fri.*

The heart of Pont Audemer is like a sweet kernel encased in the hard-to-crack shell of dusty concrete, railway sidings and traffic jams. Persist, and you will be rewarded. Old bridges cross rivulets of the river Risle, overhung by ancient beamy houses. The main street, the attractive rue République, is closed to traffic on market days. Monday is for general household goods and clothes and Friday for the *Marché maraîcher*, probably the best in the whole area for food. The stall holders seem to take particular pride in Pont Audemer in laying out their wares, and the whole street glows with neat displays of whatever is in season at the time.

In springtime on the steps of the nice old church, St. Ouen, overlooking all this activity, are flower sellers selling posies of wild daffodils for a few francs. Just the thing to brighten up the gîte. Look inside for some magnificent Renaissance stained glass (and some by Max Ingrand too).

Alas there is neither outstanding hotel nor outstanding restaurant to make a stay in the centre feasible, but in an unlikely situation just outside is a star:

➤ Auberge du Vieux Puits (HR)M
6 r. Notre Dame du Pre.(0)232.41.01.48 Fax (0)232.37.28 cl. Mon. p.m; Tues. o.o.s.; 17/12-26/1

I know several Brits who consider any visit to Normandy that omits a visit to the Vieux Puits unthinkable. It has been there as long as they can remember, dispensing good food and hospitality to generations of francophiles. I hope they might be interested in learning a little of its history, partly gleaned from recent conversations with Hélène and Jacques Foltz, the present proprietors.

The original building in fact dates from 1630, a *maison de maître*, with three wings. In the 18C it was enlarged and used as one of the

Auberge du Vieux Puits

80 tanneries which were the main commercial activity at the time of Pont Audemer, whose numerous streams were utilised to wash the skins. One of these runs, partly subterranean, around the property today.

In 1920 a former master-tanner, M. Harlay, took on the task of restoration. His respect for the original Norman character was so passionate that he spent two years searching the region for suitable materials.

In Rouen he discovered an ancient *relais de poste* due for demolition. This in fact was the Hôtel du Cygne described by Flaubert as the trysting place of Emma and Leon in *Madame Bovary*. With infinite care he carted away the old 17C well and installed it in the courtyard of his home, where it gave its name – *Le vieux puits* – to the building.

In 1934 the father of the present proprietor, Albert Foltz, fell in love with the place and opened it up as a hotel. Ten years later the bombardments of 1944 destroyed twenty bedrooms but miraculously spared the rest of the ancient ensemble, over which Albert presided lovingly until his death, decorating the rooms with a unique collection of Norman furniture, utensils and antique faience, still intact today.

Jacques and Hélène succeeded him in 1964 and in 1985 constructed a new wing, totally in harmony with the old section, and installed six new bedrooms. They too have fallen under the spell that the old house exerts and recognise that it is not simply an Auberge, it's an institution and a valuable part of the region's patrimony.

So much for the past, what about the present? The old well still takes pride of place in the willow-hung courtyard that is such an agreeable contrast to the dusty road outside. The blackened beams, low ceilings, copper utensils, fresh flowers, log fires and bonhomie continue to charm the faithful British clientele, (and those of many another nation). Jacques Foltz has resisted the temptation to 'smarten up' his restaurant, gilding the lily with tapestry chairs and velvet drapes or cocktail lounges. The floors are still bare stone, the table linen minimal, and if you want a drink you sit on hard chairs in a little side room. Ask to see the stunning room upstairs, which is used for functions.

Jacques knows better than to omit from his menu those dishes that have been best-sellers since his father's day – the duck with bitter cherries for which the restaurant is famous, roast pigeon and Trout Bovary, a local trout cooked in champagne. Menus are 200f (not dinner, not weekends). Most people eat *à la carte*, for which you should allow at least 250f.

Bear in mind that this is a restaurant-with-rooms. It is very pleasant to cross the courtyard after dinner and fall into bed, but the 12 rooms are tiny. They cost from 270-430f.

You are experiencing much more than dinner-bed-and-breakfast here – a slice of Norman history, which justifies the arrow.

Map 5D   **PONT ERAMBOURG** 61790, Calvados. 3 km E of Condé sur Noireau on D511

A pretty village in the heart of the lovely Suisse Normande. The D511 follows the river.

Au Poisson Vivant (R)S
(0)231.69.01.58 cl. Sun. p.m.; Mon.

NEW   A modern restaurant in an old building, managing to be tasteful in spite of lots of bright orange. Packed with local fans.

Menus in English are not usually good news, but here that does not apply. The 70f version offers interesting possibilities: sea trout with ginger-flavoured butter, cheese and dessert – an unusual formula. For 89f you could choose a *terrine* of wild boar, followed by red mullet on a bed of cabbage. Dover sole *aux agrumes* (i.e. with citrus fruits) is 80f, and the sauté of venison comes with fresh pasta.

Map 3E   **PONT L'EVÊQUE** 14130, Calvados. 48 km NE of Caen, 11 km S of Trouville

---

Ⓜ *Mon.*

The town was almost completely destroyed in the 1944 bombing and has never regained much character since, allowing the few fine 16C buildings that survived to deteriorate. Traffic thunders through its narrow main street, adding dust and confusion to the scene and further threatening the fabric of ancient timbers. So the best news for a long time was to find that one of the most impressive structures, the old staging post hotel, L'Aigle d'Or, which looked disgracefully shabby on my last visit, has been granted a new lease to what I hope will now be a very long life:

Auberge de l'Aigle d'Or (R)M
68 r. de Vaucelles (0)231.65.05.25 cl. Wed. o.o.s.

NEW That busy road might still cause concern but penetrate round the back into the well-preserved Norman courtyard and the scene changes. No dust but fresh white paint and black beams, no noise but bird song, no grime but many flowers. Inside the transformation continues, with everything spic and span and freshly polished, while the attractive old beams and flagstones have been judiciously retained. It's a delightful halt now, and the management, M and Mme Aimé Stephan, are obviously trying hard to make their mark and get established. Their 125f menu includes wine or cider, and lists well-presented old favourites like *pâté de canard pistaché*, farm chicken in cider and fresh pasta. An arrow to encourage to catch the excellent value while it's still going.
Menus 125 to 290f.

Auberge de la Touques (R)M
pl. de l'Eglise (0)231.64.01.69 cl. Mon. p.m.; Tues. 3/12-26/12; 2/1-26/l

Perhaps the auberge suffers from being tucked away behind the old church, beside the river from which it takes its name. Although it is long-established, although the dining room is pretty enough with its pink cloths and beams, although the 75f menu appears good value (*moules*, trout, dessert), the place is rarely full. I detect a certain lack-lustre. Am I right?

Map 5D **PONT D'OUILLY** 14690, Calvados. 19 km W of Falaise by the D511

 Sun.

Nature was kind to this little town, surrounding it by the lovely craggy countryside of the Suisse Normande, but history was not – it placed in the path of the Falaise Gap devastation, so that almost the entire town was wiped out. Mercifully the old market *halles* survived and lend a modicum of character.

Le Commerce (HR)M-S
(0)231.69.80.16 Fax (0)231.69.78.08 cl. Sun. p.m. and Mon. except July and Aug.

A solid Logis situated in the market square, with an excellent local reputation and much approved of by FE readers too. The food is predictably traditional Norman, on menus from 75f, and the 16 rooms, though small, are not expensive at 180-230f. It is quieter at the rear, with space for repose.

Auberge St. Christophe (HR)M-S
(0)231.619.81.23 Fax (0)231.69.26.58 cl. Sun. p.m; Mon.; 19/10–3/11

2 km out of town on the D23, with lovely views over the surrounding countryside from most of the bedrooms. The clientele for the hotel can sometimes be exclusively British, but the restaurant is valued by locals too and is often packed out. The seven rooms decorated in simple country style are on the small side (or cramped as one reader described them), 270f. Menus from 95f.

Map 3G   **PONT ST. PIERRE** 27360, Eure. 21 km SE of Rouen by N14 and D126

In very pretty country, green with the Andelle valley and green with the forest of Longboel. A loop of the Seine curves to within four km of the village, and this would be a good touring base.

Hostellerie La Bonne Marmite (HR)M-L
(0)232.49.70.24 Fax (0)232.48.12.41 cl. Sun. p.m.; Mon.; 20/2-10/3;25/7-13/8

NEW   Once a coaching inn, and still looking exactly like one. If it has not been used for a film set by now it should have been. Beams wherever feasible, both inside and out, and a pleasant rear courtyard. The hostellerie is well-known and so is its chef Maurice Amiot, who goes in for gastronomic competitions and often wins them. His cellar is his particular pride. The atmosphere is warm, cosy, pampered; it's the kind of place from which you see prosperous red-faced French families emerging around four o'clock of a Sunday afternoon, blinking at the sunlight and heading for a kip. The nine comfortable rooms cost 370-550f and menus start at 140f.

l'Auberge de l'Andelle (R)M
(0)232.49.70.18 cl. Tues. p.m.

NEW   From the exterior the auberge looks attractive because of the window boxes, its position between the little river from which it takes its name and an imposing château, but inside is pretty too. Two small rooms are heavily beamed. Cooking is less fussy than at the Bonne Marmite, but well-prepared and presented, based on fresh seasonal products. Menus start at 75f except at weekends, when it's 105f; you would be wise to book.

Map 3A   **PORT BAIL** 50580, Manche. 10 km S of Carteret

Such a pretty village, full of character, with wide chestnutted square, lovely old abbey church dating from the 8th and 12th centuries and an incomparable beach. If you feel the urge to be secluded you can always find a stretch of sand to meet that requirement; just lie down and watch the wind surfers doing all the work.

All the more pity then that there is now not a single hotel or restaurant that I can recommend. La Fringale is getting decidedly scruffy, though if you firmly resolve not to spend much money on a more expensive meal, their *moules marinières* are not a bad deal. You eat upstairs, with a view from the window seats or drink with the locals in the bar below. Les Pêcheurs across the road, though potentially attractive inside, is even worse gastro-wise.

Far far better to take a picnic. Turn left before the old bridge for a glorious walk along the estuary, animated with wild life and a better spot to set up a table and spread out the pâté and wine I cannot imagine.

Map 3C   **PORT-EN-BESSIN** 14520, Calvados. 9 km N of Bayeux, via the D60

Ⓜ *Sat.*

If the cultural attractions of Bayeux have been covered, it makes a head-clearing change to head for the salty invigoration of a little fishing port like Port-en-Bessin. Its little harbour is always lively and colourful, with plenty of non-tourist activity from the fishing fleet based there. Take a walk to the end of the jetties for a good gulp of ozone or climb up the cliff path to the old blockhouse for a photo-opportunity of the harbour.

This is a popular Sunday excursion and there are plenty of cafés, souvenir shops and restaurants to cater for all tastes. M. Criquet, the butcher, is recommended for a picnic stock-up of *terrines* and *saucissons*.

Bistrôt a Coté (R)M
12 r. Lefournier (0)231.51.79.12 cl. Tues. p.m.; Wed. o.o.s.; 24/12-1/2

NEW   You come to Port en Bessin to eat fish; by association you assume that the fish comes straight from the quay to your plate. Dream on!

In most of the fishy-orientated restaurants here and elsewhere along the coast it has travelled much further than that, via the deep freeze. It's all in the price and anyone who believes that fresh fish ever comes cheap nowadays is kidding himself. Here, one street back from the promenade, in this stylish little nautical-themed bistro, it is fresh and priced accordingly.

However, you are not committing yourself to big spending. If you are content with a plate of marvellous *moules* and *frites*, the bill will be 59f – far better than an illusory bargain menu for the same price elsewhere. A weekday menu here is 98f. Another option is twelve oysters and a glass of Muscadet for 82f. A sole, which is my yardstick for fish restaurants, is admittedly on the steep side at 125f, but 145f for the platter *de fruits de mer* is very fair. So are the wine prices and there is good house carafe wine available.

Map 4H **PORT MORT** 27940, Eure. 10 km S of Les Andelys on D313

Another pretty stretch of river, well worth trying.

Auberge de Pecheurs R(M)
(0)232.52.60.43 cl. Mon. p.m.; Tues.

I would never have looked twice at this rather dull-seeming restaurant on the main road had it not been for a reader's fervent recommendation. I'm glad I did. Ignore the undistinguished decor and the fake beams and concentrate on the 98f menu. It offers *mousse de canard*, fillet of ling with leek *purée*, and a dessert. If you want one of the house specialities, like the stuffed boned pigeon or the home-made *foie gras* you will have to go to 155f. Service in the pretty rear garden in summer.

Map 5D **PUTANGES PONT ÉCREPIN** 61210, Orne. 17 km SW of Falaise

---

Ⓜ *Thurs.*

The nice little twin towns of Putanges and Pont Écrepin are connected by a modern bridge, which replaces the mediaeval one blown up in 1944, over the willow fringed river Orne. The market on its banks has taken place there for over 400 years.

The Lac de Rabodanges is just a few kilometres away, and here you can bathe, picnic, take refreshment at a water's-edge café and mock the amateur wind surfers and water skiers.

➤ **Hotel Lion Verd** (HR)S
(0)233.35.01.86 Fax (0)233.39.53.32 cl. Fri. p.m. o.o.s.; 23/12-1/2

A very popular and well-documented Logis, so book well in advance. It's not surprising that it is so well-esteemed, being one of the most agreeable family-run hotels in the area, with wide gravelled terrace overlooking the river, and the big pink dining room likewise. Cooking is good and getting better all the time, the rooms, if not stylish, are undoubtedly comfortable (bag one overlooking the river) and the prices extremely reasonable. There have been reports describing Madame as *formidable* but certainly her husband (*chef*), M. Guillais, makes up for any shortcoming there.

19 rooms cost from 250-320f, with variations of bath or shower, double or twin beds.

I particularly recommend the cheapest menu at 70f which offered *terrine, poulet de Vallée d'Auge*, salad or cheese, and dessert. The *plat du jour* is a mere 35f, which suits the locals just fine. The size of the dining room reflects its deserved popularity.

I dropped the arrow for a while because of some negative reports but I think it is justified again for good value in this price range.

Map 2B   **QUETTEHOU** 50630, Manche. 28 km E of Cherbourg, 10 km S of Barfleur

---

Ⓜ *Tues.*

The Tuesday market takes place in Quettehou's wide central street and is a meeting place for the owners and tenants of the many gîtes and British-owned holiday homes in the area. It's the place to take care of the everyday nuts and bolts shopping too, with several restaurants and bars. Readers agree with me that the best is:

La Chaumière (HR)S-M
(0)233.54.14.94 Fax (0)233.44.09.87

The obvious lure of the seaside towns ensures that their hotels are often full and more expensive than bed and board inland. La Chaumière's recently acquired five bedrooms, all with bathrooms, would make a good alternative at 130-300f. But it is the restaurant that is the star turn here. M. Orange takes good care of the cooking, leaving wife and daughter to deal with front-of-house. The whole enterprise is spic, span and spotless and the food way above average. Fish is fresh from the nearest port. Unlike many holiday hotels, la Chaumiere knows that it has to rely on locals to come back and back and so the menus are varied and enticing.

Menus from 58f-125f and good carafe wine.

Map 4B   **QUETTREVILLE-SUR-SIENNE** 50660, Manche. 10 km S of
Coutances

The river Sienne is little-known, little-appreciated. That's a shame
because it is a delightful river, flowing through some of the prettiest
country in the peninsula. With an idle hour to spare, it would be well
worthwhile following its course. Here it flows wide and free; my idea
of heaven would be to buy a picnic and eat it on the banks, where
the river flows through the village, but a happy alternative would be:

Au Château de la Tournée
33.07.82.07 cl. Mon.; Sun. o.o.s.

On the D971 at a crossroads.
  A puzzle this one. Why is it not listed in any guidebook except this
one? Thought I had over-estimated it and there might be hidden
snags, but no, it's looking better than ever. You step inside from the
buzz of the main road into a lovely old room with ancient beams
and a decoration of dried hops. The *patron* collects antiques and
objets d'art; his eclectic tastes run to an amazing illuminated crêche
in the giant fireplace and a suit of armour in the overflow dining
room, but the impression is more of appreciation of fine
craftsmanship than of eccentricity. Lucien Quémener and his family
have been here for five years and built up a considerable local
clientele as well as the passing trade for which his position is ideal.
His cooking is both traditional and experimental – coming he claims
from *tous les pays du monde*. For example on the 125f menu an
original *Tatin d'Endives*, a *Papillote d'Agneau à l'Orientale* and
interesting desserts. The cheapest menu is 85f for lunch (not
Suns).
  The ten rooms are gradually being redecorated. When I visited
they cost 140f for one with shower; there is one with a bath and two
double beds and two have their own w.c.s.
  I should very much like to have some first-hand reports on what
looks like a potential winner and see if we can solve the mystery as
to why the Auberge is not better-known.

Map 6D   **RÂNES** 61150, Orne. 20 km SW of Argentan by D916

Ⓜ *Sat.*

A nothing-special little town on the main road, where it might be
useful to know of a halt that stays open on Sun. and Mon.

Le St. Jean (R)S
(0)233.39.75.16 cl. Tues. p.m.; Wed.

> A solid stone building on the corner of the market square, with a friendly bar and friendly *patronne*.
>
> Excellent value on the 65f menu, good carafe wine. House specialities are sweetbreads with asparagus, duck with cider and bass with sorrel.

| Map 4A | **REGNEVILLE-SUR-MER** 50590, Manche. 11 km SW of Coutances |

> It was a reader's prompting that led me to explore for the first time the bay of the Sienne; it's a region of vast skies, vast open spaces of sea, endless marshes; little boats lie for most of the day high and dry, tossed on to dry land like a child's abandoned toys. The sands stretch for ever and when the wind howls across the estuary any exposed skin gets prickled with the flying grit. On a sunny day, however, the palette of colours is unlimited, and walking is a delight.

l'Hostellerie de la Baie, Le Port (HR)M
(0)233.07.43.94

NEW

> It is hardly surprising that any restaurant/hotel here should take advantage of the panorama, and sure enough the Hostellerie's plate-glass windows make the most of the view of sea and sand. It's a popular destination in summer, when the terrace comes into service, but the large dining room is cosier than most seaside establishments, with beamed ceiling, copper pans and exposed stone, and if you did hit bad weather a meal inside, sheltered from the ferocity outdoors, could be very comforting. The food would certainly help. Predictably it is seafood and fresh fish that is the speciality here, with prices reasonable for the quality offered. I would always counsel eating one beautiful dish *à la carte* when it comes to fish but the menus, starting at 90f, are a viable alternative. The biggest surprise was the standard of the bedrooms. They are very well equipped, with bath, telephone etc. and freshly decorated. The sea views from their windows might well be expected to push the prices up, but No; I think 200-250f is well justified here.
>
> Didier Lecureur is a hands-on *patron*, usually behind the bar, always with a welcome. With a few more reports this could well be an arrow.

Map 2B	**RÉVILLE** 50760, Manche. 32 km E of Cherbourg, 3 km N of St. Vaast

Take a drive along the flat coast from St. Vaast to the Pointe de Saire for good views of the rock-strewn bay. There are lovely sands at the point but too many bungalows and caravans in recent years. On the way, on a sharp corner, you will pass:

Au Moyne de Saire (HR)S
(0)233.54.46.06 Fax (0)233.54.14.99 cl. Sun. p.m. from Oct-Mar. 2/1-15/2, 2/10-17/10

I had been briefed by readers to expect changes here but the reality far exceeded expectations. What had once been a cheap stopover, typical of many undemanding undistinguished Logis all over France, is now exceptionally agreeable. The youthful Marguérys have transformed drabness into lightness and brightness. The extended dining room is particularly pretty in its apricot reincarnation, and the bedrooms, though simple, are country-style fresh. The garden is new, and offers a welcome opportunity to relax for drinks or tea, and there is a private parking lot at the rear. M. Marguéry is a member of the *Jeunes Cuisiniers Restaurateurs* of the Manche and lists as specialities some far-from-simple dishes like home-prepared *foie gras*, *gravad lax*, fillet of beef in port and kidneys in a mustard sauce. Menus start at 83f.

The eleven rooms cost from 145-275f and demi pension is 200-260f. I wish there were more simple but good accommodation like this, allied to good food and a smile. An arrow for encouragement.

Map 3G	**ROUEN** 76000, Seine-Mar. 87 km E of Le Havre

Ⓜ *Every day*

No 1 choice in my book for an off-season break. There is so much to see and do – so many museums, the wonderful cathedral, the ancient churches, the Joan of Arc associations, the river traffic – that one could never be bored. And if the sun should shine, do as the Rouennais do – make for one of the multitude of chairs set out on the pavements outside a restaurant or bar, and enjoy the parade.

Most important, it is a city with a clearly-defined heart. You can hardly get lost in Rouen, you can hardly fail to find its centre, which is compact and easily walkable. Big big problem is parking. You can either cruise around and try to spot someone leaving a slot by the road (which fill up quite early in the morning) or take the easy way out (as I do) which is to follow the signs to the Parking in the Place du Vieux Marché, grab any gap you find on the way or accept the inevitable and pay up for the Parking. It's probably better anyway because your car is less likely to get bumped there and you don't have to worry about feeding the meter.

The Place du Vieux Marché marks one limit of the most interesting and popular section of the city centre; the church of St. Maclou is at the other end, with the pedestrianised rue du Gros Horloge leading up to the cathedral in between. Cover this part at all costs and then, if time allows, explore some of the side streets, especially those to the north of the cathedral, the oldest part of Rouen. The area between cathedral and river was heavily bombed and almost totally destroyed in 1944, so there is little of interest to detain you there. Stop off at the Tourist Office, in one of the city's most beautiful buildings just opposite the cathedral, to pick up maps and current programmes.

In the Middle Ages it was in the Place du Vieux Marché that public executions took place. A mosaic stone marks the place where, on May 30th, 1431, Joan of Arc was burned alive.

Nowadays the centre of the Place is occupied by a modern architectural complex of church and small covered market, open every day for high quality produce. The steps leading down to the market provide seating for students and backpackers and there is always a lively and colourful atmosphere here. It is fitting that the centre of the square should be food-orientated because the surrounds have of recent years become almost exclusively a guzzler's paradise. I never actually remembered to count the restaurants and bars round the perimeter but there must be dozens. And then there are the speciality shops selling *foie gras*, sophisticated *charcuterie*, wine, beer. It would be a difficult palate or an empty purse that could not find gastronomic satisfaction here.

Many of the charismatic old-fashioned shops that lined the rue du Gros-Horloge have closed recently, making way for more young-fashion outlets and innumerable shoe shops. The standards get higher the further away from the marketplace you stroll. Even the shopping-allergic will find plenty of interest in this, the city's most famous thoroughfare. Old cobblestones and attractive 15-17C half-timbered houses lend plenty of character and of course there is the most popular monument in Rouen, surveying the scene from its prominent position above the archway spanning the road – le Gros Horloge. The gilded single-handed clock was removed from its belfry in 1525 by the people of Rouen, and re-positioned in the specially-designed arch so that they could get a better look at its magnificent face.

The vista down the *rue* is blocked at the far end (about ten minutes stroll from the Place) by the bulk of the cathedral, set in a great square. Monet took a room in what is now the tourist office in

Le Gros Horloge

order to paint it in some of its many guises, early or late in the day or year, and then in the following year stayed in another building, now alas replaced by a particularly repellant post-war erection, so that not all the twenty different versions of the scene are angled from the same viewpoint. Sit quietly in the square for a while to take in some of the details of the exterior, but avoid buying a drink or snack here – you could do better and cheaper elsewhere.

Developed over eight centuries, the building might serve as a catalogue of ecclesiastical architectural styles. From the 11C onwards each generation contributed its finest work to the ensemble. The differences between the two main towers flanking the 16C west door are immediately striking. On the left the Tour St. Romain is a relic of the 12C church, early Gothic on a Romanesque base; the right-hand Butter Tower is pure Flamboyant Gothic. The story goes that it got its name in the 17C, when the wealthy burghers who did not want to be deprived of their butter during Lent were prepared to finance the building of the tower in exchange for official forgiveness, but as a scholarly guide pointed out to me, butter was not around at that time and fat would have been more like lard. Pity, it's a nice story. One thing I can say with confidence – the spire is the tallest in France.

Of course it is a miracle that the cathedral survived the wartime devastation and there are plenty of tales of unexploded bombs that might have wrecked it. What an *appalling* thought. This is not the place for an inventory of the interior; just take my word for it that it's worth investing in a detailed brochure, and go early or late to avoid those dreadful people – tourists.

Continue the walk by following the north side of the cathedral, the rue St. Romain, past the Archbishop's palace, which is not open to the public. The outline of the cathedral spire is framed by a window, a lonely relic of the chapel where Joan of Arc's trial was held and where her rehabilitation was proclaimed in 1456.

Cross over the busy rue de la République to find another must-see, the jewel of French Gothic architecture, the abbey church of St. Ouen, now restored and open for concerts, where the magnificent organ, one of the largest in the country, sometimes comes into its own. Stunningly beautiful choir, double clerestory, and some 14C glass.

Many people miss another treasure hidden away in the picturesque rue Martainville, the Âitre St. Maclou. There is no indication from outside that this unique curiosity is worth a visit – just a shabby doorway and an inconclusive courtyard, with art students wandering about. Proceed to the far doorway on the right however and you enter another world. Here is one of the last examples of a mediaeval plague cemetery. It takes the form of a square of grass surrounded by half-timbered galleried buildings, built in the early 16C. Look at the carvings on the pillars to discern

Cathédrale Notre Dame

the purpose of the grisly enclosure. They depict the Dance of Death, with stylised macabre motifs – skulls galore, crossbones, and sundry tools whose use it may be best not to ask. The bodies were piled up in the gallery, while the lower storey, now closed in, was an arcaded walkway. To see the happily chattering, blissfully unaware young students of the École des Beaux Arts occupying the gruesome old charnel house seems bizarrely inappropriate.

Restoration of war-time devastation has been highly successful and imaginative. It is well worthwhile exploring some of the older areas, where treasures are continually being cleaned and repaired. Walk down the rue Diélette, lined with half-timbered houses, and offering a pleasing vista of the tower of St. Ouen, awaiting restoration; note the picturesque cul-de-sac of the rue des Hauts Mariages. Look at the Palais de Justice, formerly the site of the Normandy Parliament. Shell holes from the 1944 damage are much in evidence but the restoration of the elegant building is impressive. At every visit I find another small area to admire, like the rue Eau de Robec, just south of St. Ouen. Canalised streams of water flow through this little street, lined with restored old houses, making it particularly pleasant on a hot summer's day. Few tourists seem to discover the way here. The delightful little restaurant listed below would be a good excuse for a visit. Do not fail to look up on your tours of discovery. For example in the enchanting rue Martainville, with its marvellous 15th-17C houses, there is a gold canopy with swaying tassels above some carved angels, set high in the wall of number 210.

Other high spots include (and you should certainly buy a specialist guide because there are so many to enjoy) the Renaissance Hotel de Bourgtheroulde, which has famous bas-reliefs of the Field of Cloth of Gold, La Tour Jeanne d'Arc, which is the keep of the 13C castle where she faced torture, and the Musée des Beaux Arts is one of the most important art galleries in France, particularly strong on post-Revolution artists, like Géricault and David, as well as Impressionists and Post-Impressionists.

Hotels: Rouen does have one serious deficiency – it lacks a good range of hotels. There are several in the modern re-built area that are practical, clean, inexpensive and fill the bill if a central bed is all that is required, forget the character, but you hardly need me to describe them, so I shall save the space for the more unusual and just list three that readers have confirmed are exemplary:

Hotel Viking (H)M
21 quai Havre (0)235.70.34.95 Fax (0)235.89.97.12

38 rooms 255-320f.

Hotel Québec (H)S
18 r. Québec (0)235.70.09.38 Fax (0)235.15.80.15

38 rooms from 170-330f.

Hotel Lisieux (H)S
4 r. Savonnerie (0)235.71.87.73 Fax (0)235.89.31.52

30 rooms 185-310f.

Here are two that I can personally recommend:

► **Hotel Frantour Vieux Marché** (H)M
33 r. du Vieux Palais (0)235.71.00.88 Fax (0)235.70.75.94

This is my old favourite Colin's Hotel, taken over by a chain. Disaster was my original reaction but no, nothing has changed except the management and that appears to be very friendly at the time of going to press. Conveniently situated in the SW corner of the Place du Vieux Marché, and therefore ideally placed for restaurant visits. The exterior is uncompromisingly modern – a sheet glass profile on the rue de la Pie and another behind a quiet and ancient courtyard in the rue du Vieux Palais. A different story inside where the starkness gives way to soft pastels and deep armchairs in the reception area. The bedrooms are furnished with expensive chintz drapes and bed covers to offset their simplicity. Nothing over the top, but comfortable, quiet and with parking facilities, which is a huge bonus in this situation.
45 rooms from 350-495f.
Arrowed for practical comfort, but I need constant updating please.

Hotel de la Cathédrale (H)M
12 r. St. Romain (0)235.71.57.95 Fax (0)235.70.15.54

The only hotel I found in the old quarters between cathedral and St. Maclou, and the only one with any individuality. But there's a snag to olde-worlde loadsa-character – mediaeval streets did not cater for parking 20thC vehicles.
You may stop outside in the narrow cobbled street long enough to unload luggage but then you must follow the receptionist's advice as to the best nearby parking lot.
Otherwise the hotel is good news. In the very heart of the city but with an unexpected flowery courtyard at the rear, in which to sit amid the greenery and recover after a day's foot-slogging. Nothing excessive in the way of obtrusive modernisation but the rooms are

comfortable and all different according to their original attributes. Management is friendly and most reports have been favourable.

Rooms with bath are 355f and with shower 300f. Breakfast 35f (real butter in real pots).

Restaurants: What Rouen lacks in hotels it more than makes up for in eating opportunities. You can pay your money, little or large, and take your choice from bistros to Michelin stars, from *brasseries* where you can eat whatever you fancy to specialist cafés where you eat what they are particularly good at. The rouennais love to eat out, particularly in the open air, and new restaurants are constantly opening in the hope of gaining their custom. Unfortunately they sometimes close too. The following are some of my favourites, chosen for their variety and for being the best in their class:

➤ **Les Nymphéas** (R)L
7 r. de la Pie (0)235.89.26.69 Fax (0)236.70.98.81 cl. Sun. p.m.; Mon.

The prettiest restaurant in Rouen, now owned by Patrice and Thérèse Kukurudz, late of le St. Pierre in La Bouille, where Patrice once had a Michelin star. To his intense delight this has been restored to him here.

Glass doors open on to a very pretty and colourful courtyard, perfect for summer dining. Inside is pretty too, thanks to peach curtains and walls, which lighten the effect of the dark beams. Immaculate tableware and service, especially from Thérèse, whose keen eye never misses a trick.

There is a no-choice 165f menu, which is excellent value if it happens to feature what you fancy, but my advice would be to go for the 190f menu which offers four courses from the 250f *menu gastronomique* – surely enough for most stomachs to handle, especially as the preliminary *amuses bouches* and the *mignardises* served with the coffee are too good to skip. I had a perfect *terrine* of fresh duck *foie gras*, then a sublime mixture of scallops and *langoustines* in ravioli, served with a *beurre blanc* flavoured with Noilly Prat. With the irresistible cheese board and pancakes imaginatively accompanied by grapefruit and a grapefruit sorbet, this more than filled the bill. As did the wine – *not* cheap.

The only proud possessor of two Michelin stars in Rouen is Gill on the embankment, but as his restaurant is severely stark and a touch serious, I am going to award the arrow for the restaurant I would most like to visit for a special occasion to Les Nymphéas.

l'Ecaille (R)M
26 Rampe Cauchoise (0)235.70.95.52 Fax (0)235.70.83.49 cl. Sun. p.m.;
Mon.; 5/8-25/8

This is my number one for fish. You will find it not far from the Vieux
Marché by following the rue Cauchoise in the NW corner. The
decor is an appropriate navy blue and green.

There is fish and then there is messed-about fish and I generally
prefer the former. The exception is when there is an inspired chef in
the kitchen who respects his natural ingredients and does not allow
any fancy additions to mask their intrinsic fishiness. Such a paragon
is Marc Tellier. After I had sampled his combination of red peppers
and anchovy butter with red mullet fillets, and clams and parsley
purée with John Dory I doffed my cap in respect.

The prices are good too for a fish restaurant, where cheapness
usually equates with frozen-ness. And the wine list will not break the
bank either.

The recommended menu is 145f (not Sat. p.m.; or Sun.). There
are others at 175, 245, 350 and even 450f if you insist on lobster.

Le Beffroy (R)M
15 r. du Beffroy (0)235.71.55.27 Fax (0)235.89.66.12 cl. Sun. p.m.

NEW

Chosen as the representative of the incredibly-picturesque-olde-
worlde-typically- Norman group. (Others in this category are Dufour
at 67 rue St. Nicolas and La Couronne, the oldest restaurant of
them all, in the Vieux Marché.)

Taken for granted are dark beams, big fireplace, glowing copper.
It is all very cosy and comforting, as is the traditional cooking. This is
the place to try *canard à la rouennaise* and *tarte Tatin*. Wines a bit
pricey.

I picked it because it is central, open on Mondays, and has a
good value starter menu.

Menus 100f, 200f, 275f.

Les P'tits Parapluies (R)M
46 r. du Bourg l'Abbe (0)235.88.55.26 Fax (0)235.70.24.31 cl. Sun; Mon. 1st
fortnight in August

An old favourite, to be found near the Hotel de Ville, which has
gone from strength to strength since I first wrote about it. It has now
risen to the dizzy heights of a Michelin star (and inevitably its prices
have risen too). Readers still rave about it though, describing their
meal there as 'the best of the whole holiday'. Its name comes from
the old umbrella shop that used to occupy the site, and the decor is
still nostalgically 'retro'.

The cooking, although obviously of a sustained high standard, remains unpretentious. Familiar bistro-type dishes recur, but stylishly presented. A favourite with the young, chic, and hungry. Menus from 180f (lunch only, wine included), then 190, 240f.

Brasserie de la Grande Poste (R)S
43 r. Jeanne d'Arc (0)235.70.08.70

NEW

Opposite the Palais de Justice in the main road north from the river.

I love *brasseries* – their bustle and variety – and this is a good example of the genre. It has been a Rouen institution for donkeys' years, and retains its art deco interior, with tall marble columns, swinging light fittings, etched glass, iron-based tables, banquettes, and waiters in black waistcoats and long white pinnies. It is just the place to drop into for a beer, a coffee, a cheap lunch or an evening meal when you can't be bothered to dress up or book ahead. Open all year round.

On a streaming March day I took refuge from the rain here with my notebook and a much needed *café crème* and watched the lunch customers beginning to arrive. The 'workers' all ordered the *plat du jour*, which costs 40f. Huge platefuls of casseroled rabbit and veg duly arrived. Businessmen went for the menu and consumed three or four courses with the wine that is thrown in, without apparent thought of how to stay awake during the afternoon; only wimps like me asked for the *carte* and ordered salads or a bowl of *moules*. But we were all equally well satisfied.

Another *brasserie*, recommended by a reader, is **La Walsheim** in the rue Martainville. Also usefully open every day, all hours, and with the advantage of a terrace overlooking St. Maclou.
'*On the 59f menu, I started off with six oysters, then skate with delish sauces, then crème caramel.*' J.T. Deprez.

It is hard to select favourites from the Place de Vieux Marché range, nearly all with tempting tables outside. I hear that the **Toque d'Or**, which used to be my number one choice then fell from grace, is back on form. I like **Le Rouennais** very much, one of the prettiest, looking very classy, but keeping its prices down, but if I had to plump for one it would probably be:

Bistrot d'Adrien (R)M
37 pl. du Vieux Marché (0)235.71.57.73

A very old restaurant in a very old building, but with newish management, who have wisely not changed the character.

There are three atmospheric rooms. I like downstairs by the
entrance best, noisy, always something to watch, loads of action.
Bag the window tables if you are quick off the mark, but they are
usually occupied by vociferous businessmen. Upstairs is quieter,
and so is the rear room. All have in common plain white tablecloths,
tiled floors and decorations that are eclectic to say the least. Lots of
old tin signs, like 'Byrrh' and 'Ricard' and wonderful 'Dames' and
'Messieurs', less appropriately 'Coiffeur' and railway stations A
further eccentricity is a selection of hats of all varieties from tépis to
tin, suspended on the downstairs walls.

The fare is simple, traditional. On the 98f menu I enjoyed 9
oysters (a sensible number), steak, excellent cheese board (always
a barometer of a fair restaurant) and a non-event dessert. Don't
economise by ordering carafe wine – it's disgusting. If this sounds a
dismal account, it misleads. I thoroughly enjoyed the occasion.

Menus from 78f.

➤ l'Orangerie (R)M
2 r. Cormeille (0)235.88.43.97 Fax (0)235.98.70.44

Chosen not because it is typical of a group of restaurants but
because it is so entirely different. Tucked away in a quiet courtyard
just off the Place is the old 18C Hôtel de Ville, now converted into
this charming restaurant. It has a strikingly light and airy feel, thanks
to the cream stone of the vaulted room, all newly cleaned. There
are arches, pillars, statues, balustrades and many tubs of greenery.
On fine days there are white iron chairs set outside on the cobbles,
with white parasols, white cloths, all satisfyingly cool.

The management emphasise the freshness of all their produce,
particularly fish, and I can well believe them. Nevertheless the prices
are extremely reasonable, especially for lunch when you can eat in
a section of the main restaurant called La Fringale, where two
courses cost only 68f. Otherwise it's 98f.

Arrowed for outstanding surroundings and good value.

Pascaline (R)S
5 r. de la Poterne (0)235.89.67.44

NEW An interesting formula here in a pretty little art deco bistro near the
Palais de Justice. You can order the menu if you wish (57f) but the
interesting option here is the buffets in the section called Le Bistro
Comptoir. You can take the salad buffet for 30.50f and help yourself
to as many *crudités* and salads as you can eat, or the *entrée buffet*,
which features *terrines*, *charcuterie* and fish for 43.50f or the
pâtisserie buffet for 36f. Or all three for 74.50f. I love the flexibility,
especially for a family outing.

Le Petit Bec (R)S
182 r. Eau de Robec (0)235.07.63.33 cl. Sun; evenings except Fri.

NEW   Recommended by Madame Robic in the Tourist Office – an
excellent tip-off because I not only discovered a delightful little
restaurant but a delightful new area too. Le Petit Bec is indeed petit
and is full every lunchtime by mostly young office workers. It's
pretty, painted yellow, light and airy, good for tasty light meals, like
quiches, gratins, salads and pastries, all home-made.
Menu at 72f.

➤ **Au Temps des Cerises** (R)S
4 r. des Basnage (0)235.89.98.00 cl. Mon. lunch; Sun.

NEW   The rue des Basnage runs parallel with the rue Jeanne d'Arc,
between the rue Ganterie and the rue Lecanuet.
You wouldn't think it possible to devise a menu where every item
had cheese as an ingredient and still make it interesting, would
you? Wrong, 'Cherrytime' does just that. You don't of course have
to have three courses, but if you did you might find dishes like *oeufs
cocotte au Reblochon*, or *salade de chèvre au miel chaud, faux-
filet au Boursin, fondues*, etc. all featuring *fromage blanc* flavoured
with honey accompanying ice creams for dessert. I like it for the
times when I feel just like a plateful of assorted cheeses – you can
get one here with six different prime specimens for 48f or three for
25f, served with lovely crusty bread. The decor is suitably cheesy –
huge plaster cows and old cheese boxes, and there is a very
pleasant large terrace. Lunch menu 60f otherwise *à la carte*.
An arrow for originality.

I could go on – I think **l'Episode** in the rue aux Ours (SW corner of
cathedral square) serves some of the best food in the city, but it is
tiny, invariably full and quite expensive (170f) and you definitely go
there to eat not to admire the decor; **Restaurant Philippe** in the
same road is a recent good find, much cheaper (54f), always
packed, especially at lunchtime. Any reports on these and any other
treasures would be most welcome.

Map 3G   **SAHURS** 76113, Seine-Mar. 80 km from Le Havre, 65 km from
Dieppe, 16 km from Rouen.

Access either by A 13 to Maison Brulée, then ferry from La Bouille,
or from D982 via D367 from Canteleu. From Rouen follow the river
on D37.

The Seine snakes into a great *boucle* here, almost making an island of the Forest of Roumare. It's very pleasant unspoiled countryside, with plenty of opportunities to view the mighty river.

Le Clos des Roses (HR)S
(0)235.32.46.09 Fax (0)235.32.69.17 R. cl. Sun. p.m.; Mon.

A modest Logis chosen for its easy proximity to Rouen and peaceful setting. (Not overlooking the Seine alas, but in the village).

Giselle Huet sends her up market clients here when La Bouille is full, and has never heard a grumble.

Josette Danger welcomes and her husband Gilbert produces traditional Norman fare. They have 19 rooms, of which 15 have *en suite* facilities.

Rooms 150f simple, 260f with bath.

Menus from 78f, but you'd probably want to pay a bit more to get something really interesting.

Map 3E **ST. ANDRE D'HÉBERTOT** 14130, Calvados. 9 km E of Pont l'Evêque by N175 and D17 south

---

Hard to credit that by turning just a km off the *nationale* one could arrive at such intensely rural, utterly unspoiled countryside as that which surrounds St. André d'Hébertot, a picture-postcard hamlet if ever there were one. As you mount the hill you come across a lovely old grey château, privately owned, set in sweeping parkland; its lichened walls line the village street, hard by an ancient village church. Opposite is the old priory.

Auberge du Prieuré (HR)M-L
(0)231.64.03.03 Fax (0)231.64.16.66 cl. Wed; 20/1-6/2

The building is as stunning as ever, set in green lawns sheltered by gracious trees, so quiet that you can hear yourself think, and the reception area and dining room are exactly as I remembered them – huge beams, lots of flowers, flagged floors, stone walls, old doors opening out on to the gardens. Lovely. But there have been many changes since I last wrote about Le Prieuré. It has sprouted a hideous annexe, whose rooms totally lack charm. O.K. for them to be modern but do they have to be so dark? Windows are perversely let into the roof, so there is no chance to see the beauty around – surely the whole point of coming here. And the prices have increased dramatically. That's the bad news.

Auberge DU PRIEURÉ

The good news is that the rooms in the old building are said to be unchanged. They were all full (with a seminar which does not bode well) when I visited, so I cannot confirm this and should very much like to hear from someone who can. I wrote: 'There are seven lovely bedrooms, decorated in appropriate country style, all with bathrooms and windows looking out on the garden.' I hope very much that this is still true and if it is I strongly advise a request for these rooms only.

The other good news is that there has been a swimming pool installed and that the food is vastly improved. That too has rocketed in price and so have the wines, so this is never going to be a bargain break, but the setting is so special that I think le Prieuré squeaks in. But no arrow.

Rooms 550f. Menus from 145, 180f (lunch only).

Map 4F   **ST. AUBIN LE VERTUEUX** 27300, Eure. 4 km S of Bernay

I found nowhere to stay in Bernay, so looked around the surrounding countryside drove down the D833, followed the sign on the left and discovered:

Hostellerie du Moulin Fouret (HR)M
(0)232.43.19.95 Fax (0)232.45.55.50 cl. Sun. p.m. and Mon. o.o.s.

NEW   An ancient water-mill, but not a particularly attractive building from the outside, covered in creeper and a bit gloomy. Investigate round the back however and the picture changes. Here streams from the river Charentonne trickle appealingly through the garden and a pleasant terrace set with many umbrellas and recliners makes the best of the outstandingly attractive aspect.

Once inside the mill and the 16C origins become obvious – heavy beams and low ceilings add plenty of character, as do soft table lights, fresh flowers and pretty china.

Francois Déduit cooks traditional and regional food, with more lavish use of Norman cream than is today fashionable. Take dinner here and you will be happy to stagger upstairs.

The eight rooms are somewhat disappointing in this setting in that they are more functional than charming, with showers not baths, but the view over the river makes up for a lot and they are not unduly expensive.

Menus 98, 150 and 275f.
Rooms from 280-380f.

Map 4B   **ST. DENIS LE GAST** 50450, Manche. 5 km W of Hambye on the D13, 15 km N of Villedieu.

In the heart of the pretty valley of the Sienne.

Hotel St. Evremond (HR)S
(0)233.61.44.42 Fax (0)233.61.33.77 cl. Mon. o.o.s.

NEW   A recommendation from Madame Allain (of l'Auberge de l'Abbaye at Hambye) was good enough for me. I checked out this extremely simple little hotel/restaurant and found it to be clean, bright and cheap. Rooms cost 165f with shower and the 72f menu is said to be more than adequate. Owners M. and Mme Cassis aim to please.

Map 5C	**ST. GERMAIN DU CRIOULT** 14110, Calvados. 4.5 km W of Condé-sur-Noireau on the rte. Vire, D512

Auberge St. Germain (HR)S
(0)231.69.08.10 cl. Fri. p.m.; Sun. o.o.s. 1/8–8/8; 15/12-15/1

NEW
An old-fashioned Logis, simple rooms, simple food, simple good value. Heaving on Sunday lunchtimes, with the flushed Mme. Baude endeavouring to serve, chat to regulars and cope with nosy-Parkers like me.

Her husband cooks local specialities like Haddock in sauce Normande, sauté of beef in cider, and of course tripe with calvados, on a modestly-priced 69f menu.

The rooms are basic but clean and functional – 170-225f.

Map 2A	**ST. GERMAIN DES VAUX** 50440, Manche. 29 km NW of Cherbourg, 8 km Nez-de-Joburg

Right at the tip of the Cotentin's north-western finger, near the impressive viewpoints of the Cap de la Hague and the Nez de Jobourg and 'the smallest port in France', Port Racine. A drive in this direction adds a new dimension to a knowledge of the area's witty diverse attractions.

Le Moulin à Vent (R)M
(0)233.52.75.20 cl. Sat. lunch; Sun. p.m.; Mon.

NEW
Turn right in Joburg and the Moulin is well signed off the D203. The lanes are long and narrow, the high hedges with occasional glimpses of the sea remind me of south Devon. The tower of the old windmill stands silhouetted against the rocks in a wild windswept landscape. Comfort is at hand in the shape of an excellent little restaurant, which deserves to be better known and assured of more custom, but before investigating and in order to work up an appetite, a walk along the cliff path would bring rewards in the shape of fabulous views of rollers far below. Next stop America. In winter it is untamed nature at its fiercest, but when sunshine mellows the harshness of the rocks it is a truly lovely spot, ideal for picnics if a restaurant meal is not envisaged.

An ideal introduction to a guaranteed first-class meal is to sip an aperitif in the garden, admiring the view, and choosing from the menu. The fresh bass is to be recommended, so is the smoked ham from Vire, or the tunny *tartare* with a spinach garnish. It hardly matters – everything is fresh and cooked *à point*. The decor is pink and deep red, the *patronne* friendly and helpful. Full marks all round.

Menus are 95f and 160f.

An arrow for exceptional cooking in an unspoiled beauty spot.

Map 6B   **ST. JAMES** 50240, Manche. 19 km S of Avranches by D998

Already on the hub of five roads, this little town is no doubt going to be an even more useful stop-off when the new Caen-Rennes autoroute is completed, passing a few km west. It's a pleasant-enough typically French small town, with plenty of stocking up shops and easy parking in the big square.

Normandie (HR)S
pl. Bagot (0)233.48.31.45 Fax (0)233.48.59.45 R cl. Sun. p.m. in winter

A change in management here means that the place has been smartened up but the welcome is not as friendly as it used to be. However the 14 rooms are clean and cheap at 180f up to 250f, all with showers, and the food simple but good on menus from 70f, with house wine helping to keep the bill manageable.

Map 5B   **ST. JEAN-LE-THOMAS** 50530, Manche. 17 km S of Granville

---

Ⓜ *Sat.*

Just one long main street makes up this pleasantly sleepy village. It trickles down through flowery cottage gardens to a vast sandy beach, where the ride recedes for miles. Mont St. Michel swims on the horizon, and you can hire a guide, with or without a pony, to ride across the treacherous shifting sandbanks towards the vision.

With time to spare, follow the coast road towards Avranches for more unique views of *Le Merveille*. From Bec d'Andaine stick to the minor road along the flat salt marshes, in a world of old stone barns and primitive farms, past Le Grand Port (not very grand) and Le Grouin du Sud. For refreshment there are somewhat grotty snack bars at the end of sandy lanes and several possibilities to hire a horse for a *promenade equestre* along the immense beaches.

Hotel Les Bains (HR)S
(0)233.48.84.20 Fax (0)233.48.66.42 cl. Wed.; 5/11-27/3

The daughter and son-in-law of Madame Gautier have now joined the family team; I'm not surprised that reinforcements were necessary, since the Gautier web now covers half of the village. There is the original building, with very pleasant garden and popular heated swimming pool, a large new bar and snack restaurant presided over by s.-in-l. Latish for lunch, we arrived, not hungry enough for a big tuck-in. 'Could we have just a salad or a sandwich perhaps?' 'No problem.' Pushing our luck: 'In the garden maybe, now that the rain has stopped?' 'Certainly. I'll just wipe down the tables.' 'With just a glass of wine, not a whole bottle?' 'Why not?' It was a very good salad and served with a smile.

Just across the road are two more houses annexed for additional beds and, best of all, down on the beach is the Villa Les Dunes with four more rooms and a big terrace overlooking the sea. At 292f a room, I imagine you have to be pretty quick off the mark to book this one and it was certainly occupied on my visit so I cannot report on the standard. The rooms in the hotel are pretty basic but adequately fitted with a variety of showers, baths, single, twin or double beds at 160-335. Meals are from 75f and the quality is said to be high.

'Exactly as you describe, excellent value, charming family, delicious food. Carpeted walls and dodgy plumbing, but the beds were superbly comfortable.' Sally Barlow.

Map 3B   **ST. MARCOUF DES ILES** 50310, Manche. 7 km S of Quinéville, 15 km SE of Valognes

---

I was reproached by a reader for commenting that the coast south of St. Vaast was dreary and hardly worth a detour apart from the historical interest of the landing beach, Utah. Always a martyr to duty, always ready to be corrected, I re-inspected, hoping to be proved wrong. I wasn't. Dreary it still is, in my view, and worse than ever now that I can no longer recommend the Château de Quinéville. However, for those with more tolerant tastes and an appetite, sustenance is at hand:

Le Relais des Iles (H)S (R)M
(0)233.21.00.98

NEW   Panoramic view from the dining room, where, predictably, seafood stars. Humble rooms, nice terrace. Menus from 78f.

Map 3E   **ST. MARTIN AUX CHARTRAINES** 14130, Calvados. 3.5 km NW of Pont l'Evêques on the N177

On a very busy crossroads of the nationale and the D58.

Auberge de la Truite (R)M
31.65.21.64 cl. Sun. p.m. and Mon. except July, Aug and fêtes

This is the kind of solid French bourgeois establishment where you see solid French bourgeois citizens settling down at mid-day on Sunday in keen anticipation of three hours' happy guzzling. *Chef/patron* Jean-Michel Lebon looks exactly as a *chef* should look – massively well-fed and importantly mustachioed. He also looks as though he enjoys his *métier* and the results thereof. Commendably he is not above experimenting with the *cuisine du terroir et de la mer* which he advertises: oysters are mixed with salmon and served in a light pastry crust, saddle of lamb comes with ravioli made from lentils. The dining room sparkles with polished brass, polished glasses, polished cutlery. This is serious, well-dressed, well-mannered eating, and good value at the price.
    Menus from 90f-195f.

Le Bistro des Chartrains (R)S
(0)231.65.20.36 cl. as above

NEW   For less serious, less well-dressed, but hopefully equally well-mannered eaters M. and Mme Lebon suggest a new alternative. Attached to the Auberge, round the corner is this attractive bistro, with checked cloths, buffet service, cheerful faces and cheerful prices. Reports please.
    Menus from 50f, carafe wine.

Map 5D   **ST. MARTIN DE MIEUX** 14700, Calvados. 5 km S of Falaise on the D511, signed Putanges

➤ **Château du Tertre** (HR)L
(0)231.90.01.14 Fax (0)231.90.33.16 cl. Sun. p.m.; Mon.; 5/1-15/2

NEW   A stunning 18C château, where the world if not his wife seemed to have slept: Marcel Proust, Gustave Flaubert, Guy de Maupassant, to name but few, have lingered here in the park of 40 acres, and loaned their names to the bedrooms.
    The rooms are charmingly furnished and equipped, each one individually styled. Worth the price tag of 490-880f for a special

occasion (or even 1,100f for an apartment for a very special occasion).

The gardens are lovely. There is a large vegetable plot to supply the chef with nothing but the freshest, a duck pond, lots of roses and a croquet court.

The standard of chefs is top bracket, trained at some of the best restaurants in France. You will not be fobbed off with expensive ingredients lazily prepared. Rather expect dishes like crab in a pastry case on a bed of white cabbage, John Dory, roast, with *andouille* from Vire, a miraculously tender pigeon with a sauce made from the apéritif Quinquina. You might expect a bill far in excess of the reality, which is 160f or 190f including wine!

Too good to miss – at least try it for a meal if not for a luxurious bed. Arrowed for the best luxury combination in the district.

Map 5B   **ST. PIERRE-LANGAIS** 50530, Manche. 8 km SE of Granville on the D973

Just a hamlet on a crossroads, at which you turn left (if heading south), following the signs to the ruined abbey of la Lucerne d'Outremer (a pleasant peaceful spot if you're in picnicking mood).

Le Jardin de l'Abbaye (R)M
(0)233.48.49.08 cl. Mon. 6/2-28/2; 25/9-11.10

NEW   On the way to the abbey, at La Croix Barée, you will come across what looks like an old stone cottage, as pretty as a picture with roses round the door and a neat garden. This is the restaurant. Inside is elegant *rustique*, just two small rooms and attractive table settings, fresh flowers, fireplace.

The character of the cooking is like that of the cottage – simple, well-presented, derived from good local materials. The 95f menu is a bargain, but there are others up to 300f.

A find, this one. More reports please for a possible arrow.

Map 5B   **ST. QUENTIN-SUR-LE-HOMME** 50220, Manche. 5 km SE of Avranches by D103 and D78

Just a pleasant tiny village, in whose centre is:

Le Gué du Holme (HR)M
*Le Bourg (0)233.60.63.76 Fax (0)233.60.06.77 R. cl. Sat. lunch and Sun. p.m.
in winter; 28/2-13/3*

A chunky stone building with orange blinds and geraniummed window boxes with a pleasant garden behind for summer snacking. Annie and Michel LeRoux have worked hard to upgrade their ten bedrooms, which are now very comfortable and well equipped at 380-490f, and the menus, from 140f, feature plenty of local seafood. Much favoured by Avranchin businessmen for lunch. It would certainly make a peaceful and agreeable base for a visit to Mont St. Michel or en route to Brittany.

Map 2B   **ST. VAAST-LA-HOUGUE** 50550, Manche. 30 km E of Cherbourg

 Sat.

Gets bigger and busier. Some hold that the marina and its inhabitants have swamped the character of the little town and its residents, but there's still enough fishy activity in evidence to lend loads of atmosphere. The red-faced weather-beaten fishermen still mend their nets on the quay side and gossip with their *copains* before wobbling home on antique bicycles, fortified by a stiffener or three at one of the many local bars on the quayside. There is still a very sizeable fishing fleet competing for attention with all the glossy yachts of many nations; the quiet backstreets are still lined with modest grey stone cottages that have no truck with the tourists.

The surroundings are just as lovely, just as unspoiled. Offshore island Tatihou with its marine museum can be reached on foot at low water and another not-to-be-missed walk leads along the stone sea wall, battered by waves in rough weather, along the little isthmus that links the former island of La Hougue, with its landmark fort, to St. Vaast. From here you can view the whole coastal panorama around the vast bay, past the landing beaches to Grandcamp-Maisy, and the islands of St. Marcouf. Do not fail to call in at the bijou Mariners' Chapel, with its heart-rending wall plaques in memory of beloved husbands, fathers and sons *Péris a mer*.

Parking can be a problem, especially on Saturdays. It's a great market but not for the car-encumbered.

St. Vaast

Hotel de France, Restaurant des Fuchsias (HR)M
*20 r. Mal-Foch (0)233.54.42.26 Fax (0)233.43.46.79 R. cl. Mon. from mid
Sept-April, Tues. lunch from Nov.-April and 7/1-22/2. H. cl. Mon. from mid
Sept-April, 7/1-22/2*

An enduring favourite with the Brits because of its comfiness, sheer
prettiness and the cornflakes on the breakfast buffet, and with the
French for the good value and excellent food.

The eponymous fuchsias have recovered their vigour after the
frost blight and rampage as brilliantly as ever up the facade of the
little hotel in the main street. They are the theme that runs
throughout the public rooms. The curtains are fuschia-ed, the china
too, the table linen is pink and the *trompe l'oeil* mural in the large
new conservatory features the flowers prominently. Charming.

Their use as a house emblem was the idea of the young Madame
Brix, daughter-in-law of the original owners who now leave most of

the day-to-day concerns of the hotel in the capable hands of the charming Isabelle.

The conservatory dining option, light, bright and cheerful, is in complete contrast to the older, more traditional restaurant, all dark beams and cosiness. The cooking is really very good indeed and the portions on the menus generous. On the 120f version I ate *soupe de poisson*, six creamy St. Vaast oysters and a divine *croustillade de truite de mer* – a crispy golden parcel of filo pastry encasing sea trout cooked *à point*. In the surrounding sauce were infantile vegetables, broad beans and carrots, fresh from the family farm. Normandy cheeses and a *crème brulée* flavoured with chicory (as in coffee not salad). Husband's 165f version yielded *langoustines* in raspberry vinegar, fillet beef and a feathery *tarte aux pommes*. There is a perfectly good 76f menu and others up to 260f. Demi-pension here would make good sense.

In a separate building at the end of the pretty garden are some extra rooms, furnished with flowery chintzes, cane furniture and modern bathrooms. Those overlooking the garden are particularly agreeable, especially in summer when a magnificent Kiftsgate rose garlands the maple tree in airy white swathes. These are the most expensive at 410f (320f p.p. demi-pension); we had one overlooking the road last time and there was little traffic noise, but on market days there might well be early morning activity. This cost 355f. In the main building there are decisions to be made – bath or shower, twin or double, overlooking garden or courtyard? They range from 146f-355f and demi pension here is from 220f-320f p.p.

I like almost everything about the F. et F. – the food, the good value and the charm of the management. Definitely the arrow stays.

La Granitière (HR)M
(0)233.54.58.99 Fax (0)233.20.31.49 H. cl. Tues.; 15/2-25/3. Dinner available in summer by arrangement

As the name implies, a granite house. Substantial, immaculately presented, on the main approach road to the port. There are now eleven spacious well-equipped rooms, furnished with repro antiques, all with luxurious bathrooms of the maroon/dark blue persuasion. Most readers have been pleased with the comfort on offer, but one found the owners 'tight-lipped'. There's certainly not the atmosphere of the Fuchsias here but the mod-cons might be considered just as important. Rooms 285-458f. Meals 85-190f.

Restaurants there are aplenty, mostly along the quayside, predictably specialising in fish. Readers have recommended most of them and it's just a question of walking along, viewing the menus and the clientele and deciding which one appeals. You will get what you pay for. I have a new favourite:

La Chasse Marée (R)M
8 pl. du Gén. de Gaulle (0)233.23.14.08 cl. Tues.; 3 weeks in Nov-Dec and 2 weeks in Jan-Feb.

A smart little bistro, distinctive with its navy blue and white striped awnings. Inside all is nautical chic – simple but not designed for fisher folk. The fish here comes sophisticated – *fricassée de saint Jacques et crevettes*, *choucroute de poissons* – or straightforward – a perfect *sole meuniere* – on menus at 98f and 140f or, of course, as is often preferable in fish restaurants, on the *carte*.

| Map 1F | **ST. VALERY-EN-CAUX** 76460, Seine-Mar. 32 km W of Dieppe, 32 km E of Fécamp |

Ⓜ *from June to September, Fri.*

The steep chalk cliffs slope down to enclose the harbour of this little fishing town. Its centre was razed in 1940 and the re-building is dull, apart from an eccentric church in the market place, whose windows pitch down to the ground. Worth looking inside – far better than you might think. A forest of masts rises from the yachts tied up in the mouth of the river and fish is sold straight from the fishing boats along the quays. The beach is stony and seemingly forever windswept, but St. Valery still attracts its share of holiday makers and there are plenty of cafés in the flowery main square to cater for them.

The other side of the harbour suffered less damage and dignified old houses still look down upon the water. I had never thought to look for a hotel up here before, but recently discovered:

Hotel Henri IV (H)S
16 rte. du Havre (0)235.97.19.62

NEW On the main road but with an unexpected courtyard at the rear; most rooms look out over the harbour (make sure you ask for one of these). The friendly owners serve breakfast in the courtyard and encourage their guests to use it for relaxing and for picnic lunches. The rooms, some with baths and some with showers, are bargains at 180f-280f, with real furniture not all plastic.

Could be an arrow with a bit more feedback.

Les Terrasses (HR)M-S
Front de Mer (0)235.97.11.22 Fax (0)235.97.06.83

> Better than its bleak modern facade facing north on the windy sea
> front might suggest. Readers have leapt to its defence when I
> described it as austere. The twelve rooms have been re-furbed and
> now have cheerful fabrics and bathrooms apiece. Try and get one
> facing the sea of course. 220-350f. The dining room makes the
> most of the marine view and is heavily booked at the weekends.
> Seafood figures prominently and menus start at 90f.

Map 2F   **ST. WANDRILLE-RANÇON** 76490, Seine-Mar. 4 km NE of
Caudebec by the D37

> A pretty village, embalmed in the peace that seems to emanate
> from the abbey in its centre, to which I strongly recommend a visit.
>   The abbey is named after the 7C Count Wandrille, who, on the
> day of his marriage to a young and lovely bride, gave up his life at
> the court of King Dagobert to consecrate his life to God. His wife
> entered a convent and Wandrille joined a group of hermits and was
> subsequently ordained at St. Ouen in Rouen. His saintliness and
> magnificent physique earned him the nickname of God's Athlete.
>   Even on a busy Sunday afternoon the silence in the abbey
> grounds was striking. The ruins of the soaring slim columns which
> used to support the 14C nave are still impressive, as are the
> wonderful Renaissance stone carvings, in total contrast to the
> simplicity of the tiny chapel, built by the monks after the 1944
> bombing. Inside are bare hard benches, flowers and white walls,
> hung with some amazing modern paintings, which I like very much
> indeed. There is a pleasant walk to St. Saturnin chapel built at the
> edge of the abbey park.

Auberge Deux Couronnes (R)M
35.96.11.44 cl. Sun. p.m. and Mon. 2/9-21/9

> A charming typically Norman old building opposite the abbey gate.
> Two small and cosy beamed dining rooms are always packed at
> weekends, and the *Complet* sign goes up regularly (so book). .
>   The food is traditional Norman, as you might expect, well-cooked
> and presented, on good menus, from 125f and there is carafe wine.

Map 5B	**STE. CÉCILE** 50800 Villedieu-les-Poeles, Manche. 2 km E of Villedieu.

The Manoir is well signed on the D554, off the Caen road

Le Manoir de l'Acherie (HR)M-S
(0)233.51.13,87 Fax (0)233.61.89.07 cl. Sun. p.m.; Mon.; except July and Aug.

An old stone house, peacefully set in a pleasant garden. There are two cosy dining rooms with log fires and dark beams and the bedrooms look out on to lots of greenery. The food is said to be very good but I thought the 88f menu looked a bit boring and it would be necessary to go onto the 125f or 175f for an interesting meal. Demi-pension is from 305-340f per person.

Rooms range from 250f to 300f for one with bath, or 330f for twin beds.

Readers have been well satisfied with the quiet relaxation on offer and this is a reliable and friendly stop.

Map 1G	**STE. MARGUERITE-SUR-MER** 76119, Seine-Mar. 12 km W of Dieppe signed from the D75

Take the road signed to the Phare d'Ailly, a pleasantly wooded route towards the sea, with good walks towards the beach at Vasterival.

→ La Buissonière (R)M
rte. du Phare d'Ailly (0)235.83.17.13 cl. Sun. p.m.; Mon.; 15/12-15/3

NEW Utterly charming, utterly unexpected. La Buissonière looks like a private home, a kind of chalet bungalow, white, brown shuttered, flowery garden, parasols and deckchairs on the lawns. And indeed that is what it was until its nice owner decided to share her cooking skills with the public. Now you can sit in her light and airy dining room or on the terrace overlooking the rhododendrons at the rear and sample the fare of someone who is clearly in love with her craft.

The menus are innovative and always changing according to the season and the market. The cheapest is 115f, which represents excellent value.

An arrow for something different.

Sées.

Map 6E   **SÉES** 61500, Orne. 23 km SE of Argentan; 22 km N of Alençon

(M) *Sat.*

Quite a sizeable town, once a bustling Gallo-Roman provincial
centre, now a sleepy backwater, with narrow quiet streets of old
houses and several squares. It centres on the gorgeous 13th
century cathedral 'one of the finest examples of Norman Gothic'
enthuses Michelin, and the Bishops Palace on the other side of the
place. *Son et Lumière* floods the cathedral, and the whole town, on
summer evenings.

Le Dauphin (HR)M
*31 pl. des Halles (0)233.27.80.07 Fax (0)233.80.33 cl. Sun. p.m.; Mon. o.o.s.;
Feb.*

An ancient *relais de la poste* next to the market halls. The building,
picturesquely beamed, has been wisely restored. The 7 rooms are
not large, but attractively furnished and equipped, some with four
poster beds – 300-560f, the latter price for an apartment. Cooking
is good – Norman specialities on menus that start at 110f (75f for
lunch) – a *langoustine* soup, shoulder of lamb stuffed with
mushrooms, cheeses and desserts, served in a pretty dining room
– tapestry chairs, pink and black curtains.
It's all better than I've made it sound, probably because it was
closed last time I visited and I was unable to add anything to
previous impressions. Readers confirm that it is a comfortable and
reliable stop.

Le Cheval Blanc (HR)S
*1 pl. St. Pierre (0)233.27.80.48 Fax (0)233.28.58.05 cl. Thurs. p.m.; Fri.; 15/2-
28/2; 7/11-30/11*

Long, black and white, in yet another square. A cheaper alternative,
with convenient opening times. 9 simple rooms, 205f with shower,
250f with bath. They have a useful quick lunch formula – 59f buys
an *entrée* from the menu and the *plat du jour*. Otherwise the menus
are 69f midweek and 89f weekend. Nice owners.

If an *omelette* or *crêpe* is all you can cope with for lunch, there's a
popular new *crêperie*, 'Au Normandy' opposite the cathedral.

Map 6B   **SERVON** 50170, Manche. 9 km SE of Mont St. Michel, 4 km SW
           of Pontaubault

Auberge du Terroir (HR)S
(0)233.60.17.92

NEW   If you wished to combine a visit to the Mount with a peaceful rural
           overnight stop this is the place. The auberge is aptly named,
           situated in deep countryside, a pleasant old stone ex-farm building,
           with white paint and geraniummed window boxes. White tables wait
           in the gardens for exhausted pilgrims. The rooms in the Annexe just
           across the (minor) road cost 240f and are all named after
           composers – Beethoven, Debussy, etc. In the main building, still
           with showers but older, they are 190f. The auberge is well-known
           locally for the cooking of its *chef-patron* Thierry, and on the day I
           had allocated to eat there it was fully booked with a party, so all I
           can tell you is that menus run from 79-220f and looked promising.
               Could be an arrow – let me know.

Map 5E   **SILLY-EN-GOUFFERN** 61200, Orne. 10 km from Argentan, well
           indicated off N26

           In deepest countryside, down lengthy green rides through the
           forest. Utterly peaceful.

Pavillon de Gouffern (HR)M
(0)233.36.64.26 Fax (0)233.36.53.81

NEW   Included for its position and lovely leafy grounds, this old hunting
           lodge could have been restored with more taste and less obvious
           commercial consideration. The flags of many nations that flutter at
           its gate seem totally out of harmony with the surroundings.
           However, although the 19 bedrooms are disappointingly
           characterless, they are undeniably comfortable, with every mod con
           and gloriously rustic views. Over-priced at 450f. The trellised, light
           and airy dining room overlooks the garden; on its 145f menu were a
           hare *terrine*, *brochettes* of pork and a dessert.

Map 1F   **SOTTEVILLE-SUR-MER** 76740, Seine-Mar. 25 km W of Dieppe

           Not a lot to recommend Sotteville as a beach resort. Not a lot of fun
           sunbathing on those cobbles. Press on to Veules, or halt for
           refreshment at:

Les Embruns (R)M
(0)235.197.77.99 cl. Sun. p.m. and Mon. o.o.s.; 30/9-7/10; 20/1-12.2

NEW
A tiny beamed restaurant, where the cost of your main dish determines the price of the whole meal. There is a commendably short menu, with main courses costing between 72f and 97f. For example a guinea fowl stuffed with wild mushrooms is 77f and you could choose, say, a *gratin* of mussels and shrimps on a leek *purée* and a dessert, all included in that price. Good value, good choice.

Map 3C   **SULLY** Calvados. 3 km NW of Bayeux by D6

On the little road that leads to Port en Bessin.

➤ **Château de Sully** (HR)L
(0)231.22.29.48 Fax (0)231.22.64.77 R. cl. Mon. except evenings in high season; R. and H. closed 15/11-15/3

NEW
Bayeux is surrounded by luxury château hotels, but this is the one I like best. At L prices one expects near-perfection and I think Sully is the château that comes nearest to meeting that demand. It's a stunning 18C mansion set in 15 acres of grounds, with the huge advantage of a large covered swimming pool. Its fortunes, since it was converted into a hotel, have been mixed; British investment was involved at one time, but there were problems. The new management, headed by Inka and Antoine Brault, both graduates of the prestigious hotel management school of Lausanne, have now got the mixture right, profiting from the previous expenditure, adding professionalism, and retaining a friendly atmosphere. There are only 23 rooms, which helps to keep the personal touch, and they are exquisitely furnished and equipped. The prices I was given personally were cheaper than those on the tariff, so it might be worth checking. They ranged from 480f for a really luxurious double to 350f for the cheapest on offer, tucked away in the roof with mansard windows. At this price I could put up with a bit less light, considering that all the other amenities of the hotel would be at my disposal, but of course it is always a good idea to go for the best you can afford for a special occasion (Bridal suite 720f). It would definitely be a special occasion here, with so many attractions nearby – the coast, Bayeux, and the lovely local countryside.

The dignified amber-coloured dining room is a fitting setting for Luc Mobihan's cooking, which has won him a Michelin star. Again the prices are fair. Menus start at 130f and rise to 270f for the lobster brigade.

An arrow for the very best.

Map 4D   **THURY-HARCOURT** 14220, Calvados. 26 km S of Caen

Ⓜ *Tues.*

A sad shadow of its pre-war self, but a useful first or last night stop, in the heart of the enchanting Suisse Normande.

Relais de la Poste (HR)M
r. de Caen (0)231.79.72.12 Fax (0)231.39.53.55 cl. Sun. p.m. o.o.s.; Mon.; 15/1-15/2

A long-established solid hotel in the centre of town. The 12 rooms are comfortable and have not increased vastly in price so that they are now affordable at 300-420f.
  Good Norman cooking on menus from 138f, in a delightful vaulted dining room.

Map 3E   **TOUQUES** 14800, Calvados. 3 km SE of Deauville by N834

Ⓜ *Sat.*

Do not make the mistake of supposing that Touques is just a suburb of Deauville. T'other way round if anything, since Touques has been around since mediaeval times. In the 11C it was an important port on the mouth of the river from which its name derived. Thomas à Becket built a church here, the Dukes of Normandy were regular visitors. The few ruins that remain of William the Conqueror's castle at Bonneville-sur-Touques are witness to the town's early eminence. A bigger contrast to its more popular parvenu neighbour cannot be imagined.
  The town, alas, without direct access to the beach, was allowed to fade somewhat until recently, when a clever pedestrianisation and planting policy makes it distinctly more attractive. Deauville it can never ape, but I have a feeling that Touques is up and coming and would provide a reasonable alternative to staying on the coast.

Le Village (HR)M
64 r. Louvelet Briere (0)231.88.01.77 Fax (0)231.88.99.24 cl. Tues. p.m. and Wed.; o.o.s.; Jan.

NEW
A pleasant little hotel in the town centre, opposite the Mairie. It is for its restaurant that it is particularly well-known. Gérard Cenier pleases locals and Deauville visitors alike with his cooking which he describes as *soigné*. You should book if you want to eat at popular times. The dining room is certainly more *soigné* than one would

imagine from the exterior, with attractive stone walls and elegant place settings.

There are 8 comfortable rooms above. It might be wise to ask for one *au calme*.

Rooms 300f.

Menus from 135.

Map 3C **TRACY-SUR-MER** 14117, Calvados. 2.5 km SW of Arromanches, 7 km N of Bayeux, signed off the D156

Just a hamlet in peaceful green fields.

Hotel Victoria (H)M
24 Chemin de l'Eglise (0)231.22.35.37 Fax (0)231.21.41.66 cl. Fri in April, May and Sept and from 30/10-1/4

NEW A nice old grey stone manor-house, covered with roses, dating probably from the last century and now a useful haven from the tourist activities from which it derives its customers. There is a flower-filled courtyard, a large garden and enclosed car park. The fourteen rooms, built for a more stately age, are spacious and gracious and cost 330f with shower or 430f with bath. The lack of a restaurant is hardly a deterrent, with so many enticing alternatives nearby.

Map 4B **TRELLY** 50660, Manche. 12 km S of Coutances

The hotel is actually in the hamlet of Le Chevalier, well-signed from both the D7 and the D971, in the green heart of Normandy. Set in a maze of narrow leafy lanes is the aptly named

➤ **La Verte Campagne** (HR)M
(0)233.47.65.33 Fax (0)233.47.38.03 cl. Sun. p.m.; Mon.; 7/1-31/1

NEW OWNERS Anywhere as pretty as this usually has a snag – often the price or the attitude of the owners. Not so here. I re-visited with great trepidation because although I was terrified of the previous owner, the doughty Madame Meredith, I always loved staying in her charming home.

It's an 18C erstwhile farmhouse, smothered with climbing roses, as picturesque as can be, utterly peaceful. Inside is cool, dim, stone-walls, big fireplaces, fresh flowers, copper – you know the kind of thing – all immaculately presented. The new young owners have wisely changed nothing here.

Upstairs is pretty well as I remembered it too, except that some of the rooms have been redecorated. Madame Meredith was always full so I could never look at rooms other than mine, the only single and of course the smallest. This time I was able to see the other six, all lovely. I particularly liked the one decorated in red Toile de Jouy, twin beds, with bath opposite, which I would gladly have paid 380f for. What has changed is the food. The youthful Pascal Bernou has been a chef for 15 years, working in Michelin-starred restaurants, but this is the first time he has been *chef-patron*. A Michelin star in 1996 was his reward for innovative and skilled cooking, served in the charming dining room. Rooms from 200-380f, menus from 135f. Demi-pension would be a wise choice here, at 280-350f per person.

A truly lovely place to stay – one of my favourites in all Normandy. Arrowed for delightful situation, owners and food.

Verte Campagne, Trelly

Map 1H   **LE TRÉPORT** 76470, Seine-Mar. 30 km N of Dieppe

Lively, cheerful, good-humoured. The fish and little but the fish. Terrible beach but plenty of ozone. It's pleasant enough to stroll out along the wooden pier to the lighthouse, or along the prom and up to the viewpoint on the impressively sheer cliffs.

It's also pleasant to acquire an appetite by strolling along the quayside inspecting the menus of the almost exclusively fishy restaurants. Well they may throw in a token *bifsteack* or lamb chop but it would take a real pisciphobe to choose meat here. The limited closing dates are a good indication that the customers are not just summer tourists.

Don't necessarily go for the cheapest; with so much competition for customers there's going to be corners cut to get the prices down. With fish you get what you pay for, sometimes less but never more. There are usually special promotions – lobster at so much a gram, which always leaves me choosing something else because I can't work it out.

Spoiled for choice but my favourites are:

Le St. Louis (R)M
43 quai Francois 1er (0)235.86.20.70 cl. 15/11-15/12

NEW   Quite smart inside, with well-set tables. Absolutely classic fish dishes like a wing of skate with *beurre noisette*, a steak from a wonderful turbot hoiked out of the Tréport waters very recently or a pristinely fresh sole. What more could one ask? Menus from 160f.

La Matelote (R)M
4 quai Francois 1er (0)235.86.01.13. cl. 18/12-3/1

NEW   More adventurous perhaps, in a decor that is modern, navy-blue, fishing-net- bestrewn. Scallops are combined with sweetbreads, the fillets of sole are served in a sauce thick with seafood. Pleasant service. Menus at 89f. (Lunch mid-week), then 92f. (except dinner at weekends), 125f.

Map 3E   **TROUVILLE** 14360, Calvados. 3 km E of Deauville, 41 km S of Le Havre, 47km NE of Caen

---

Ⓜ *Wed. and daily in July and August*

The beautiful new Pont de Normandie has brought Trouville within easy reach of Le Havre, making it equidistant between the two main ferry ports.

No distance at all across the other bridge to its more elegant sister, Deauville, but there is little family resemblance. When Deauville dies out of season or when the weather is too inclement for the delicate Parisians to venture out and brave the sea breezes, Trouville gets on with its workaday existence as a busy and colourful fishing port. The catch, enviably fresh, ends up on the fish market stands and it makes a diverting little exercise to walk along and speculate what you would buy if you had the excuse.

While Deauville is jet-set, Trouville is family-set. The kids get the beach and Dad gets the casino, at the mouth of the river, the smarter end of town, where dignified Edwardian villas, some reincarnated as hotels, line quiet streets. I get the distinct impression that the town is smartening itself up. There is a whole new area of pleasant pedestrianisation and interesting little shops and cafés just behind the main drag.

Hotel Carmen (HR)S-M

24 r. Carnot (0)231.88.35.43 Fax (0)231.88.08.03 cl. mid Jan – mid Feb. No meals Mon. p.m. or Tues.

Readers have been well satisfied with this little hotel in a side street near the casino, run by M. and Madame Bude. Demi pension is obligatory in high season, but this is no great hardship since the standard of cooking is way higher than you might expect from a two-star hotel.

17 rooms are modestly comfortable, with a wide price range to cover most tastes and pockets, from 200-360f.

Menus 95f. Half pension 240-330f.

Along the boulevard facing the fish market is a string of fishy restaurants, serving similar food at similar prices. If you wish to eat at a table outside one of these on a sunny Sunday, you should have booked. Otherwise it's musical chairs, strolling casually up and down, observing who is at the coffee stage and making a strategic dive at the right moment. Our favourite has always been Les Vapeurs, a veteran of some 70 years, run like a Parisian *brasserie*, with impatient waiters in black-and- white uniform. We were thwarted at our last attempt and knew better than to believe the frantic *maitre d'* when he promised us a table in half an hour. We got lucky a few doors away at La Marine and squeezed in gratefully, ready to accept second-best. But in fact the food was every bit as good and the waiters less cocky. I pigged out on oysters and Husband was very happy with his 85f worth of *moules*, fried plaice and *crême caramel*. All irreproachable and generous. A visit to the loo gave me the chance to notice a nice stone-walled room inside, complete with *vivier*, and another upstairs, so good news for cloudy days too.

As we left, around 3 o'clock, our table was eagerly appropriated yet again, making me wonder why our British fishing ports don't offer the same formula – fresh fish, simply cooked, eaten in the sunshine (and don't plead the weather – this was March).

Menus from 85f.

La Petite Auberge (R)M
7 r. Carnot (0)231.88.11.07 cl. Tues. p.m.; Wed. 2/1-17/1

A change from the noisy row of restaurants on the front, this one is quieter, more *rustique*, serving regional food and of course good fish. Readers have approved this long-standing recommendation and it is very popular with the locals.

Menus from 110f.

Chez Nicolas (R)S
32 r. des Bains (0)231.88.56.10

NEW   Just a few blocks back from the river, in the newly smartened up area. A change from the salty scene, this is a new bistro, tiny, usually full, cooking traditional Norman food, not necessarily fishy (though they do specialise in oysters and six best St. Vaast will cost you 42f). If you take the 68f menu, you get six for the first course anyway, plus skate/boeuf bourguinon and dessert. Nice atmosphere.

Menus from 68f.

Bistrot les 4 Chats (R)S
8 r. d'Orleans (0)231.88.94.94 cl. Wed. and Thur.

NEW   Another innovation, in the same area. This is a menu-on-blackboard, scrubbed tables, arty kind of bistro, specialising in tapas. It does have a *carte* too, listing inexpensive dishes and snacks. Different, young at heart, and fun.

Map 2F   **VALMONT** 76540, Seine-Mar. 10.5 km SE of Fécamp via the D150, which follows a green and fertile valley

---

Dominated by a castle on a rocky spur; the Romanesque keep and a Louis XI wing are open to the public and certain other rooms house temporary exhibitions. The Benedictine Abbey of Valmont, founded in the 12C, became the private residence of cousins of

Delacroix in the 19C and the artist used to stay here. The graceful Lady Chapel (or the 'Six o'clock chapel' because the monks celebrated mass here at that time) has remained intact among the ruins.

l'Agriculture (HR)S-M
pl. du Docteur Dupont Hotel (0)235.29.03.63 Restaurant (0)235.29.84.25 Fax (0)235.29.45.59 R. cl. Sun. p.m.; Mon.; 15/1-14/2

NEW   Several readers' reports first alerted me to the value to be found here in this solid stone building on the main road. The restaurant is a few hundred yards away on the other side of the road, a more modern, glass-sided building, looking out onto the garden. It is a surprisingly large room, which I'm told gets very busy at weekends and, when I visited, stiflingly hot (but it was an unusually sunny day). Apart from that quibble the news was good. Michel Guérin is a friendly and helpful *patron*, as well as being a fine cook, and his menus, starting at 59f for mid-week lunch, are good value. Others are at 95-195f.

Behind the hotel is a pleasant terrace on which to relax, and there is safe parking and a room for the handicapped. All the eighteen rooms are pleasantly furnished with real furniture and good value at 230-340f. It's the kind of place where demi-pension would be a good idea, at 220-280f per person.

Map 3B   **VALOGNES** 50700, Manche. 20 km SE of Cherbourg

 Fri.

Valognes clings to its old title 'The Versailles of Normandy' but that's pushing it a bit. The events of 1944 destroyed for ever most of the dignified 18C houses that hitherto lined the quiet streets. The one or two that were spared, like the Hotel de Beaumont or the Hotel de Granvol-Caligny, only emphasise the contrast between what was and what is now, in the concrete reincarnation. However it is still an important market town for the surrounding agricultural area, with a huge market filling the square on Fridays. Because of its position it would make a useful overnight stop, if only there were any recommendable hotels. The best I can offer are the Haut Gallion in the rte. de Cherbourg (40 rooms at 280f) or the Louvre in the rue Religieuses (22 rooms from 160-265f), but without much enthusiasm for either.

The restaurant scene is not much better in the town itself. In the square by the church is La Galetière, a pizzeria approved of by readers, and Le Versailles Normand, a useful *brasserie*. But there is a new possibility just outside the town on the Carentan road:

Beaurépaire (R)M
(0)233.40.20.30 cl. Sun. p.m.; Mon.

NEW

Opened in 1994 and still looking a bit raw, although old stone has been used to renovate and extend the old farm-house. The garden needs to fill out too and then it will all be very pretty and colourful. Inside the restaurant is elegant and soothing, with a high gallery for extra seating. Cooking is said to be very superior, easily the best in the town. The 140f menu yielded scrambled eggs and oysters, *noisettes d'agneau aux herbs poivrées*, cheese and dessert – good value in view of the high standard of surroundings and covers. More reports most welcome.

Map 3H   **LE VAL ST. MARTIN** 27700 Le Thuit, Eure. 3 km N of Les Andelys on D313

The best way to approach Les Andelys is to follow the river. There are pastures between the road and the river (and sometimes it must be said ugly camping sites) and to the left the chalk escarpment is carved into bizarre shapes, towering high. Just pootle gently along, past a few scattered houses and in no time you will be in Les Andelys, with no traffic fret.

Le Manoir de Clairval (HR)M
2 r. de Seine (0)232.54.37.17 Fax (0)232.54.37.45 R cl. Tues. and Wed.

NEW

A new enterprise which I think might prove very useful. The Manoir is a dignified white building overlooking the river (with a few caravans in between) which has recently been turned into a hotel. The grounds are scruffy, the taste inside the lovely rooms is dubious, but look at the price – 295f for a spacious double room with shower, or 350f with bath. Ceilings are high, windows down to the ground; one might wish the furniture were antique rather than job lot, but for this sum, so near the delectable Les Andelys, that would be asking too much.

This would be a good kid-stop, with a big untamed garden, and no main roads to worry about. It would also be a very peaceful halt for those with a long journey ahead of them. There is a restaurant, with menus from 98f, about which I know nothing. Reports welcome.

Map 1G   **VARENGEVILLE** 76119, Seine-Mar. 11 km W of Dieppe

The coast road westwards from Dieppe, the D75, reveals a very different Seine Maritime from the acres of flat farmland that form the greater part of the landscape. There are gorgeous views of the spectacular chalk cliffs that painters have loved to portray for generations; far below the foam of the rollers and the curve of the bays are further temptations to stop the car and get out the camera. Pourville-sur-Mer and Quiberville are now caravanned plots on the landscape but the fishing boats still pull up on to the cobbled shores and these are good stops for a lunch of a dozen oysters and a glass of Chablis.

Buffeted by the sea breezes, graveyard running down to the very edge of the high cliffs, stands the ancient church where Braque is buried. Inside his Tree of Jesse, burning blue, attracts a steady stream of visitors. On the same lane is the Parc des Moutiers, a Gertrude Jekyll garden surrounding a rambling Lutyens house. The upper part of typical Jekyll – a series of 'rooms' approached via pergolas, with a good display of old shrub roses. Behind the house the grounds fall away dramatically and there are extensive walks through the woods and to the church.

Inland deep valleys carve their way through the wooded landscape down to the sea. Sheltering in one such is Vasterival, well-signed 3 km west.

➤ **Hotel de la Terrasse** (HR)M-S
(0)235.85.12.54 Fax (0)235.85.11.70 cl. 8/10-15/3

High above a lovely beach of sand, stones and rocks stands this popular little hotel, now in the hands of the fourth generation of the same family. The young Delafontaines are systematically brightening up the decorations, so that although the paint still peels a bit from the staircase, the bedrooms are painted in cheerful colours and some of them have views down to the sea.

It's a family hotel in every sense and booked up during the school holidays for months ahead. There's a cosy relaxed atmosphere about the place, which does not mean clutter and unruliness. Cooking is above average and readers have nothing but praise for the establishment and its owners. Menus from 85f. 22 rooms from 250-310f.

There are lovely walks from the hotel, to the lighthouse at Ailly and down to the beach; just one word of warning for the infirm, who might imagine that the sea is readily accessible. In fact it is a steep ten minutes away.

Arrowed for position, owners and good value.

Les Pucheux (R)S
1 r. du Dr Pierre Girard (0)235.97.19.28

NEW   Basically a *crêperie*, but a good one, with simple grills too.
Pleasantly beamed and cosy, in the main street.

Les Tourelles (R)S
13 r. du Dr. Pierre Girard (0)235.57.18.56 cl. Tues. o.o.s.

NEW   Another pleasant little restaurant in the main street, claiming *"etude
de menus adaptés à tous les budgets"*. Certainly you could have
just one dish here – say a sole for 72f, or the menu for 59f. Good
charcuterie, to eat here or take away.

Map 5G   **VERNEUIL SUR AVRE** 27130, Eure. 50 km S of Rouen

Ⓜ *Sat.*

On Normandy's border, defined by the river Avre, and subsequently
fortified in the 11C to hold the frontier against France. Several
splendid old houses in the area between the Tour Grise, the drum
tower, and the 15C church of La Madeleine, three storeys high,
crowned by a double diadem of lantern and Flamboyant tower. The
centre of the town, as it should be, is the wide market square, full of
colour on Saturdays.

A good choice for a weekend or en route stop-off, with the
ramparts to explore, the river Avre nearby, and a trusty favourite in
which to stay.

➤ **Le Saumon** (HR)S-M
89 pl. de la Madeleine (0)232.32.02.36 Fax (0)232.37.55.80 cl. 20/12-31/12

Le Saumon is looking very smart these days, newly painted deep
cream, proudly occupying the central position in the market square.

Inside the bedrooms too have been freshened up. 290f buys a
very nice twin bedded room overlooking the action in the square
(don't worry, Verneuil goes to bed early). More modern ones are in
the annexe at the rear, suitable for the handicapped.

The breakfast room has not changed – still the pretty blue and
white iris pattern on the walls – and neither has the salon, with a
faded flowery paper; the dining room has attractive green and
yellow trellised walls; M. Simon is chef and cooks very satisfactory
meals on a 155f menu *terrine* of *langoustines*, veal liver pan-fried in
cider vinegar, salad or cheese and dessert. Mid-week, not very

hungry, broke? Go for the 65f menu with *plat du jour* and *crème caramel*.

The arrow stays – the formula works well and readers have been very happy.

} Le SAUMON – Verneuil.

Le Clos (HR)L
98 r. de la Ferte Vidamé (0)232.32.21.81 Fax (0)232.32.21.36 cl. Mon.; 15/12-15/1

When I compare the standard of luxury here with a similarly priced establishment in England, there is no doubt that Le Clos is the handsome winner. Outside it is an eccentric turreted, lozenge-brick patterned Belle Époque manor house, on the outskirts of the town. Inside, the gates and the very air smells expensive. Nothing but the best, in dining room – china, silver, napery, flowers, antiques – and of course the cuisine; in bedrooms – not large but attractively decorated in light pastels, each with a jacuzzi in the marble bathroom – and terrace – expensive recliners and flowers likewise. All this for 800f for the room and from 180f for dinner. Watch the wine bill and you've got a good deal. Readers have concurred.

At the other end of the scale, if you're looking to re-coup a little, there is a new wine bar in a pedestrianised alley off the main square. **Les Moulettes** in the rue Moulette will fix you up with an omelette/salad/cheese platter, with a glass of wine.

Map 4H   **VERNON** 27200, Eure. 63 km SE of Rouen

Ⓜ *Sat.*

On the banks of the Seine. There are some attractive old houses near the 12C Notre Dame, and the Saturday morning market is a particularly good one, with all the bars surrounding the market square doing a thriving trade. Head here if you are looking for a sandwich lunch.

The other two local rivers, the Epte and the Eure, offer pleasant excursions and are good for picnic sites.

But Vernon's special interest for tourists is its proximity to Monet's garden in Giverny just across the river. It is therefore surprising and disappointing that there is little to recommend in the town to house the pilgrims. The two big hotels in the town centre were never great, and even one of those has now been demolished to make way for an apartment block. Look elsewhere I'm afraid. I did find two good restaurants, one an old favourite and one new:

La Poste
26 av. Gambetta (0)232.10.63 cl. Sun. p.m.; Mon.

Readers have been unanimously in favour of this one, in the town centre. Particularly busy on market days, but fewer stall holders now seem to be customers, perhaps because it's looking a bit too smart for them nowadays.

The prices are creeping up too, with the cheapest menu at 119f – *timbale* of *foie gras*, *entrecôte*, salad and dessert.

Les Fleurs (R)M
r. Carnot (0)232.51.16.80 cl. Sun. p.m.; Mon.

NEW   The rue Carnot is probably Vernon's most attractive road, with some half timbered houses and semi-pedestrianisation. It's the first turning to the left after you cross the Seine.

Two comfortable little dining rooms are usually full. Menus start at 110f, but the 140f version looked more interesting – oysters, veal in cider, cheese and a *poire Tatin*.

Map 1F   **VEULES-LES-ROSES** 76980, Seine-Mar. 26 km W of Dieppe

Ⓜ *Thurs.*

I thought I knew Veules pretty well, having dined and rhapsodised many times about its famous, rosetted restaurant Les Galets. But I think I must have always arrived in the dark or just driven down to the beach, which is nothing much, and dismissed the claims that this is the prettiest village on the coast. This time I found I could agree with that. I started further back, parking by the church in order to visit the Thursday market which the Tourist Office had promised me. No market (July and August only), but that left the whole morning free to explore.

The Tourist Office's other recommendation proved altogether more worthwhile. It was to follow the signs for the *Circuit de la Veules*, the little river, *le plus petit fleuve de France* since its source and estuary are both in Veules-les-Roses. Utterly charming to zig-zag across the main road and to discover little wooden bridges, water mills, cress fields, and some chocolate-box thatched cottages. We ate our picnic alongside one of these, and found a paddle in the fresh clear water irresistible. But there is more good news back in the town, which is undergoing a transformation from sleepy to buzzing.

➤ **Douce France** (H)M and **l'Assiette** (R)S

NEW   We journalists love nothing better than a scoop, so picture my glee on discovering this very special establishment only three weeks after it had opened. The conversion of some of the thirteen rooms contrived out of an old presbytery and stables set back from the main street were not even finished. The transformation has been thorough and tasteful. The typical but heavy Norman brown cross-timbering of the facade around the courtyard has been muted to a soft sage green which gives an almost Scandinavian look.

One of the most valuable bonuses, fully exploited, is that the little river Veules flows right through the property. A charming *salon de thé* has been established overlooking the rushing water and there are more basket chairs and tables in the courtyard for use when ever the weather allows. Some of the rooms have a private terrace with the same soothing aspect.

The accommodation takes the forms of small apartments, fitted with a smart kitchenette, fridge, microwave, cutlery and china; the opportunity to prepare one's own breakfast and snacks could knock pounds off the bill. The rooms vary and some in the roof are a bit dark, but most have little sitting areas, and luxury bath/shower rooms and are decorated with cheerful modern fabrics and expensive tiled floors.

For this standard you might expect a price at least double of the reality, which is from 330f. Go for the 380f version if you can which will give you another bedroom (so you could sleep four) and much more space.

The restaurant is good news too, featuring *Les Assiettes: Poissons Marinés* (45f), *Maraîchère* (29f), *Jambon de Parme* (45f), platters of salads, with 13 different accompaniments, hot and cold. Or you could have just lobster *bisque* for 30f or a platter of local cheeses for 35f. Leave room for super desserts, around 25f extra. Wine by the glass – hooray! A real find. Go soon before the rest of the world discovers the bargain.

Arrowed of course.

Map 5B   **VILLEDIEU-LES-POËLES** 50800, Manche. 34 km S of St. Lô

Ⓜ *Tues.*

It's not hard to discern what is Villedieu's speciality. The wide main street is lined with shops selling the copper pans which gave the town its name (poëles = frying pan). They have been made here since the 12C and the giant copper milk vats (*cannes*) to be found not so long ago outside every Norman farm came from here.

Today the craftsmen concentrate on rather less bucolic items like industrial boilers, or, increasingly, the tourist gew-gaws that are on sale in the shops. The Villedieu part of the name was bestowed on the town by the Knights of Malta; every four years since 1655 there is a great procession, known as the Grand Sacre, recalling the town's early history. The first Commandery of the Knights of St. John of Jerusalem was established here in the 12C by Henry Beauclerk, successor to William the Conqueror.

The Knights of St. John also founded a bell foundry here and you can visit this unique workshop, which still produces bells for churches and ships world-wide. You can also visit the copper workshop where the history of copper-making in Villedieu is demonstrated, and the Museum of Copperware and the Lacemakers House, which displays specimens of old lace-making frames and bobbins as well as the lace itself.

So, all in all, it's an interesting old town, with quiet inner courtyards like the Cour des Trois Rois and the Cour aux Lys, and a Flamboyant Gothic church built on the site of an earlier church erected by the Knights. Copper features even here, in the shape of vases flanking the 18C tabernacle. The Tuesday market which overflows from the main street is well worth a visit.

Le Fruitier (HR)M
pl. des Costils (0)233.90.51.00 Fax (0)233.90.51.01

Almost unrecognisable nowadays from the simple back-street hotel
that readers alerted me to some ten years ago as an alternative to
the then dominating Hotel de France in the main street. Blonde
Madame Lebargy has worked hard to achieve this transformation
into an increasingly up-market proposition, facing onto the car-park
square (but there is a private car park too). It's all very glossy
nowadays, especially in the new reception area, which boasts a
fountain. It's also very pink, extending to the pink leather seating,
the pink bar and even a pink lift. Not necessarily what one might
think appropriate for a small country town, but undoubtedly
upwardly mobile.

The 38 rooms are really very comfortable and well-equipped, with
good bathrooms, and the cooking is accomplished and generous,
served in an elegant dining room decorated with trellis *trompe l'oeil*.
In fact the whole deal is excellent value. Rooms 270f , menus from
79f (and you can happily stick with the cheapest one).

'*As good as ever but one wishes one could get a smile out of
the very efficient Mme Lebargy. Though only classified as two-star
we think this hotel is definitely superior to many three-stars but
apparently Mme L. doesn't wish to upgrade. Excellent
accommodation, beautifully prepared food on the 79f menu and a
fantastic breakfast by French hotel standards – self service choice
including fruit juices, cereals, eggs, croissants.*' Roger Lushington.

Map 2F   **VILLEQUIER** 76490, Seine-Mar. 45 km E of Le Havre

---

From Caudebec take the D81, following the Seine and 3 km further
on is the village infamous for the fact that Victor Hugo's daughter
drowned there. There is a pleasant walk along the riverbank but
otherwise the village is spoiled by heavy traffic.

Grand Sapin (HR)M-S
*(0)235.56.78.73 Fax (0)235.95.69.27 cl. Tues. p.m. and Wed. o.o.s.; 15/11-
1/12*

An old-fashioned long-established restaurant with five bedrooms
overlooking the river. Readers have been happy to overlook the
fading decor and concentrate on the view from their rooms and
from the long terrace. The restaurant is very popular at weekends
and for celebrations. Twice we have been turned away because it

was taken over entirely for a party, so don't rely on getting a table without booking.

Rooms 250-290f, menus from 65f weekdays, up to 190f.

Map 2F   **YVETOT** 76190, Seine-Mar. 51 km NE of Le Havre by N15, 36 km NW of Rouen by A15

A largish market town in the centre of the farming territory of the Caux plateau. Its modern concrete buildings lack eye appeal and it is hard to believe that from the 14thC to the Revolution the town was an independent territory with its own king. It was also famous as the legendary capital of an imaginary kingdom in a song by Béranger. The Max Ingrand glass in the hard-to-miss free-standing belfry is now easily the town's most interesting feature.

I personally would not choose to stay here, with the delightful alternative described below as an option, but I do have good reports of the Hotel Havre in the main Place Belges (35.95.16.77, rooms 220-350f).

At Val-au-Cesne, 4 km SE by D5.
Really pretty countryside, with steep green valleys running down to the Seine,

➤ **Auberge du Val-au-Cesne** (HR)M
(0)235.56.63.06 Fax (0)235.56.92.78

I vowed that I would not overwork the word idyllic in this book, but I have no option but to squander it here. The old black-and-white timbered auberge set in a flowery garden is pure picture book, inside as well as out. Beams galore, guinea fowl pecking happily away on the lawns, big fireplaces, shining copper, candles, flowers. An artist was conveying the scene to canvas and I wondered if the result will be too chocolate-box to be credited.

The five rooms are in an equally pretty annexe; those on the ground floor have tiny private terraces. I particularly liked the twin bedded room with the pretty blue chintz, but they are all charming. 350f.

The food doesn't let the side down. Jerome Carel produces a menu in harmony with the building and with Normandy – we ate a *quiche* full of local *langoustines*, a Rouennais duck and an apple *feuilleté*. In summer meals are served on the terrace and in winter by the roaring log fire in the warm and cosy dining room. The menu price has not been communicated but you should allow around 260f *à la carte*.

Auberge du Val au Cesne
Yvetot

Wines and spirits by John Doxat

Bonne cuisine et bons vins, c'est le paradis sur terre.
(Good cooking and good wines, that is earthly paradise.)

King Henri IV

OUTLINE OF FRENCH WINE REGIONS

Bordeaux
Divided into a score of districts, and sub-divided into very
many *communes* (parishes). The big district names are
Médoc, St Emilion, Pomerol, Graves and Sauternes. Prices
for the great reds (châteaux Pétrus, Mouton-Rothschild,
etc.) or the finest sweet whites (especially the miraculous
Yquem) have become stratospheric. Yet château in itself
means little and the classification of various rankings of
châteaux is not easily understood. Some tiny vineyards
are entitled to be called château, which has led to disputes
about what have been dubbed 'phantom châteaux'.
Visitors are advised, unless wine-wise, to stick to the
simpler designations.

Bourgogne (Burgundy)
Topographically a large region, stretching from Chablis
(on the east end of the Loire), noted for its steely dry
whites, to Lyons. It is particularly associated with fairly
powerful red wines and very dry whites, which tend to
acidity except for the costlier styles. Almost to Bordeaux
excesses, the prices for really top Burgundies have gone
through the roof. For value, stick to simpler local wines.

Technically Burgundies, but often separately listed, are
the Beaujolais wines. The young red Beaujolais (not
necessarily the over-publicised *nouveau*) are delicious,
mildly chilled. There are several rather neglected
Beaujolais wines (Moulin-à-Vent, Morgon, St Amour, for
instance) that improve for several years: they represent
good value as a rule. The Mâconnais and Chalonnais also
produce sound Burgundies (red and white) that are usually
priced within reason.

Rhône
Continuation south of Burgundy. The Rhône is particularly
associated with very robust reds, notably Châteauneuf-du-
Pape; also Tavel, to my mind the finest of all still *rosé*

wines. Lirac *rosé* is nearly as good. Hermitage and Gigondas are names to respect for reds, whites and *rosés*. Rhône has well earned its modern reputation – no longer Burgundy's poorer brother. From the extreme south comes the newly 'smart' dessert *vin doux naturel*, ultra-sweet Muscat des Beaumes-de-Venise, once despised by British wine-drinkers. There are fashions in wine just like anything else.

Alsace
Producer of attractive, light white wines, mostly medium-dry, widely used as carafe wines in middle-range French restaurants. Alsace wines are not greatly appreciated overseas and thus remain comparatively inexpensive for their quality; they are well placed to compete with popular German varieties. Alsace wines are designated by grape – principally Sylvaner for lightest styles, the widespread and reliable Riesling for a large part of the total, and Gerwürtztraminer for slightly fruitier wines.

Loire
Prolific producer of very reliable, if rarely great, white wines, notably Muscadet, Sancerre, Anjou (its *rosé* is famous), Vouvray (sparkling and semi-sparkling), and Saumur (particularly its 'champagne styles'). Touraine makes excellent whites and also reds of some distinction Bourgueil and Chinon. It used to be widely believed – a rumour put out by rivals? – that Loire wines 'did not travel': nonsense. They are a successful export.

Champagne
So important is Champagne that, alone of French wines, it carries no AC: its name is sufficient guarantee. (It shares this distinction with the brandies Cognac and Armagnac.) Vintage Champagnes from the *grandes marques* – a limited number of 'great brands' – tend to be as expensive in France as in Britain. You can find unknown brands of high quality (often off-shoots of *grandes marques*) at attractive prices, especially in the Champagne country itself. However, you need information to discover these, and there are true Champagnes for the home market that are *doux* (sweet) or *demi-sec* (medium sweet) that are pleasing to few non-French tastes. Champagne is very closely controlled as to region, quantities, grape types, and is made only by secondary fermentation in the bottle. From 1993, it is prohibited (under EEC law) to state that other wines are made by the 'champagne method' – even if they are.

Minor regions, very briefly

Jura – Virtually unknown outside France. Try local speciality wines such as *vin jaune* if in the region.

Jurançon – Remote area; sound, unimportant white wines, sweet styles being, the better.

Cahors – Noted for its powerful *vin de pays* 'black wine', darkest red made.

Gaillac – Little known; once celebrated for dessert wines.

Savoy – Good enough table wines for local consumption. Best product of the region is delicious Chambéry vermouth: as an aperitif, do try the well distributed Chambéryzette, a unique vermouth with a hint of wild strawberries.

Bergerac – Attractive basic reds; also sweet Monbazillac, relished in France but not easily obtained outside: aged examples can be superb.

Provence – Large wine region of immense antiquity. Many and varied *vins de pays* of little distinction, usually on the sweet side, inexpensive and totally drinkable.

Midi – Stretches from Marseilles to the Spanish border. Outstandingly prolific contributor to the 'EEC wine lake' and producer of some 80 per cent of French *vins de table*, white and red. Sweet whites dominate, and there is major production of *vins doux naturels* (fortified sugary wines).

Corsica – Roughish wines of more antiquity than breeding, but by all means drink local reds – and try the wine-based aperitif Cap Corse – if visiting this remarkable island.

Paris – Yes, there is a vineyard – in Montmartre! Don't ask for a bottle: the tiny production is sold by auction, for charity, to rich collectors of curiosities.

HINTS ON SPIRITS

The great French spirit is brandy. Cognac, commercially the leader, must come from the closely controlled region of that name. Of various quality designations, the commonest is VSOP (very special old pale): it will be a cognac worth drinking neat. Remember, *champagne* in a cognac connotation has absolutely no connection with the wine. It is a topographical term, *grande champagne* being the most prestigious cognac area: *fine champagne* is a blend of brandy from the two top cognac sub-divisions.

Armagnac has become better known lately outside France, and rightly so. As a brandy it has a much longer history than cognac: some connoisseurs rate old armagnac (the quality designations are roughly similar) above cognac.

Be cautious of French brandy without a cognac or armagnac title, regardless of how many meaningless 'stars' the label carries or even the magic word 'Napoleon' (which has no legal significance).

Little appreciated in Britain is the splendid 'apple brandy', Calvados, mainly associated with Normandy but also made in Brittany and the Marne. The best is *Calvados du Pays d'Auge*. Do taste well-aged Calvados, but avoid any suspiciously cheap.

Contrary to popular belief, true Calvados is not distilled from cider – but an inferior imitation is: French cider (cidre) is excellent.

Though most French proprietary aperitifs, like Dubonnet, are fairly low in alcohol, the extremely popular Pernod/Ricard *pastis*-style brands are highly spirituous. *Eau-de-vie* is the generic term for all spirits, but colloquially tends to refer to local, often rough, distillates. Exceptions are the better *alcools blancs* (white spirits), which are not inexpensive, made from fresh fruits and not sweetened as *crèmes* are.

Bringing Back Those Bottles

When thinking of what to bring back from France in the way of alcoholic beverages, apart from considerations of weight and bulk conditioned by your mode of travel, there are a few other matters to bear in mind. Within the theoretically unlimited import for personal consumption of products which have paid any national taxes in the country of origin ('duty free' is a separate subject), there are manifest practical as well as some semi-official restrictions.

In wine to choose sensibly is not inevitably to go for the least expensive. Unless you envisage having to entertain a lot of relatives, beware the very cheapest of French table wines! Though France produces many of the world's greatest, her prolific vineyards also make wines to which no British supermarket would allocate shelf-space. Quality does count along with value. Primarily what you are saving by purchasing in France is the comparatively high excise duties imposed in Britain against the minimal ones in France. However, the British tax is just the same on a bottle of the most ordinary *vin ordinaire* as on the rarest of vintage claret. When it comes to the latter, buying fine vintage wines in France does not automatically mean obtaining a bargain, unless you are an expert. There are not that many specialist wine merchants in France, a commerce in which Britain excels.

To summarise: it is undoubtedly sound, middle range wines that are the most sensible buy.

If you like those famous liqueurs, such as Bénédictine, Chartreuse, the versatile Cointreau, which are so expensive in Britain, shop around for them: prices seem to vary markedly.

I have briefly dealt elsewhere with French spirits. If you are buying Scotch whisky, gin or vodka, you may find unfamiliar names and labels offering apparent bargains. None will harm you but some may have low, even unpleasant, taste characteristics. It is worth paying a trifle more for well-known brands, especially de-luxe styles. Though they are little sold in Britain, former French colonies distill several excellent types of rum (*rhum*).

I deem it a good idea to make an outline list of intended purchases, after deciding what you can carry and how much you wish to spend. As to wines, do you want mainly red, or only white, or what proportion of both types? Can you afford champagne? Best to buy that in visiting the region where you should have the opportunity to taste and possibly find a bargain. What about other sparklers? What do you require in dessert wines, vermouths, liqueurs, spirits? Does your list work out at more cases (12 bottles) than you can easily transport? A conspicuously overloaded vehicle may be stopped by police as a traffic hazard. Now you have a list of sorts. What about cost? For essential comparisons, I would put against each item the maximum (per bottle) I would be prepared to pay in Britain. Certainly carry a pocket calculator so, as you examine potential purchases, you can easily work out what you are saving.

Condensed glossary
of French wine and ancillary terms

Alsace – See Wine Regions.

Abricotine – Generic apricot liqueur: look for known brands.

Alcool blanc – Spirit distilled from various fruits (not wine); not fruit-flavoured cordials.

Aligoté – Light dry Burgundy.

Anis – Aniseed, much flavoured in Pernod-type aperitifs.

Anjou – See Loire (Wine Regions).

Aperitif – Literally 'opener': any drink taken as an appetiser.

Appellation (d'origine) Contrôlée – or AC wine, whose label will give you a good deal of information, will usually be costlier – but not necessarily better – than one that is a VDQS 'designated (regional) wine of superior quality'. A newer, marginally lesser category is VQPRD: 'quality wine from a specified district'. Hundreds of wines bear AC descriptions: you require knowledge and/or a wine guide to find your way around. The intention of the AC laws was to protect consumers and ensure wine was not falsely labelled – and also to prevent over-production. Only wines of reasonable standards should achieve AC status: new ones (some rather suspect) are being regularly admitted to the list.

Armagnac – See Hints on Spirits.

Barsac – Very sweet Sauternes of varying quality.

Basserau – A bit of an oddity: sparkling red Burgundy.

Beaumes-de-Venise – Well-known *vin doux naturel*; see Provence (Minor Regions).

Beaune – Famed red Burgundy; costly.

Bergerac – Sound red wine from south-west France.

Blanc de Blancs – White wine from white grapes alone. Sometimes confers extra quality but by no means always. White wine made from black grapes (the skins removed before fermentation) is *Blanc de Noirs* – Carries no special quality connotation in itself.

Bordeaux – See Wine Regions.

Bourgeuil – Reliable red Loire wine.

Bourgogne – Burgundy; see Wine Regions.

Brut – Very dry; description particularly applicable to best sparkling wines.

Brut Sauvage – Dry to the point of displeasing acidness to most palates; very rare though a few good wines carry the description.

Cabernet – Noble grape, especially Cabernet-Sauvignon for excellent, if not absolutely top grade, red wines.

Cacao – Cocoa; basis of a popular *crème*.

Calvados – See Hints on Spirits.

Cassis – Blackcurrant; notably in *crème de cassis* (see Kir).

Cave – Cellar.

Cépage – Indicates grape variety; e.g. *Cépage* Cabernet-Sauvignon.

Chablis – See Burgundy (Wine Regions). Fine Chablis are expensive.

Chai – Ground-level storehouse, wholly employed in Cognac and sometimes in Bordeaux and other districts.

Champagne – See Wine Regions. Also specially note *Méthode Traditionelle* below.

Château(x) – See Wine Regions (Bordeaux).

Châteaneuf-du-Pape – Best known of powerful Rhône red wines.

Chenin-blanc – Grape variety associated with many fine Loire wines.

Clairet – Unimportant Bordeaux wine, its distinction being probable origin of English word Claret.

Clos – Mainly a Burgundian term for vineyard formerly (rarely now) enclosed by a wall.

Cognac – See Hints on Spirits.

Corbières – Usually a sound south of France red wine.

Côte – Indicates vineyard on a hillside; no quality connotation necessarily.

Côteau(x) – Much the same as above.

Crème – Many sweet, sometimes sickly, mildly alcoholic cordials with many local specialities. Nearer to true liqueurs are top makes of *crème de menthe* and *crème de Grand Marnier* (q.v.). See also Cassis.

Crémant – Sparkling wine with strong but rather brief effervescence.

Cru – Literally 'growth'; somewhat complicated and occasionally misleading term: e.g. *grand cru* may be only grower's estimation; *cru classé* just means the wine is officially recognised, but *grand cru classé* is most likely to be something special.

Cuve close – Literally 'sealed vat'. Describes production of sparkling wines by bulk as opposed to individual bottle fermentation. Can produce satisfactory wines and certainly much superior to cheap carbonated styles.

Cuvée – Should mean unblended wine from single vat, but *cuvée spéciale* may not be particularly special: only taste will tell.

Demi-sec – Linguistically misleading, as it does not mean 'half-dry' but 'medium sweet'.

Domaine – Broadly, Burgundian equivalent to Bordeaux *château*.

Doux – Very sweet.

Eau-de-vie – Generic term for all distilled spirits but usually only applied in practice to roughish *marc* (q.v.) and the like.

Entre-deux-Mers – Undistinguished but fairly popular white Bordeaux.

Frappé – Drink served with crushed ice; viz. *crème de menthe frappé*.

Fleurie – One of several superior Beaujolais wines.

Glacé – Drink chilled by immersion of bottle in ice or in refrigerator, as distinct from *frappé* above.

Goût – Taste; also colloquial term in some regions for local *eau-de-vie* (q.v.).

Grand Marnier – Distinguished orange-flavoured liqueur. See also *crème*.

Haut – 'High'. It indicates upper part of wine district, not necessarily the best, though Haut-Médoc produces much better wines than other areas.

Hermitage – Several excellent Rhône red wines carry this title.

Izarra – Ancient Armagnac-based liqueur much favoured by its Basque originators.

Juliénas – Notable Beaujolais wine.

Kir – Well-chilled dry white wine (should be *Bourgogne Aligoté*) plus teaspoon of *crème de cassis* (q.v.). Made with champagne (or good dry sparkling wine) it is Kir Royale.

Liqueur – From old *liqueur de dessert*, denoting post-prandial digestive. Always very sweet. 'Liqueur' has become misused as indication of superior quality: to speak of 'liqueur cognac' is contradictory – yet some very fine true liqueurs are based on cognac!

Litre – 1.7 pints; 5 litres equals 1.1 gallons.

Loire – See Wine Regions.

Méthode Traditionelle – Most widely used description of superior sparkling wine made as is champagne, by fermentation in bottle, now that any labelling association such as 'champagne method' is banned.

Marc – Mostly coarse distillations from wine residue with strong local popularity. A few *marcs* ('mar') – *de Champagne, de Bourgogne* especially – have achieved a certain cult status.

Marque – Brand or company name.

Meurseult – Splendid white Burgundy for those who can afford it.

Minervoise – Respectable southern red wine: can be good value as are many such.

Mise – As in *mise en bouteilles au château* ('château-bottled', or ... *dans nos caves* ('in our cellars') and variations.

Montrachet – Very fine white Burgundy.

Moulin-à-Vent – One of the rather special Beaujolais wines.

Muscadet – Arguably the most popular light dry Loire white wines.

Muscat – Though used for some dry whites, this grape is mainly associated with succulent dessert-style wines.

Nouveau – New wine, for drinking fresh; particularly associated with now tiring vogue for *Beaujolais Nouveau*.

Pastis – General term for powerful anis/liquorice aperitifs originally evolved to replace banned *absinthe* and particularly associated with Marseilles area through great firm of Ricard.

Pétillant – Gently, naturally effervescent.

Pineau – Unfermented grape juice lightly fortified with grape spirit; attractive aperitif widely made in France and under-appreciated abroad.

Pouilly-Fuissé – Dry white Burgundy (Macon); sometimes over-valued.

Pouilly-Fumé – Easily confused with above; a very dry fine Loire white.

Porto – Port wine: usually lighter in France than the type preferred in Britain and popular, chilled, as an aperitif.

Primeur – More or less the same as *nouveau*, but more often used for fine vintage wine sold *en primeur* for laying down to mature.

Rosé – 'Pink wine', best made by allowing temporary contact of juice and black grapes during fermentation; also by mixing red and white wine.

Sauvignon – Notable white grape; see also *Cabernet*.

Sec – 'Dry', but a wine so marked will be sweetish, even very sweet. *Extra Sec* may actually mean on the dry side.

Sirop – Syrup; e.g. sugar-syrup used in mixed drinks, also some flavoured proprietory non-alcoholic cordials.

Supérieur(e) – Much the same as *Haut* (q.v.) except in VDQS.

VQRPD. – See AC above.

Vin de Xeres – Sherry ('vin de 'ereth').

Glossary of cooking terms and dishes

(It would take another book to list comprehensively French cooking terms and dishes, but here are the ones most likely to be encountered.)

Aigre-doux	bittersweet
Aiguillette	thin slice (*aiguille* – needle)
Aile	wing
Aiolli	garlic mayonnaise
Allemande (à l')	German style, i.e.: with sausages and sauerkraut
Amuse-gueules	appetisers
Anglaise (à l')	plain boiled. *Crème Anglaise* – egg and cream sauce
Andouille	large uncooked sausage, served cold after boiling
Andouillettes	ditto but made from smaller intestines, usually served hot after grilling
Anis	aniseed
Argenteuil	with asparagus
Assiette Anglaise	plate of cold meats
Baba au rhum	yeast-based sponge macerated in rum
Baguette	long, thin loaf
Ballotine	boned, stuffed and rolled meat or poultry, usually cold
Béarnaise	sauce made from egg yolks, butter, tarragon, wine, shallots
Beurre blanc	sauce from Nantes, with butter, reduction of shallot-flavoured vinegar or wine
Béchamel	white sauce flavoured with infusion of herbs
Beignets	fritters
Bercy	sauce with white wine and shallots
Beurre noir	browned butter
Bigarade	with oranges
Billy By	mussel soup
Bisque	creamy shellfish soup
Blanquette	stew with thick, white creamy sauce, usually veal
Boeuf à la mode	braised beef
Bombe	ice-cream mould
Bonne femme	with root vegetables
Bordelais	Bordeaux-style, with red or white wine, marrowbone fat
Bouchée	mouthful, e.g. vol-au-vent
Boudin	sausage, white or black
Bourride	thick fish-soup
Braisé	braised

Brandade (de morue)	dried salt-cod pounded into a mousse
Broche	spit
Brochette	skewer
Brouillade	stew, using oil
Brouillé	scrambled
Brûlé	burnt, e.g. *crème brûlée*
Campagne	country style
Cannelle	cinnamon
Carbonnade	braised in beer
Cardinal	red-coloured sauce, e.g. with lobster, or in *pâtisserie* with redcurrant
Cassolette or cassoulette	small pan
Cassoulet	rich stew with goose, pork and haricot beans
Cervelas	pork garlic sausage
Cervelles	brains
Chantilly	whipped sweetened cream
Charcuterie	cold pork-butcher's meats
Charlotte	mould, as dessert lined with sponge-fingers, as savoury lined with vegetable
Chasseur	with mushrooms, shallots, wine
Chausson	pastry turnover
Chemise	covering, i.e. pastry
Chiffonade	thinly-cut, e.g. lettuce
Choron	tomato Béarnaise
Choucroute	Alsatian stew with sauerkraut and sausages
Civet	stew
Clafoutis	batter dessert, usually with cherries
Clamart	with peas
Cocotte	covered casserole
Cocque (à la)	e.g. *oeufs* – boiled eggs
Compôte	cooked fruit
Concassé	e.g. *tomates concassées* – skinned, chopped, juice extracted
Confit	preserved
Confiture	jam
Consommé	clear soup
Cou	neck
Coulis	juice, purée (of vegetables or fruit)

Court-bouillon	aromatic liquor for cooking meat, fish, vegetables
Couscous	N. African dish with millet, chicken, vegetable variations
Crapaudine	involving fowl, particularly pigeon, trussed
Crécy	with carrots
Crème pâtissière	thick custard filling
Crêpe	pancake
Crépinette	little flat sausage, encased in caul
Croque-Monsieur	toasted cheese-and-ham sandwich
Croustade	pastry or baked bread shell
Croûte	pastry crust
Croûton	cube of fried or toasted bread
Cru	raw
Crudités	raw vegetables
Demi-glâce	basic brown sauce
Doria	with cucumber
Émincé	thinly sliced
Étuvé	stewed, e.g. vegetables in butter
Entremets	sweets
Farci	stuffed
Fines herbes	parsley, thyme, bayleaf
Feuilleté	leaves of flaky pastry
Flamande	Flemish style, with beer
Flambé	flamed in spirit
Flamiche	flan
Florentine	with spinach
Flûte	thinnest bread loaf
Foie gras	goose liver
Fondu	melted
Fond (d'artichaut)	heart (of artichoke)
Forestière	with mushrooms, bacon and potatoes
Four (au)	baked in the oven
Fourré	stuffed, usually sweets
Fricandeau	veal, usually topside
Frais, fraîche	fresh and cool
Frangipane	almond-cream pâtisserie
Fricadelle	Swedish meat ball
Fricassé	(usually of veal) in creamy sauce
Frit	fried
Frites	chips
Friture	assorted small fish, fried in batter
Froid	cold
Fumé	smoked
Galantine	loaf-shaped chopped meat, fish or vegetable, set in natural jelly

Galette	Breton pancake, flat cake
Garbure	thick country soup
Garni	garnished, usually with vegetables
Gaufre	waffle
Gelée	aspic
Gésier	gizzard
Gibier	game
Gigot	leg
Glacé	iced
Gougère	choux pastry, large base
Goujons	fried strips, usually of fish
Graine	seed
Gratin	baked dish of vegetables cooked in cream and eggs
Gratinée	browned under grill
Grecque (à la)	cold vegetables served in oil
Grenadin	nugget of meat, usually of veal
Grenouilles	frogs; cuisses de grenouille – frogs' legs
Grillé	grilled
Gros sel	coarse salt
Hachis	minced or chopped
Haricot	slow cooked stew
Hochepot	hotpot
Hollandaise	sauce with egg, butter, lemon
Hongroise	Hungarian, i.e. spiced with paprika
Hors-d'oeuvre	assorted starters
Huile	oil
Île flottante	floating island – soft meringue on egg-custard sauce
Indienne	Indian, i.e. with hot spices
Jambon	ham
Jardinière	from the garden, i.e. with vegetables
Jarret	shin, e.g. jarret de veau
Julienne	matchstick vegetables
Jus	natural juice
Lait	milk
Langue	tongue
Lard	bacon
Longe	loin
Macédoine	diced fruits or vegetables
Madeleine	small sponge cake
Magret	breast (of duck)
Maïs	sweetcorn
Maître d'hôtel	sauce with butter, lemon, parsley
Marchand de vin	sauce with red wine, shallots
Marengo	sauce with tomatoes, olive oil, white wine

Marinière	seamens' style e.g. *moules marinière* (mussels in white wine)	*Pot-au-four*	broth with meat and vegetables
Marmite	deep casserole	*Potée*	country soup with cabbage
Matelote	fish stew, e.g. of eel	*Pralines*	caramelised almonds
Médaillon	round slice	*Primeurs*	young veg
Melange	mixture	*Printanier (printanière)*	garnished with early vegetables
Meunière	sauce with butter, lemon	*Profiteroles*	choux paslry balls
Miel	honey	*Provençale*	with garlic, tomatoes, olive oil, peppers
Mille-feuille	flaky pastry, (lit. 1,000 leaves)		
Mirepoix	cubed carrot, onion etc. used for sauces	*Pureé*	mashed and sieved
Moëlle	beef marrow	*Quenelle*	pounded fish or meat bound with egg, poached
Mornay	cheese sauce		
Mouclade	mussel stew	*Queue*	tail
Mousseline	Hollandaise sauce, lightened with egg whites	*Quiche*	pastry flan, e.g. *quiche Lorraine* – egg, bacon, cream
Moutarde	mustard		
		Râble	saddle, e.g. *râble de lièvre*
Nage (à la)	poached in flavoured liquor (fish)	*Ragoût*	stew
		Ramequin	little pot
Nature	plain	*Râpé*	grated
Navarin (d'agneau)	stew of lamb with spring vegetables	*Ratatouille*	Provençale stew of onions, garlic, peppers, tomatoes
Noisette	nut-brown, burned butter	*Ravigote*	highly seasoned white sauce
Noix de veau	nut (leg) of veal	*Rémoulade*	mayonnaise with gherkins, capers, herbs and shallots
Normande	Normandy style, i.e. with cream, apple, cider, Calvados	*Rillettes*	potted shredded meat, usually fat pork or goose
Nouilles	noodles		
		Riz	rice
Onglet	beef cut from flank	*Robert*	sauce with mustard, vinegar, onion
Os	bone		
		Roquefort	ewe's milk blue cheese
Paillettes	straws (of pastry)	*Rossini*	garnished with foie gras and truffle
Panaché	mixed		
Panade	flour crust	*Rôti*	roast
Papillote (en)	cooked in paper case	*Rouelle*	nugget
Parmentier	with potatoes	*Rouille*	hot garlicky sauce for *soupe de poisson*
Pâté	paste, of meat or fish		
Pâte	pastry	*Roulade*	roll
Pâté brisée	rich short-crust pastry	*Roux*	sauce base – flour and butter
Pâtisserie	pastries		
Paupiettes	paper-thinslice	*Sabayon*	sweet fluffy sauce, with eggs and wine
Pavé	thick slice		
Paysan	country style	*Safran*	saffron
Périgueux	with truffles	*Sagou*	sago
Persillade	chopped parsley and garlic topping	*St-Germain*	with peas
		Salade niçoise	with tunny, anchovies, tomatoes, beans, black olives
Petits fours	tiny cakes, sweetmeats		
Petit pain	bread roll	*Salé*	salted
Piperade	peppers, onions, tomatoes in scrambled egg	*Salmis*	dish of game or fowl, with red wine
Poché	poached	*Sang*	blood
Poêlé	fried	*Santé*	lit. healthy, i.e. with spinach and potato
Poitrine	breast		
Poivre	pepper	*Salpicon*	meat, fowl, vegetables, chopped fine, bound with sauce and used as fillings
Pommade	paste		
Potage	thick soup		

Saucisse	fresh sausage	*Thé*	tea
Saucisson	dried sausage	*Tiède*	luke warm
Sauté	cooked in fat in open pan	*Timbale*	steamed mould
Sauvage	wild	*Tisane*	infusion
Savarin	ring of yeast-sponge, soaked in syrup and liquor	*Tourte*	pie
		Tranche	thick slice
Sel	salt	*Truffes*	truffles
Selle	saddle	*Tuile*	tile, i.e. thin biscuit
Selon	according to, e.g. *selon grosseur* (according to size)		
		Vacherin	meringue confection
Smitane	with sour cream, white wine, onion	*Vallée d'Auge*	with cream, apple, Calvados
		Vapeur (au)	steamed
Soissons	with dried white beans	*Velouté*	white sauce, bouillon-flavoured
Sorbet	water ice		
Soubise	with creamed onions	*Véronique*	with grapes
Soufflé	puffed, i.e. mixed with egg white and baked	*Vert(e)*	green, e.g. *sauce verte*, with herbs
Sucre	sugar (*sucré* – sugared)	*Vessie*	pig's bladder
Suprême	fillet of poultry breast or fish	*Vichysoisse*	chilled creamy leek and potato soup
Tartare	raw minced beef, flavoured with onions etc. and bound with raw egg	*Vierge*	prime olive oil
		Vinaigre	vinegar (lit. bitter wine)
		Vinaigrette	wine vinegar and oil dressing
Tartare (sauce)	mayonnaise with capers, herbs, onions	*Volaille*	poultry
		Vol-au-vent	puff-pastry case
Tarte Tatin	upside down apple pie		
Terrine	pottery dish/baked minced, chopped meat, veg., chicken, fish or fruit	*Xérès*	sherry
		Yaourt	yoghurt

FISH – Les Poissons, SHELLFISH – Les Coquillages

Alose	shad	*Daurade*	sea bream
Anchois	anchovy	*Écrevisse*	crayfish
Anguille	eel	*Éperlan*	smelt
Araignée de mer	spider crab	*Espadon*	swordfish
		Étrille	baby crab
Bar	sea bass	*Favouille*	spider crab
Barbue	brill	*Flétan*	halibut
Baudroie	monkfish, anglerfish	*Fruits de mer*	seafood
Belon	oyster – flat shelled	*Grondin*	red gurnet
Bigorneau	winkle	*Hareng*	herring
Blanchaille	whitebait	*Homard*	lobster
Brochet	pike	*Huître*	oyster
Cabillaud	cod	*Julienne*	ling
Calamar	squid	*Laitance*	soft herring-roe
Carpe	carp	*Lamproie*	lamprey
Carrelet	plaice	*Langouste*	spring lobster, or crawfish
Chapon de mer	scorpion fish	*Langoustine*	Dublin Bay prawn
Claire	oyster	*Lieu*	ling
Coquille St-Jacques	scallop	*Limand*	lemon sole
		Lotte de mer	monkfish
Crabe	crab	*Loup de mer*	sea bass
Crevette grise	shrimp	*Maquereau*	mackerel
Crevette rose	prawn	*Merlan*	whiting

Morue	salt cod	*St-Pierre*	John Dory
Moule	mussel	*Sandre*	zander
Mulet	grey mullet	*Saumon*	salmon
Ombre	grayling	*Saumonette*	rock salmon
Oursin	sea urchin	*Seiche*	squid
Palourde	clam	*Sole*	sole
Pétoncle	small scallop	*Soupion*	inkfish
Plie	plaice	*Thon*	tunny
Portugaise	oyster	*Tortue*	turtle
Poulpe	octopus	*Torteau*	large crab
Praire	oyster	*Truite*	trout
Raie	skate	*Turbot*	turbot
Rascasse	scorpion-fish	*Turbotin*	chicken turbot
Rouget	red mullet		

FRUITS – Les Fruits, VEGETABLES – Les Légumes, NUTS – Les Noix

HERBS – Les Herbes, SPICES – Les Épices

Ail	garlic	*Courgette*	courgette
Algue	seaweed	*Cresson*	watercress
Amande	almond	*Échalote*	shallot
Ananas	pineapple	*Endive*	chicory
Aneth	dill	*Épinard*	spinach
Abricot	apricot	*Escarole*	salad leaves
Arachide	peanut	*Estragon*	tarragon
Artichaut	globe artichoke	*Fenouil*	fennel
Asperge	asparagus	*Fève*	broad bean
Avocat	avocado	*Flageolet*	dried bean
Banane	banana	*Fraise*	strawberry
Basilic	basil	*Framboise*	raspberry
Betterave	beetroot	*Genièvre*	juniper
Blette	Swiss chard	*Gingembre*	ginger
Brugnon	nectarine	*Girofle*	clove
Cassis	blackcurrant	*Girolle*	edible fungus
Céléri	celery	*Grenade*	pomegranate
Céléri-rave	celeriac	*Griotte*	bitter red cherry
Cêpe	edible fungus	*Groseille*	gooseberry
Cerfeuil	chervil	*Groseille noire*	blackcurrant
Cerise	cherry	*Groseille rouge*	redcurrant
Champignon	mushroom	*Haricot*	dried white bean
Chanterelle	edible fungus	*Haricot vert*	French bean
Châtaigne	chestnut	*Laitue*	lettuce
Chicorée	endive	*Mandarine*	tangerine, mandarin
Chou	cabbage	*Mangetout*	sugar pea
Chou-fleur	cauliflower	*Marron*	chestnut
Choux de Bruxelles	Brussels sprouts	*Menthe*	mint
		Mirabelle	tiny gold plum
Ciboulette	chive	*Morille*	dark brown crinkly edible fungus
Citron	lemon		
Citron vert	lime	*Mûre*	blackberry
Coing	quince	*Muscade*	nutmeg
Concombre	cucumber	*Myrtille*	bilberry, blueberry
Coriandre	coriander	*Navet*	turnip
Cornichon	gherkin	*Noisette*	hazelnut
Courge	pumpkin	*Oignon*	onion

Oseille	sorrel	*Pomme*	apple
Palmier	palm	*Pomme de terre*	potato
Pamplemousse	grapefruit	*Prune*	plum
Panais	parsnip	*Pruneau*	prune
Passe-Pierre	seaweed	*Quetsch*	small dark plum
Pastèque	water melon	*Radis*	radish
Peche	peach	*Raifort*	horseradish
Persil	parsley	*Raisin*	grape
Petit pois	pea	*Reine Claude*	greengage
Piment doux	sweet pepper	*Romarin*	rosemary
Pissenlit	dandelion	*Safran*	saffron
Pistache	pistachio	*Salsifis*	salsify
Pleurote	edible fungi	*Thym*	thyme
Poire	pear	*Tilleul*	lime blossom
Poireau	leek	*Tomate*	tomato
Poivre	pepper	*Topinambour*	Jerusalem artichoke
Poivron	green, red and yellow peppers	*Truffe*	truffle

MEAT – Les Viandes

Le Boeuf	Beef	*Le Porc*	Pork
Charolais	is the best	*Jambon*	ham
Chateaubriand	double fillet steak	*Jambon cru*	raw smoked ham
Contrefilet	sirloin	*Porcelet*	suckling pig
Entrecôte	rib steak		
Faux Filet	sirloin steak	*Le Veau*	Veal
Filet	fillet	*Escalope*	thin slice cut from fillet
L'Agneau	Lamb	*Les Abats*	Offal
Pré-Salé	is the best	*Foie*	liver
Carré	neck cutlets	*Foie gras*	goose liver
Côte	chump chop	*Cervelles*	brains
Epaule	shoulder	*Langue*	tongue
Gigot	leg	*Ris*	sweetbreads
		Rognons	kidneys
		Tripes	tripe

POULTRY – Volaille, GAME – Gibier

Abatis	giblets	*Lièvre*	hare
Bécasse	woodcock	*Oie*	goose
Bécassine	snipe	*Perdreau*	partridge
Caille	quail	*Pigeon*	pigeon
Canard	duck	*Pintade*	guineafowl
Caneton	duckling	*Pluvier*	plover
Chapon	capon	*Poularde*	chicken (boiling)
Chevreuil	roe deer	*Poulet*	chicken (roasting)
Dinde	young hen turkey	*Poussin*	spring chicken
Dindon	turkey	*Sanglier*	wild boar
Dindonneau	young turkey	*Sarcelle*	teal
Faisan	pheasant	*Venaison*	venison
Grive	thrush		